GOOD SEX.
GREAT SEX.
THE CHOICE IS YOURS.

The best aphrodisiac?

(a)   Spanish fly
(b)   South American tree bark
(c)   a well-told erotic tale

Multiple male orgasms?

(a)   happens all the time
(b)   what do you mean, not to you?
(c)   very rare . . . but you'll both have fun trying

Is bald—down there—better?

(a)   you mean I'm not the only one with this preference?
(b)   what, are you crazy?
(c)   what's the safest way to shave?

Talking turn-ons?

(a)   dirty words
(b)   foreign accents
(c)   telling stories in the dark

Is she faking?

(a)   if you think she is, she is
(b)   no, never, no way
(c)   you probably can't tell, but the better question is "Is there anything I can do to make it better for you?"

Share a fantasy?

(a)   be gone, freak
(b)   yes, but not with him (or her)
(c)   yes, next time when the two of you are making love

A Main Selection of the Venus™ Book Club and a Featured Alternate of Doubleday Book Club® and of The Literary Guild®

TOTALLY PRIVATE

Answers to the Questions
Lovers Long to Ask

Joan Elizabeth Lloyd

WARNER BOOKS

A Time Warner Company

Copyright © 2001 by Joan Elizabeth Lloyd

Warner Books, Inc., 1271 Avenue of the Americas, New York, NY 10020

Visit our Web site at www.twbookmark.com.

For information on Time Warner Trade Publishing's online program, visit www.ipublish.com.

 An AOL Time Warner Company

Printed in the United States of America

First Printing: September 2001

10 9 8 7 6 5 4 3 2 1

Library of Congress Cataloging-in-Publication Data

Lloyd, Joan Elizabeth.
  Totally private : answers to the questions lovers long to ask / Joan Elizabeth Lloyd.
     p. cm.
  ISBN 0-446-67718-3
     1. Sex instruction. 2. Sexual excitement. I. Title.
HQ31.L665 2001
 306.7—dc21   2001017944

Cover design by Diane Luger
Cover photograph by Herman Estevez
Book design by Nancy Sabato

*This book is dedicated to all the wonderful people who've
written to me over the years. I've enjoyed your comments,
answered your questions, and sympathized with your problems.
I hope I've helped and, please, keep writing.*

*And to John Aherne whose suggestions, comments, and criticisms
are right on target and always helpful.*

Contents

Introduction

Since the publication of *Nice Couples Do* in 1991, I've received hundreds of letters from all over the world asking my advice on an amazing variety of sexual issues. In 1996 I started my own website at http://www.JoanELloyd.com, and in the years since I've had more than a million visitors. Thousands have written to me with questions and comments of all kinds and on an incredible variety of topics.

Now I've combined these letters and lots of research with my own personal opinions and the result is *Totally Private*. Think about this book as a discussion of sexual issues just between the two of us. Share what you like with your partner and with your friends. Or keep it totally private.

As the title implies, letters written to me are expected to be totally private and anonymous. However, others can often benefit from a writer's experience. I have disguised all letters by rewriting and removing or changing any personal references and changing all names. I've kept the flavor of the letter but made it totally private. The letters reflect the opinions and experiences of their authors: I don't necessarily agree with or specifically recommend anything within the letters themselves. They are included for informational purposes only.

In many sections, I recommend professional help. I'm only a person who's been there, done that. I am not a doctor, nor do I want anyone to think I've been educated in sexuality. Remember, this book is for fun and for general information. For specific problems, see a doctor.

Much of what you'll read is my personal opinion. Is cybersex cheating? Are threesomes possible in a loving relationship? Does size matter? Occasionally, where I feel that it's important for you to be able to separate my opinion from fact, I use the Internet abbreviation IMHO, which means In My Humble Opinion. Of course, all of the letters I quote express the personal feelings of their authors.

The letters I receive are from a very diverse audience. You'll see that some are written by half of a married couple, others refer to "my boyfriend" or "my girlfriend." Unmarried lovers have as many problems as married ones.

As you can imagine, dividing this book into topics posed an immense problem; so many of the topics overlap. The section on orgasm suggests masturbation, which is covered in another chapter. Fetishes, fantasies, and communication are all interlocked. So let your fingers do the walking through the book. Read from front to back, or begin with a topic of particular interest. I thought about adding an index, but that seemed so scholarly, and this isn't intended to be a treatise on sexuality. It's a discussion of sexual issues, with lots of facts and opinions thrown in. So read, wander, and enjoy.

You'll notice that the letters I quote are "signed." I have changed all the signatures and there's no particular ethnicity involved. Questions have come from all over the world, from Ahmeds and Tonys, Pavels and Jacques, Ramons and Peters. They come from Marys, Marias, Moiras, Mariquitas, and Maryas. No one's real name is used. Everything is anonymous and countryless, and, in many cases, ageless.

One last thing. My next book will include responses to a yummy sex survey you can find at the end of *Totally Private*. I'd love to include your opinions, thoughts, and feelings, so please, when you're finished reading, fill out some or all and send them to me.

So now it's up to you to turn the page, read, learn, and enjoy. Remember, it's all Totally Private.

About Bodies

Women's Bodies

Dear Joan,
Okay, I'll come right out with it. I'm fat. I'm about fifty pounds over-weight, and although I keep trying to slim down, it never seems to work out. My husband loves me the way I am and wants to make love often, sometimes with the lights on. I'm embarrassed by the way I look and I want to make love in the dark.

Now he's gone further. He wants me to buy some sexy lingerie and I just can't deal with it. Please help me.
Mandy

Dear Mandy,
I get several letters a week from women like you who have allowed the size of their body to get in the way of great sex. They tell me that their breasts droop, they have a scar, they are too flat-chested or too big-busted, they have flabby thighs or a thousand other problems.

In a short letter I can't counter the thousands of commercials and stories that insist that the only successful women are the ones who weigh one ten, with semi-large breasts that stand up even when the woman is lying down, slender thighs, and long hair that looks like a shampoo commercial. Sorry, we real women don't look like that. At least I don't, and none of my friends do either. And we have great sex lives despite everything!

I'll admit that you've hit one of my hot buttons. This entire campaign to make us feel bad about ourselves makes me angry. I'm about ten pounds overweight, with thighs filled with cellulite. I've gone from a size ten to a fourteen over the past twenty years, slowly gaining with age, and I've got drooping breasts, which I've had since the birth of my first child.

I can still remember my six-month checkup after her birth. I was just twenty-one and I clearly recall sitting on the obstetrician's exam table putting my bra back on and listening to the doctor mumble while writing on the chart. Abdomen—normal. Breasts—pendulous. I was crushed. Pendulous, droopy breasts. I was doomed never again to be perky, if I ever was.

I'm as guilty as the next woman of that bad body image thing. I still gaze at my breasts in the bathroom mirror after my shower, wishing. Now, however, they have company. Now my tummy sags a bit, my ass is a few inches lower than it was years ago, and my thighs are definitely squishy and lumpy. And I *know* about all the propaganda we're fed and I'm *still* susceptible to those bad feelings.

I recall an article I read many years ago when Farrah Fawcett was in her heyday as Jill Monroe on *Charlie's Angels.* Remember? She of the great body and big hair? She of the poster with the gorgeous smile and prominent nipples? The article I read said she thought she had fat thighs. I laughed out loud.

So give up, ladies. You'll never be perfect. And I'll bet you that your husband doesn't care. That shouldn't give you license, however, not to make the most of what you have. Use a bit of makeup, some perfume. Comb your hair and, in general, make yourself look attractive, most of all because that way you'll *feel* attractive. That's the key. You need to *feel* attractive.

Almost more important than the way we feel about ourselves is that we're passing this body image obsession on to our daughters. What a pity. I listen to women out in the mall with their school-age daughters, moaning about their weight, lamenting the inability of their diet to cope with ice cream and chocolate cookies. No wonder so many teenaged girls have eating disorders. Much is learned from their mothers. If you want to diet, fine, just don't make it the center of your life, and keep your mouth shut in front of your kids.

So, Mandy, relax and let your husband love you. Buy a sexy nightie and hide it in the bathroom. One evening, slip into the bathroom and turn out the lights so you don't chicken out. Then put the nightie on and ask your husband to dim the lights. Then walk out into the bedroom. The look on your husband's face should convince you of how delicious he thinks you look. Then his actions should match his look.

Since this is such a hot button topic, I posted some information on women's body image and our obsession about weight on my Web page. Here are just some of the responses.

Dear Ms. Lloyd,
I am a big, tall man and I have always been fond of large women. My wife has gained some weight recently (she has never been a small woman) and now she's quite heavy. I have to tell you that I find her as sexy and attractive as the day we met. The way a woman feels about herself directly affects how she looks. If you can, tell ladies who have problems with the way they look not to be ashamed of their body. There is nothing more sexy and provocative as a woman who carries herself with pride, holds her head up, and has a playful spirit. There is nothing worse than seeing a beautiful tall woman wearing flat shoes and hunched over trying to hide her height or a big woman who confines herself to fashions that make her look like a mountain with a head. Stand tall! Wear bright colors! Wear sexy lingerie! Show off your body. There are a lot of men like me who appreciate you.
Jared

Dear Joan,

I am a fat twenty-something married woman who comes from a family of very weight-obsessed women. I have never been exactly skinny, but I was always in great physical shape and played sports and was very popular in high school.

I met the man of my dreams in my first year of college, and for some reason I started gaining weight. I was horrified. That was several years ago, and to date I have gained over fifty pounds. Saying that I felt worthless does not even cover it. My family still reminds me all the time that I am not attractive, and every time I look in the mirror I know that. Despite diets and exercise, I still gain about five pounds a month. I went to many doctors, and they all gave me the same diet, which I have been using for two years.

I finally went to a shrink and discovered lots about myself that I won't go into here, but suffice it to say that there were lots of emotional reasons for my weight gain—first and foremost my family. Let me tell you that, over the year since, my attitude has changed entirely.

Needless to say the "dream man" wasn't long for my world. Obviously my looks had a lot to do with the reasons that we were together, but I now know that my size wouldn't have mattered if he had really loved me.

I've met several wonderful guys since, men who like me for who I am, not what I look like. My attitude has improved dramatically, and I think that's why men are attracted to me, regardless of my weight. Yes, I still try to lose weight, but it's not the center of my life anymore.
Maggie

Dear Joan,

I've been learning slowly that feeling bad about your body has nothing to do with what you really look like. I'm five feet three and I once was a little ninety-pound, skinny, gawky young girl.

I'm now one fifty-five and have begun that natural aging process that makes my body soft and a bit flabby.

I had a revelation some months ago. I realized that somewhere between being unhappy and skinny at ninety pounds and unhappy and droopy at one fifty-five, I must have passed through my ideal weight. And I never knew it! I was too busy feeling bad about myself. Somewhere I missed lots of good feelings by always focusing on the negative.

Anyway, I've done a lot of thinking, and I now realize that, although I may not have a board-flat stomach anymore and I may have a bit too much skin under my arms, I can be happy with myself. I've changed my entire attitude. That's not to say that I don't often look in the mirror and wish I were different, but that doesn't affect me the way it used to. I can lament, without feeling bad about ME. I'm terrific!!!

So for those of you who might be unhappy with your appearance, I say, Look deep inside. Look into your heart and ask yourself, "Am I happy with who I am?" If the answer is yes, put that damned scale away. If you're not happy, find out why—it's probably not just your weight. But whatever you do, every time you look in the mirror, smile real big and tell yourself that you are fantastic!!

Sally

Dear Joan,

I too have always been body-conscious, and I've tried many dramatic weight-loss systems and fad diets. I dieted, exercised, and got nowhere. It was important to me to get thinner, so at thirty-six I discovered that it took a conscious effort on my part, combining the right nutrition and exercise. I lost seventy-five lbs. and, sadly, I lost my husband of seven years in the process. Amazingly enough, he's now with a woman who is the size I used to be. I guess during my obsession about my weight, I forgot about him.

What all this has taught me is that I have to be who I am for

me, and not for anybody else. It took me far too long to figure that out.
Terri

Dear Joan Lloyd,
I'm a forty-year-old man and I wanted to comment on women and this body image thing. I listen to talk shows and I'm amazed at how many women feel really bad about themselves. During my dating years, I went out with all kinds and sizes of women: fat, thin, short, and tall. And to me they were all beautiful. Of course I wasn't physically attracted to every woman I saw, but I found (and I still believe) that physical appearance, although it might attract me at first, wasn't what held my interest. Appearance had little if any affect on my desire to have a second date with a woman.

The most wonderful woman I ever dated was chubby and beautiful. Her smile was alive and charming, and she had a heart of gold. I knew that I would rather spend my entire life with somebody like that at my side than with a "perfect ten" who would constantly ask me, "Is my butt getting too big?"

You probably guessed that the chubby woman is now my wife. Since our marriage, she has changed her hairstyle, lost weight, gained weight, and now she's settled somewhere in the middle. All I care about is that she's happy. This whole hang-up that women have with their bodies just makes me ill. I don't care how big your butt is, just be your own beautiful self. And stay away from those horrible diet pills—is it really worth poisoning yourself just to look thinner?
Charlie

Dear Joan,
I'm a forty-two-year-old man and I'm really bothered by my wife's attitude. She is concerned about her size and weight, and I cannot convince her that she is perfect to me. I love her look, her smile, her eyes—well, everything about her. Maybe she

doesn't care that I find her lovely. Maybe she's more concerned about how she looks to other people than to me. I find myself comparing her appearance with that of other women, but I use *her* as the benchmark of good looks and not them. If a woman doesn't look like her in some aspect then that's a minus. I wish I could convince my wife of this since it adversely affects our love life. I am sure I am not the only male who feels this way.
Jacques

So, Mandy, I hope you've gotten the message. Despite all the things out there pushing women to be unhappy unless they look like the model who's dishing out the low-calorie TV dinner or eating the whole-bran cereal, try to feel good about yourself. It's the attitude, not the looks, that will hold a man.
Joan

Dear Joan,
You say that a woman's personality should count more than her physical appearance, but I just don't get turned on by fat women. Like all men, I often mentally undress women. But doing that with an overweight woman just leaves me cold. I could likely become close friends with a woman like that, but not ever a lover. Is there something wrong with me?
Burt

Dear Burt,
I understand that you'd prefer to date a *Playboy* centerfold, and if you can find one, go for it. If not, you're going to spend a lot of cold nights waiting, and you'll miss a lot of wonderful people.

You say that you could become friends with a less attractive woman; maybe that's okay. Long-lasting love affairs depend on friendship to keep them going. So if you start there, you're one step up. And when you and your "friend" discover that your friendship is becoming more than just that, undressing her will be wonderful and

your worries about her appearance the furthest thing from your mind.
Joan

Dear Mrs. Lloyd,
I am a man of average height and weight. When I'm with the guys, I join them in whistling at thin women and pretend to agree with their disparaging comments about "porky" women. But when I'm alone, I like to look at my erotic magazines that feature overweight women. These are the pictures I use when masturbating.

When I date big women, I am always afraid to be seen by my friends. They would probably laugh at me. What do you think?
Chris

Dear Chris,
I think that you're perfectly normal. No one can control who turns them on, your friends' opinions notwithstanding. It's conventional wisdom that men are turned on only by gorgeous girls. If that were true, there would be zillions of single men, since there are too few cover girls to go around. Stop being afraid of who you're seen with and enjoy your dates. I know that's easier said than done, but after the first time, you'll discover that your buddies' opinions are so much less important than your own.

One more point. Are you sure that the "guys" like only skinny women with big breasts like they say they do? Maybe some of them are putting on a show because they are afraid that the "guys" will laugh at them. The fact is that sexual tastes are as variable as there are people in the world. Men like women who are small, big, skinny, fat, strong, weak, dominant, submissive, and so on and so on. Don't swallow that line the "guys" are handing you.

And if your friends criticize your date, maybe you should reconsider their friendship.
Joan

Dear Joan,

I am thirty years old, five feet five, and I weigh one thirty. I'm a 34C, with a small waist and great hips. I wear a size 8. In addition to those stats, I have a small bone structure and an extremely fast metabolism. I couldn't gain weight if my life depended on it.

Lots of women hate me for my looks and my ability to get dates. Well, I don't find that I get any more second or third dates than other women. Listen, ladies, I get lots of first dates, I'll admit it. I'm attractive and I've got my choice of men. But many of those men just want to be seen with someone who looks like me. With those guys I soon find out that we have nothing in common and we don't have more than one or two dates. The men who stay in my life for longer than a month are interested in me as a person, not as a perfect body, just as they would be with any other woman.

Please stop worrying about women like me, and be your own charming, interesting self.
Doreen from Michigan

Dear Doreen,
Bravo!! I couldn't have said it better myself.
Joan

Dear Ms. Lloyd,
I know you have to be politically correct and all and say that men don't care about looks, but it's really all bull. No real man wants to waste time with a "dog." I'm six two, all muscle, and I go out only with babes: tall, blond, and stacked. Who cares what their personality is like, as long as they know how to give good head?
Vincent

Dear Vincent,
I don't think it's just political correctness. Real men want a woman they can talk to, share interests with, enjoy in and out of bed. Of course, since you're such a hunk, I'm sure you have your pick of women to date. I wonder, however, whether you have any long-term

relationships. I also wonder what you and your date do before it's time for sex, and afterward. I would guess that your evenings must be pretty dull if good head is all you care about. But if that's what makes you happy, go for it.
Joan

Dear Joan,

I'm twenty-seven and I'm skinny. I'm not fashionably slender, I'm skinny. My clothes don't fit right and I'm totally flat-chested. I sit with friends at lunch and eat everything, trying to gain weight. All I get are glares from women picking at salads. I guess they're jealous, but there's nothing here to be jealous of.

Frankly I am sick to death of people who cannot accept the way I am because of *my* size. Women think they're complimenting me when they tell me how thin I am and how they wish they could eat the way I do. Nonsense. It's just as difficult being in this body as it is being in theirs!! If anyone wants to be like me they can have it. I have never liked being thin and never will. Trust me, it's no picnic.
Marsha

Dear Marsha,

I've never thought about this problem from your point of view, and thank you so much for opening my eyes. I've always envied tiny, underweight women as much as the next person, never realizing that many of them have as much of a problem with their self-image as anyone else. Boy, it's sad that the forces of body-evil out there are trying so hard to make us all unhappy so they can sell diet drinks, exercise equipment, and pills of every sort.

On behalf of all of us who have unwittingly insulted you, I sincerely apologize.
Joan

Dear Joan,

I'm a nineteen-year-old male, long curly hair, sharp, silver-gray eyes, six feet two inches tall . . . and I weigh a good two hundred sixty pounds. This may not actually sound too bad, but it's enough to make me feel insecure about myself. I'm a college sophomore and I have had a few dates, but no relationship has lasted for an extended period of time. I couldn't figure out why, until one day I accidentally overheard one of my former dates bad-mouthing my size to one of her girlfriends.

I don't understand why it is such a factor for many women when they choose a guy. So, women, don't feel alone on this one, since we men get flack for our size as well.
Kirby

Dear Kirby,
Suffice it to say that you just haven't met the right woman yet. I know that sounds trite, and I guess it is, but sometimes the best advice is the oldest and most obvious. Be who you are. Find women who can look beyond the physical and find the person beneath. Only relationships based on common interests and shared ideals flourish in the long run.

While you're looking, keep yourself well groomed and wear clothing that compliments your size. Be proud of the person you are, and you'll find that many women respond as much to attitude as to appearance.
Joan

Vaginas

Dear Joan,
I've been having a problem I hope you can help me with. I'm a twenty-four-year-old woman and I'm kind of new at sex. My problem is that I don't seem to get soaking wet the way I read in books. Is there some problem with me? What should I do?
Delia

Dear Delia,

Probably not. If you are experiencing any other physical problems, consult your doctor. Lack of lubrication can be a symptom of diabetes or other systemic condition. You might mention it at your next gynecological checkup, just to be on the safe side.

If you're in generally good health, however, your lack of lubrication is probably just the way your body is. The fluids are produced naturally by the mucous membranes that line the vaginal canal. Some women produce copious amounts of fluid, others very little. Since lubrication is a result of hormone changes during arousal, the amount of wetness can vary from one time in your monthly cycle to another as well.

Wetness is also a function of your level of arousal. As foreplay proceeds, your body produces lubricating fluids to ease penetration, but it's not automatic or immediate. It can take from ten to twenty minutes for some women to get moist, so relax and enjoy the buildup.

If lack of lubrication is harming your sexual encounters, there is an obvious solution. Use a water-based lubricant, such as K-Y Jelly or Astroglide, both available in your local drug or variety store. It feels wonderful and makes sex slippery and delightful. By the way, your partner should enjoy the slithery sensation as well.

One last thing. Don't believe all that is written in romance novels. Real women don't necessarily respond the way those ladies in the books do. Remember that they seem to be able to make love on the carpet in front of the fireplace without any carpet burns or messy wet spots. Enough said.

Joan

Dear Joan,

I don't necessarily smell so sweet "down there." Do you recommend douching before a date with my boyfriend?

Annette

Dear Annette,
No. The vagina cleans itself naturally and healthfully, all by itself, even during menstruation. Careful daily washing is usually sufficient to keep your body clean and good-smelling. Douching can increase your risk of infection by removing the natural disease-fighting organisms. So shower and enjoy.
Joan

Dear Joan,
A quick question. Can douche prevent conception?
Milly

Dear Milly,
No!!!!!!
Joan

Dear Joan,
Okay, I'll admit my ignorance. Exactly where is the clitoris?
James T.

Dear James,
The clitoris is a pea-sized structure located at the front of the vaginal area, just where the inner lips meet. When a woman isn't aroused, it can be quite difficult to find, since it retreats beneath a pad of tissue called a hood. When a woman gets excited during sex, the clitoris swells and protrudes from its covering. Stroking the clitoris gently can bring a woman great sexual pleasure, but let your lady guide you in this. Like any other part of the body, some women's clitorises are very sensitive, others find it takes quite a bit of pressure to give pleasure. This also varies during arousal. Many women, myself included, find that too much rubbing, particularly when very excited, can be irritating. Let her reactions guide you.

And once you've found the clitoris, James, don't decide that it's all you have to know about arousing a woman. It's a wonderful part of foreplay, but it's not the only part. Don't ignore all the other erotic

parts of a woman's body: lips, breasts, legs, arms, hands, neck . . . You get the idea.
Joan

Penises

Dear Joan,
This is really embarrassing, but I don't have anyone else to talk to. I'm a twenty-year-old guy, and about a week ago I was with my girlfriend and we were making out. Anyway, my cock got hard, but when we were ready to do it, it wasn't. I couldn't get it inside, and despite all my efforts, I was done for the evening. Since then I've been with her once more and the same thing happened. She's been really nice about it and doesn't mention it at all, but I'm really terrified. Is this permanent? Please help!!!
PJ

Dear PJ,
What you are probably battling is the occasional impotence that most men experience from time to time. I remember a male friend of mine saying that he was with a group of guys in their twenties and thirties and this topic came up. One man, after much stuttering and stammering, admitted that he was experiencing problems having sex with his wife. Several of the men nodded, so he said, "Okay, have any of you had problems getting or keeping an erection?" Almost every man said yes. He was amazed at how common a problem it was.

As to your difficulties, you'll probably realize that you were under a lot of stress at that time: work, classes, home problems, slight illness, and, of course, performance anxiety. Any of those conditions and dozens more can affect your ability to get or maintain an erection. Once the problem appears, it becomes its own source of stress and thus everything gets worse.

The cure? It's easy to say and much more difficult to do. You have to relax. It will help, as well, if you do discuss it with your girl-friend. After all, she knows there's a problem and is probably frustrated at not knowing how to help you. Explain to her that you've been experiencing some stress-induced problems and that you'd like to spend time with her without any plans for intercourse. Suggest that, since there are so many ways to please a woman that don't require an erect penis, you want to make love to her with your hands, mouth, and such. Not only will that take the pressure off your body to perform, but your girlfriend, who sounds like a wonderful woman, supportive and generous, will be enjoying the experience thoroughly. Let her help by suggesting things she'd like: an erotic massage, a sensual joint bubble bath . . . well, you get the idea.

Eventually, I think you'll find that the problem corrects itself. Of course, if it persists or there is any pain, swelling, or discharge, seek medical help.
Joan

Dear Joan,
I'm really troubled. My girlfriend and I have been doing it for several months now, and it's really pretty good. She seems happy and she comes most of the time we make love. However, I know my penis is smaller than the guy she used to date. Although she seems to come just about every time, I still worry that I'm not really satisfying her. What is the normal size of a penis, both in length and distance around? Mine's only five inches when I have an erection, and it's about three inches around.
Steve

Dear Steve,
There's an old saying: If it ain't broke, don't fix it. You say that your girlfriend seems satisfied, so you certainly must be doing things right. Keep doing what you're doing and stop worrying about the size of your penis. It's obviously making her happy. Did you know that most women don't climax from thrusting alone anyway, so the size of the organ is not terribly relevant?

Okay, I know you want an answer to your other questions: Does size really matter? How big should my penis be? You aren't alone in wondering, and worrying. I think I get questions from men about the size of the penis more often than any other. Men seem obsessed by the physical properties of their organ, and I'm sure that worry detracts from their sexual pleasure and maybe their partner's pleasure as well. The best news I can give you is that men's fears are, for the most part, groundless.

From all I've read, the average erect penis is between five and seven inches long. The record, by the way, documented by a Dr. Robert Dickenson early in the twentieth century, was thirteen inches long. Girth? Most men have penises between two and four and a half inches in circumference, with some as large as six inches. Okay, guys, go measure.

That doesn't address the unspoken issue, however, and that is, Do women care?

Amazingly enough to men, most women neither care nor notice the size of a man's equipment after some initial curiosity. I've asked many women, and none of them seem to prefer to have intercourse with men who have larger penises. Most aren't even aware of the "normal" man's size. If the lovemaking is good, they're happy. If not, women seldom if ever discuss the size of a man's equipment—only his talent in bed.

Did you know that a woman's vaginal channel has nerve endings only in the first two inches? The remaining length is unable to feel anything anyway, so whatever length you have over the first two inches is a nonevent. As for girth, a woman's body is so flexible that it can expand to fit almost any size, and relax to hold even slender penises snugly.

A personal recollection: In the early 80s, before we needed to be concerned about AIDS, I indulged in a series of one-night stands and short-term relationships. I once spent the night with a man of amazing proportions. Although I seldom noticed the size of a man's organ, his was hard to miss, and of course he made sure I knew how "well hung" he was even before he removed his pants. I didn't have a ruler handy (evil grin) but he was larger than any man I've been with, before or since.

He, of course, was very proud of his amazing proportions. Unfortunately, he also believed that his size made up for any lack of finesse and consideration on his part. We got right to intercourse (and it wasn't lovemaking by any stretch of the imagination) with few preliminaries, and he failed to notice that I wasn't nearly lubricated enough, especially to allow penetration of his extra-large equipment.

To make a very long experience short, by the end of the evening I was unsatisfied and sore, so sore in fact that I visited my gynecologist the following day. The doctor insisted on giving me a gigantic shot of penicillin, "just in case." Needless to say, that was the first and last evening I spent with Mr. Extra-large.

The moral of the story is, stop worrying about the size of your instrument and concentrate on the talent with which you play it. Become a good, considerate, communicative lover and your date will not even notice the size of your equipment.
Joan

Dear Joan,
My penis is only five inches long when erect and about three and a half inches when not. I know that's really small. Well, I'm willing to try anything to make my penis bigger—hormones, surgery, anything. What should I try first?
Pete

Dear Joan Elizabeth Lloyd,
I know you get all kinds of questions, and I hope you won't laugh at me. I've heard that hypnosis can increase the size of my penis. Is that true?
Danny

Dear Joan,
My penis is only four inches long, and I know that's too small to please a woman. Is there anything I can do to make my cock larger?
Stan

Dear Stan (and everyone else with a similar question),

Most men's magazines and lots of adult websites advertise one product or another "guaranteed" to increase the size of the penis. Pills, herbal rubs, hypnosis, and even medical procedures are hyped to men who still believe that size matters. Do they work? Most don't, but even those men who succeed in getting something to happen only add a fraction of an inch.

I thought you might be interested in this letter.

Dear Joan,

I thought this tale might amuse you and help others who wonder about the size of their cock. This all happened several months ago.

For about six weeks I had been using a cream guaranteed to increase the size of my penis. I hadn't noticed anything happening, but I kept at it. Well, my wife arrived home unexpectedly one afternoon and found me rubbing the cream on. At first she thought it was a lubricant I was using to masturbate with. To cover my embarrassment, I told her what I was doing. She laughed. Actually laughed at me. I was mortified, until she told me that she had never even thought about the size of my penis. She reassured me that she loved making love with me and had no complaints at all about my size.

The ending of the story is that, since my cock was well lubricated, she spent the next hour proving to me how much she liked my penis just the way it was.

Thanks for listening,
A Guy from Kansas

So, Stan, IMHO, attempts at making your penis larger are a waste of time, energy, and money. I recently read an article on surgical penile enlargement in a men's magazine. It pointed out that, unlike breast enhancement surgery for women, with this surgery, men can't choose the size they want to be. A man can only gain an inch or two in length and less than an inch in girth. Seems like a lot of pain for a quite small gain. I think the time, energy, and even money would be much better spent on making yourself a better lover. Take time to flirt, tempt, and generally seduce your partner. Touch, stroke, and tease until the size of your equipment is the last thing on her mind. Just remember that it's not the size of the violin but the talent of the virtuoso.

I hope this helps.
Joan

Dear Ms. Lloyd,
I've been reading a lot about penis pumps and how they can make it bigger and harder. I know you've never tried one yourself (grin), but do you know anything about them? Do they work? Is it painful?
Lee

Dear Lee,
As you so correctly point out, I have no direct experience, but I have a few letters that might help. I can't, of course, vouch for the truth of any of the statements, but the letters seemed honest and informative, so I've included a few here for you.

Dear Joan,
My name is Andy and I'm a thirty-one-year-old man. Several years ago I decided to try a penis pump to increase the size of my cock. I really wanted the pump to work to make me bigger and sexier, so I did quite a bit of research before buying and trying. I read all the articles I could find, and all the advertisements; I watched videos and visited several websites (mostly devoted to gay men). I also visited a few chat rooms where men who used pumps gathered. All very interesting and educational.

I learned that most of the users of penis pumps were originally looking for a permanent increase in penis size, but finally understood that it just doesn't happen that way. If you get any permanent increase in size at all it will be only fractions of an inch with dedicated use for many, many months. Not what I had in mind when I began my search, but I pressed on.

I was told that, although most gains are temporary, there is a short-term increase in length and girth. For example, an erect seven-inch cock that is five inches around can increase to eight inches in length and six inches around with forty-five minutes of careful pumping.

Here are some of the things I learned about the pump itself. First, you have to have a good-quality cylinder that is the right size for the man's penis. Second, the pump has to have a safety bleed valve and a good pressure gauge calibrated in inches of water. To get the desired results, I also learned that I had to shave my balls and pubic area and use lots of lubricant on my entire cock and groin area to get a good vacuum seal.

I was still willing to give it a try, so with that information in mind I bought a really good pump and tried it out. Following the instructions, I started at a low pressure and built carefully to five inches of pressure. I once tried going to a pressure higher than the recommended limit of seven inches and I got several bruises as blood vessels in my skin burst. I'll never do that again. I gather that you can even get something called a "donut" below your corona from a swollen foreskin.

After several weeks of using the pump, I came to these conclusions. First, despite claims, the increase is not permanent. Like a lot of pumpers, I liked the feel of my swollen cock, and I must admit that a pumped cock hangs heavier for a while. And hang it does, because any pumping of reasonable length diminishes erectile function for a few days after the pumping session. Hmm. I stopped using it when this happened to me, since this wasn't what I had in mind at all.

Well, I still have the pump, a good one that cost me $150.00. For a while, I used it as a sex toy, and it always gets me super hard, but as I think about it now, I realize that I haven't used it in over a year. I guess the extra inches are just

not worth the fuss and risk. A hand, mouth, or vagina is ever so much better.
Andy

Dear Joan,
I recently tried a penis pump and found out that I do not like it. Although I guess most men want some kind of permanent enlargement, I just wanted the pump as a sex toy. I thought it might make me temporarily harder or bigger, better able to satisfy my wife. We also thought it would add some kind of spice to our love life.

When it first arrived my wife and I couldn't wait to give it a try. We got it out of the box and started kissing and fondling each other. After I had gotten hard we decided to see what it could do. At first it was just uncomfortable, but as I continued to use it, it actually started to hurt. It pressed into my pubic hairs and groin area too much. We released the pressure and then gave it a few more tries. No luck. I never got any real pleasure from it at all.

In my opinion it was a total waste of money, but you never know until you try. We'll keep looking for ways to add that little something extra.
Anthony

I hope these letters answer most of your questions, Lee.
Joan

Dear Joan,
I have wanted to write to you for quite a while on the subject of small penises. My husband and I have been married for almost eight years, and we have a pretty good sex life, with one exception. His penis is quite small, only about five inches, and it just isn't enough for me. Before I met him, I went with a guy who was really large. I never measured, but I would estimate that he was about nine inches erect. I guess my body just grew accustomed to his size.

When I started to go out with my now husband, it was unsatisfying, but I thought my body would adjust to him as it had to my "big guy." It didn't. Let me say right here that he's a great lover and he seldom leaves me unsatisfied. He's got great hands and a very talented mouth, so I usually climax. I just miss that wonderful "filled" feeling.

Any suggestions?

Bea

Dear Bea,

You freely admit that you've got a truly satisfying love life, which is so much more than many women can say. You've got a guy who sounds like a keeper. Do. If you occasionally long for a larger penis, get a gigantic dildo and play, either alone or with him. That might just scratch that itch.

Joan

Dear Joan,

I don't know whether you can answer this question, but when my penis is hard it curves to the right. Is there anything wrong with me? Will my lovers notice?

Thanks for any help.

Stuart

Dear Stuart,

If you aren't having any pain during intercourse, or at any other time, I wouldn't worry about it. Many penises curve naturally, and it shouldn't make any difference in your sexual response or hers. If it has always curved it will probably stay that way forever. If something has changed recently, however, although it can correct itself naturally in time, you might want a urologist to check just in case.

If you are having any pain or any difficulties during intercourse, the curvature of your penis might be a result of something called Peyronnie's disease, a condition that a urologist, a doctor specializing in problems with the urinary tract, should be made aware of.

The cause of Peyronnie's disease isn't known, and treatments vary from doing nothing to radiation to steroids to surgery. No one is sure whether any of these treatments actually cures the condition or improvement is a result of a spontaneous remission. Only your doctor can be sure of the cause of this problem and recommend treatment.
Joan

Dear Joan,
I've never had relations with a woman, but I'm worried. My penis curves downward and my balls seem to be larger than others I've seen. Why is that? Should I expect any problems during sex?
Dennis

Dear Dennis,
Your penis probably curves downward for the same reason a nose curves up or down. It's just the way your body was made. Likewise the size of your testicles. Genitals are no different than any other part of the body. They just are the way they are. As I've written to others, if you have any pain, discharge, or swelling, either during intercourse or at any other time, seek medical advice. Otherwise, just accept the way your body is and enjoy it. I know your lady-friends will.
Joan

On Circumcision

Dear Joan,
I'm a forty-two-year-old uncircumcised man and I was wondering whether the fact that I'm not circumcised makes a difference in the way a woman feels while we're making love. No one I've ever been with has ever commented on it, but I notice that the first time with a woman, she's very curious about my foreskin, since I guess it's unusual. Does it feel different for a woman? Is there anything I should do differently when we're making love?
Eugene from Paris

Dear Eugene,

Since I'm of an age where most of the men of my generation were circumcised as a matter of course just after they were born, I've been with only one man who was not circumcised, and that was a long time ago. I don't remember noticing anything different, but who knows?

Let me give you a few facts, then I'll add some letters from visitors to my website. As most people already know, circumcision—the removal of the foreskin—is a practice that goes back to antiquity. However, like breast-feeding and the use of pacifiers, circumcision goes into and out of fashion. It was widespread in the forties, fifties, and sixties, when doctors and parents were convinced that it was a good idea for hygiene. Now, circumcision rates in America are below sixty percent, and elsewhere, the number of boys who are circumcised at birth varies tremendously from country to country.

What should you do differently? For the uncircumcised man, careful cleaning is important. I've received several letters from women who enjoy performing oral sex but find that their uncircumcised partner has an unpleasant odor. Enough said. Other than that, nothing different is necessary during lovemaking.

As for the feel of a circumcised penis, here are some responses from visitors. The mix of responses is, I think, a reflection of the fact that everyone is different and responds differently to varied situations. And, of course, anything new is exciting.

Dear Mrs. Lloyd,

My former husband was circumcised, my current lover is not, and I can tell you that uncircumcised is absolutely the FINEST! I just love the way my guy's foreskin slides down when he gets hard and ready for me. There is something very primal and exciting in that.

I love to play with the foreskin when I give him oral sex, too. I just call it an "added attraction." So don't let anyone tell you that uncut is necessarily messy or dirty. It's not. Hygiene is dependent on the individual, and of course good habits are important.

My lover is squeaky clean and a real joy. Give me an uncircumcised man any time. And I find that since his sexual responses are greater, I find myself coming just over his pleasure.
Annette

Dear Joan,
My husband was uncircumcised when we were first married and we enjoyed wonderful lovemaking. Since he had had an injury to his foreskin years before we met and it caused him increasing discomfort, his doctor eventually recommended that he be circumcised. After he had the surgery, our lovemaking became even better. I like the feel of the ridges on the head of his penis when he enters me, and when I nibble the head of his penis there seems to be more enjoyment for him. So yes, we both felt the difference.
Marcy

Dear Joan,
I've been with a lot of guys, some circumcised, some not, and I really don't notice any difference when we make love. Some men are good lovers and some aren't, and the way their penises are "arranged" doesn't matter to me at all. I have lots of girlfriends, and we've had some pretty frank discussions on all topics. One day recently the subject of circumcision came up, and it was really interesting. Some of my girlfriends say it feels different, but most don't, and they argued about it for a long time. "It feels better." "It doesn't feel any different." I guess it's all a matter of taste.
Petra

Dear Joan,
I was a little taken aback and surprised when I first discovered that my boyfriend hadn't been snipped, but then I discovered that the foreskin was wonderful for spontaneous hand jobs, as there is no other lubrication required. He is aware of the poten-

tial odor and other problems, so he takes really good care of himself and I never have a problem with how he tastes or smells. In truth, the actual sex doesn't really feel all that different, as once he's truly hard, the extra skin pulls down towards the base and out of the way.

I have a theory that uncircumcised men have more sensitivity on and around the head of their penis because the foreskin protects it when wearing jeans, etc. I know that my nipples aren't as sensitive as my vagina, maybe also due to constant contact with my bra and other clothing. I haven't been able to prove whether it's true or not, but I sure do enjoy playing with him.
Jenny

So, Eugene, does it feel different? I guess it depends on the individual. I'm sorry I can't give you a definitive answer.
Joan

Dear Joan,
I'm an uncircumcised man and I'm wondering about adult circumcision. Is it painful? Will it feel different for me when I make love?
Kurt

Dear Kurt,
The best thing for you to do is talk to a doctor, either your internist or urologist, about the process and the changes it might bring. Let him or her explain, in detail, what to expect as far as the actual procedure, the recovery, and the effect on your love life. Don't be embarrassed to ask all kinds of questions, and keep asking until you're satisfied with the answers. You can also do some research online. Use any search engine, and look for "circumcision." You'll probably have to wade through lots of X-rated sites advertising photos of both circumcised and uncircumcised men, but eventually you should find lots of good information.

A word on surfing the Net for information. Please be careful to check the source of any material you find. Remember that sites hosted by the best hospitals will be mixed with Joe Blow's opinion and, even worse, John Smith's misinformation. Take care.

I thought I'd also send you two letters from visitors to my website who had it done. They had far different experiences.

Dear Joan,

Until the age of almost forty I was uncircumcised. Sex was great and I never thought about having myself changed. Then I met my current wife, and for religious reasons she asked me to be circumcised. I loved her and had no problem with undergoing the simple procedure.

I had the operation, which was no problem at all. I did have one small problem during the healing process; I found that it was difficult to control my erections due to the new sensations, including the stitches. After a few weeks, however, my penis was fully healed and we could finally make love.

Wow, what a feeling. I could feel a lot more, and I got so hard that it seemed that my penis hardly fit in my skin. After a while the excitement of this diminished somewhat.

I have to say that masturbation is also different. Before, I would rub the head of my penis while rolling my foreskin up and down, and obviously that is no longer possible. I now masturbate holding the shaft of my penis, and the tightness of my skin on the head is very exciting. My wife definitely prefers the new model and says that she now can feel the head of my penis better than before. And what's more, we both love the look of my new penis!

Tony

Dear Joan Elizabeth Lloyd,

Several years ago I decided to have my penis cut. You know, have the foreskin removed. I visited the doc and he said it was going to be a simple procedure, and I know that it is for many men. It wasn't for me. For some reason the local anesthetic didn't work properly and it hurt like hell. The healing was slow and, according to the doc, more painful than it should have been.

I guess it's pretty simple for most people, but for me it was a nightmare. I had a friend tell me that the definition of minor surgery is "someone else's." Well, this was mine and it certainly wasn't minor.
Carl

Kurt, I guess it depends on who you ask, but the majority of letters have been from men who had little problem with the procedure. Check it out with your doctor, and good luck with it.
Joan

Dear Joan,
I'm not circumcised and I'm worried. When I get aroused my foreskin doesn't pull all the way back and sometimes it's a bit uncomfortable. What can I do?
Mark

Dear Mark,
My best advice for you is to see a urologist. If the lack of complete retraction didn't give you any pain or other problems, I would suggest just ignoring it, but if you're having any kind of discomfort, seek professional help. It seems to me that a doctor can make a tiny slit in the foreskin to allow it to comfortably retract.
Joan

Dear Joan,
My boyfriend is not circumcised. During lovemaking, I like to play with the foreskin and slide it back and forth over the head of his penis. Am I doing any harm? My boyfriend seems to enjoy it, but I worry.
Samantha

Dear Samantha,

I don't think you're doing any harm. The foreskin is lined with a mucus membrane which helps to lubricate the end of the penis. As long as he enjoys it, go for it.

Joan

Joan,

My new boyfriend isn't circumcised and I notice that when I try to perform oral sex, there's a bad smell. From everything I read, it's just because he's not cleaning himself well enough. How can I tell him? I really care for him and I want to do these things, but I'm really repelled by the odor.

Jane

Dear Jane,

Telling a man that he's not "kissing sweet" is always difficult. You might blame it on your unusually heightened sense of smell that's "Always given you a problem." If that's too difficult, try making love in the shower or tub. You can wash his penis as part of foreplay and then perform oral sex. He might get the message.

You also might cover the odor with chocolate syrup or whipped cream. However, there's no substitute for just telling him. Since most men, your lover included, really enjoy receiving oral sex, I would think that if there's something he needs to do to make it easier for you, he'll probably be more than willing.

Remember to be sure not to blame him. Keep it light so he doesn't get his feelings hurt or get defensive.

If it doesn't improve, I'm sorry to say that you might have to leave oral sex out of your lovemaking.

Joan

On Vasectomies

Dear Joan,

I'm considering having a vasectomy. I've visited my doctor and got-

ten all the information I can. There's one thing they don't tell you. Can you tell me whether a woman can notice the difference when she gives head?
Tommy

Dear Tommy,
In my varied past, I've probably been with men who had had vasectomies, but I've never been able to tell that from the look or taste. I have gotten a few letters from other women on that subject.

Dear Joan,
My husband had a vasectomy after the birth of our last child and it was the best decision that we have ever made. I'm here to report that almost nothing is different! I truly enjoy oral sex and was somewhat concerned about possible changes, but if there is a difference in taste or amount, I can't tell. The only difference is the appearance. Due to lack of sperm, his semen is now practically clear instead of milky white.
Shirley

Dear Joan,
My now ex had a vasectomy after our third child was born. It was a while before we could do anything after the procedure, and when we finally did get back to our "playtime" I did not find any difference in the taste or quantity. He did seem to be more sensitive in the scrotum area (where the cuts are made). I hope this information helps those with questions.
Pam

Dear Joan,
Yes, come does taste different after a vasectomy! Not better or worse, just different. If you have difficulty with the taste you might want your lover to drink pineapple juice, as it makes his come taste sweeter, but it takes a few weeks.
Eunice

Tommy, if you want to have it done, do it, and don't worry about the taste. It's obvious that the change, if there is one, is minor and certainly not unpleasant.
Joan

Male Nipples

Dear Joan,
Here's a strange question for you. In novels, men always seem to have sensitive nipples. Well, I've never noticed any man I've been with who's enjoyed any kind of nipple play. Have you?
Jeanine

Dear Jeanine,
I'll admit that I've never been with a man with sensitive nipples either. I did get a letter recently from a man who tells me his are very sensitive. I asked him to elaborate, and here's the letter he sent to me.

> Dear Joan,
> My nipples weren't always sensitive, but over years with my wife, they've become really hot. In the beginning she loved to play with them and it didn't really do anything for me. But as time passed, they began to get really erect when she did, and now all she has to do to get me in the mood is tweak me. Maybe it's just habit, or knowing that she's telling me she's in the mood for lovemaking. Who knows? Who cares?
> *Art*

And here's one from a woman whose husband enjoys nipple play.

> Dear Joan,
> My husband just loves to have his nipples played with. At first I

was surprised when his nipples became erect just like mine do, but I learned that his body seems to react the same way mine does in lots of ways. When he's excited his nipples swell, and so does another part of him (giggle). So now I tweak his nipples to get him hot.

One more thing we enjoy. Slow dancing in the living room, naked to the waist with our nipples rubbing together. What a blast!

Marla

Some men obviously get a thrill from having their nipples played with, so try it and see what reaction you get.

Joan

About Relationships

Chapter 2

The Fine Art of Sexual Communication

Dear Joan,

I have a problem that I'm just not sure how to tackle. I've thought a lot about it but I just can't work up the nerve. My husband loves to squeeze my breasts while we're making love, but he does it much too hard. In all other ways he's a considerate lover. I've said ouch softly but I don't want to give him the idea that I don't like what he's doing. I don't want to insult or discourage him. What can I do?

Abby

Dear Abby,

You don't like what he's doing and that's no crime. No one was born knowing what to do or how to do it, so your husband is probably just going on what's always worked. Since you haven't told him not to squeeze so hard he assumes you like it. I can understand how difficult it is to tell a partner something negative, but it's not as bad as you might think.

No one likes to be criticized, and usually when something negative comes up, we get defensive and turn off. Often we resist so hard that we actually forget about the problem and do it again. So if whatever you need to tell someone is couched in positive terms, it can come out sounding like praise, not criticism.

So how can you wrap the negative in the positive? "Honey, I love it when you touch me softly, like this." Then show him how you like to be touched. "Oh, it feels so good when you . . ." "Mmm, that would feel even better if you . . ." That way you've avoided the negative and told him how good it is when it's right.
Joan

Dear Joan,
I was the one who asked you about my husband squeezing my breasts too hard. Well, I did what you suggested, and told him that night that it would feel even better if he stroked me gently. He looked surprised. "I thought you liked it this way." I swallowed hard and told him that I did like it, but if he were a bit less forceful I would like it better. He was great. He actually asked me how he should touch me. "Like this?" Well, it was great.

What happened later was even better. Afterward, when we were cuddling, he asked me whether there was anything else that he was not doing as well as he might. I couldn't think of anything, so I asked him right back. He told me a few things I didn't do the best way when I stroke his cock. I was hurt for a second; then I realized that he was telling me exactly the kind of thing I had been trying to tell him. We talked for quite a while, and since then our sex life has been even better.

I can't thank you enough for opening up so much new communication. And Charlie thanks you too.
Abby

Dear Joan Elizabeth Lloyd,
My wife isn't as creative as I am in bed. She's pretty much a plain sex, missionary position woman. I'd like to try some new things, like

maybe buying a toy or asking her to masturbate me, but I don't know how to tell her without hurting her feelings. I think she might be receptive if I could just find a way to bring the subject up. At least I hope so. But I don't want her to think that she's not good enough for me just the way she is. I just think there might be much more fun to be had. Can you help?
Kent

Dear Kent,
I think I have a way for you to tell her your desires without getting her too upset. I call it "bookmarking." The first step is to find a story or a scene in a novel that revolves around the new game you'd like to play. You can look in a book of stories like my *Bedtime Stories for Lovers,* or you might be able to find something on the Internet and print it out. Start small, with something not too far from what you two do now. Then slip a bookmark in the section you found. Don't write any notes, just give her the tale and ask her to read it when she's alone. That way she can read in private, without you watching her reactions and her body language.

Give her time to read by leaving her alone. Go out for a walk, or leave the tale for her when you're not going to be home for a while. Once she's read the story, ask her what her reactions were. If she seems really negative, you might have to move on to something else or, better still, ask her to suggest something she'd like to try. If she's neutral, or even excited by the reading, ask her whether she'd be interested in playing with you. Tell her that the story is really a description of a situation you'd like to try. See what happens.

Here's another idea. Tell a story in the dark one evening while lying on the bed before making love. It might begin, "Maybe we're in a deserted cabin in the mountains, and it's snowing and we can't get back to the lodge until the next day. We've got plenty of wood for the fire and lots of food and wine. We are lying on a thick furry rug in front of the fire." Then ask her what you two do now. Alternate paragraph by paragraph. You can guide the story around to what curls your toes and see how she reacts. If you are holding hands, you can tell still more from her grip. You can even ask her to squeeze your hand if something sounds scary but tempting. You can also see where she aims the story. Maybe she's telling *you* something.

Is communicating information about new bedroom sports risky? Yes. But it's not as risky as most people think. And think of the rewards. The two of you might have had the same fantasy for years. How sad if neither of you ever found a way to share it.

So be brave. She might want to tell *you* something but didn't have the courage either!
Joan

How Often Is Too Often?

Dear Joan,
My husband wants to make love almost every night, and that's just too much for me. How often is too often and how can I get him to slow down?
Jeanne from Missouri

Dear Jeanne,
I really can't answer this question. "How often is too often" is purely a matter of what two people want. Your problem seems to be that your desires and his are in conflict. You would like to make love less often than he does and that's a real and serious problem. Let me try to help.

Let's say you want to make love twice a week and he wants to do it six times a week. First, negotiate. Talk it out, seriously but not during the act of lovemaking. Get away from the house, on neutral turf, so to speak. Go out to dinner, but no alcohol, since this is going to be a really intense talk. Then it's up to you to bring up the subject. Discuss it as though your desires were a mismatch, not that someone's right and someone's wrong, since there is no right and wrong here. Try to agree on, say, three or four nights a week. You each will have to give a little, but that's the nature of compromise. Masturbation between times can make the compromise a bit more palatable too.

If you can't do that, get a small token you can pass back and forth. Whoever has the token can use it to make love whenever he or she likes, but then the token gets turned over to the partner. If he uses it the night after you've just made love, that's fine, and you have to be flexible. If you choose to wait several days, he has to learn patience. It's important for you two to agree that this is for the purposes of compromise, not punishment. Don't decide that you'll hold out for two weeks just to be nasty or that he'll ask for sex an hour later just because he can.

So many things in marriage are compromises; sometimes sexual frequency has to be as well.

Joan

How Brief Is Too Brief?

Dear Joan,
My wife has been telling me lately that we've been having quickies. She says it in jest, but I don't think she's really joking. How long is a quickie?
Harve

Dear Harve,
A quickie is a short sexual encounter, one that is, for the most part, shorter than one partner wishes it had been. It's not the time involved but the end result that's the indicator. I sometimes find that I just want to tear Ed's clothes off and do it NOW. As long as he's in the same mood, our lovemaking might last only a few minutes. Is that a quickie? I guess, but it leaves both of us satisfied. If it hadn't, one of us would have asked for more.

I think what your wife is telling you is that sometimes she's not satisfied. She might be reluctant to talk about it, to ask for more at the time, but she's nudging you nonetheless. The next time you two make love, use your instincts and try to ascertain whether she's ready for you. Before you penetrate, discover whether she's well lubricated, a good indication of whether she's excited. Another way to judge her level of arousal is to find out whether her nipples are erect yet. Is her breathing fast and hard? Is her pulse pounding? Use all your senses. Is she urging you onward with her hands, her mouth, her body, or does she seem to be trying to hold you back?

And when you're finished, she might not be. Be alert to all the signs that tell you she's satisfied. Is her body quiet? Is her breathing slowing? If you suspect she has not climaxed, use your hands, mouth, or toys to help her over the edge.

Joan

Spicing Up Your Sex Life

Dear Joan,

My husband and I have been married for almost twenty years, and the sex has gotten pretty dull. I don't want to make a big deal out of this, but I really think it could be so much better with a bit of creativity. But I don't know where or how to start.

Please give me some pointers. Thanks.

Jessie from Oregon

Dear Jessie,

There are so many things you can try. Start small. Rather than making love hanging from the chandelier, suggest that you'd like to make love in the morning rather than at night. If you usually make love with the lights on, turn them off, or vice versa. Switch sides of the bed so it feels different. Change your shampoo or body wash so you smell different. Suck on a peppermint candy so you taste different. Keep your creative eyes open for habits you can shake up. Read a good book about spicing up your love life. If I may sound self-serving,

I can recommend my *52 Saturday Nights.* You can even pick up ideas from erotic novels, like my book *Midnight Butterfly.*

Whatever you suggest, mention it as if it's a game, not an earth-shattering problem. "I just feel like doing something different." Give it a try and I think you'll be surprised at his reaction.
Joan

Dear Joan Elizabeth Lloyd,
Okay, here's my problem. My husband isn't the least bit romantic. He's never brought me flowers or made plans to take me out to dinner. I've talked to him about it but he doesn't seem to understand what I'm talking about. We never seem to have any fun anymore. I don't know what to do, it's just dull, dull, dull. Help!!!
Jill

Dear Jill,
Yours is a common problem and I have a suggestion. You're asking him to "be romantic," but you have to realize that he probably hasn't a clue what you're talking about. It's not that he doesn't want to make you happy, but you're not asking for anything specific enough for him to get a hold of. So ask for exactly what you want. "Darling, I'd love it if you brought me flowers or a box of candy." That's finite and he can deal with that. "I wish we could plan an evening out without the kids. I'd love to go out with just you. Would you help me make it happen?" Again, that's a specific plan.

Make a big fuss over whatever he does. I know it's not as wonderful when you have to ask for what you want, but realize that this is really difficult for him. Tell him how his ideas are really great and how much the flowers or the date night turned you on. He'll love that, and be more anxious to do it again. You might even find that next time he'll think of things without your input.

Once you've done that a few times and he's feeling a bit more confident, here's a next step. Make a definite date each week. Begin with getting a baby-sitter for, let's say, every Saturday night. Then buy a small token, a little animal or key chain. Take it and tell him that since it's yours now, you'll plan the first night out. Then plan it. Do something he will enjoy, not something for just you. After that evening, give him the token and tell him it's his turn to plan something. Give him a few concrete suggestions so that first time goes well. Be supportive of whatever he chooses. One negative remark and he won't do it again, so loosen up and enjoy whatever he selects. Then take the token back.

If that's too difficult for your husband, write out a series of evenings you'd enjoy. You can do that alone, or the two of you can spend an evening creating fun nights out. Then put each one on a separate piece of paper, fold them up small, and drop them into a jar or bowl. Then, each week, one of you can pick a scenario and be in charge of making it happen.

You get the idea, I'm sure. Take turns. Dinner and a show, or bowling. A drive or a long leisurely dinner at an expensive restaurant. Maybe even a reservation at the No-tell Motel with wine and a new nightie. Splurge. There are few things more important than keeping your sex life, and thus your marriage, in good shape.
Joan

Sex and Pregnancy

Dear Joan,
I was wondering if you get many letters from pregnant women or their partners. I'm seven months pregnant and wonder how other couples are coping with sex during pregnancy. As for myself, I'm still very active and my husband and I enjoy it almost more than before. He is, however, concerned that as pregnancy progresses, sex will become difficult or painful. The baby doesn't seem to be putting any uncomfortable pressure anywhere that inhibits sex, but we've heard that it gets worse. What can you tell me about pregnancy sex?
Mamie

Dear Mamie,

My children are in their thirties, but I remember my pregnancies quite well. Our sex life was as good as it had been before, and although it became a bit awkward, we found ways. I must admit that, over the years, I've forgotten most of the details, so I thought some letters from other women about pregnancy would answer your question better than I could.

Dear Joan,

My name is Sherry and I am a twenty-seven-year-old, six-months-pregnant woman. So far sex has been excellent for me since conception. I am horny almost all the time so it really doesn't take much to get me going. We find that just about any position works, all of them feel good, and most all of them produce great orgasms. As for advice for other pregnant women . . . I would have to say, "Ladies, indulge yourself while you can." Afterward things get really difficult.
Sherry

Dear Joan,

This is with regards to sex and pregnancy. When I was pregnant I seemed to be extremely horny! As my pregnancy progressed it only got better. I never gave my poor husband a break. I actually had sex up to the day before my son was born. I was several days late and my body wasn't going into labor, so my midwife suggested good sex to stimulate things. Well, maybe it did, because my baby was born the next day, but, of course, we had been having sex almost every day before that.
JaneAnne

Dear Joan,

With both my pregnancies the doctor told me sex was fine as long as it was not uncomfortable. With my first, I was always in the mood, sometimes to the point of wanting to murder my husband for coming home late from work!! Talk about hormones, I was dying for sex.

With my second, however, things were a little different. I had a two-year-old to take care of and that second pregnancy was more uncomfortable. I didn't feel very well most of the time. Sex was still fun, though, and it made me feel that I wasn't alone in my misery. We cuddled and he supported me. Making love was still wonderful. Even during that time I never experienced any discomfort as long as I was on top. Being on top allowed more control of depth, as once I started to dilate and drop, I was a bit tender. At that time I definitely didn't want a lot of thrusting, just loving and touching.
Allie

Dear Joan,
After I had my daughter by C-section, I was ready for sex within three weeks! The doctor told me that the biggest reason they usually advise waiting so long is that there is a big chance of harming a woman's insides, which are often messed up during delivery. For me that wasn't the case. They said it would be okay, that I just needed to take care not to tear the incision. So we took it very slow, and if it hurt, we stopped. It was wonderful to make love again after doing without for several weeks.
Selma

Dear Joan,
For me, sex was fine all the way through pregnancy. I only stopped during week thirty-six to avoid the possibility of premature labor, as semen is thought by some researchers to take a woman who is on the edge of labor right over the top. Of course others think that you can't trigger labor unless the body's ready for it, but we decided not to take chances. Anyway, that meant I went without for about a week before I gave birth to a perfect little boy.

As for positions, I found that if I lay on my side with one leg

over his hips while he lay on his side, that was the perfect position for us, especially when I got really big. I hope this helps anyone who's wondering about sex during pregnancy.
PJ

Mamie, I hope these letters have helped to answer some of your questions. I would be sure to ask your doctor about anything that concerns you. I wish you the best of everything during your pregnancy, and I hope your family grows as you want it to.
Joan

Sex and the Kids

Dear Joan,
I have a problem. I guess that's WE who have a probem, and it's only partly sexual. I'm hoping you can help. My husband and I used to have a great sex life, until the kids came along. Now it's a quickie once, or maybe twice on the weekend. We both work, so we're both tired and cranky in the evenings. By the time we get the kids in bed and the housework done it's just too late and we're too exhausted. Please, can you help us put some life into our marriage?
Connie and Dave

Dear Connie and Dave,
Having small children is the death of good sex in many households. I was there myself for many years. Although I'm now a grandmother, I remember the endless chores that got in the way of intimacy. My then husband and I thought more about the lawn than we did about our sex lives. It got predictable and, okay I'll admit it, boring, even tedious at times. Back then we didn't consider sex that crucial; the kids were the most important things in our lives.

Now, I would hope, couples know better. A good and rewarding relationship between parents is fundamental to a good family structure. Happy parents raise happy kids. You need good sex, and you both deserve it. It's time now for you both to put forth the effort that it takes to improve it. And it does take effort.

When was that last time you had great sex together? If it's measured in weeks, that's really sad. If it's measured in months, that's even worse. Don't get scared; great sex doesn't have to take hours and move the earth, just be satisfying for both of you.

Here's what I recommend:

Get a baby-sitter, preferably once a week. If you can't afford one, send the kids to their grandparents or make an arrangement with the next-door neighbors, overnight if at all possible. Maybe you can set it up so that they take your kids every other Saturday and you take theirs on the alternate weeks.

Now that you have the kids out of the way, make some plans. Do something that will help to bring you closer together. Go for a long walk together or linger over dinner, either at the local Chinese place or, if you can afford it, at a fancy restaurant. Get out of the house; that's a must. Get out of the environment where you're Mommy and Daddy and into one where you're a man and a woman. If you can't afford dinner out, pack a picnic and eat in the park.

Try not to just go to a movie or play. That's such passive entertainment, leaving no real time to talk, and that's what this "date" is all about. Talking. Talk about things you both are interested in outside the home and family. Don't talk about the kids; talk about TV shows, politics, sports, whatever you both enjoy. Lighten up! As the evening progresses, if the talk turns to sexy topics, great. That's the idea.

When I suggest this, many people say that sex should be spontaneous, and this sounds too calculated. You're right, it is planned, and it has to be. You've got so many other things to contend with, you have to plan an evening out. But there's nothing necessarily wrong about planning. Remember when you were dating? You had a date for, say, Saturday evening. You thought about it all week, debated what you would wear, where you would go. Did that ruin the kissing and loving that came later? I don't think so. Actually, all that anticipation probably made it better. I remember it did for me, and still does.

Ed and I like to vacation. Between his job and my various enterprises, we too suffer from noise. The outside world is often too much with us, so we try to get away often, if only for a weekend. We plan. Actually, Ed does most of the planning. But one thing we know is that the loving will be particularly good because we'll both be more relaxed.

Recently we went to Disney World with my daughter, son-in-law, and my two grandchildren. We loved watching the children's reaction to their first trip to the Magic Kingdom. We also, of course, had our own room, a sweetheart suite at a nothing-but-suites hotel. We had looked forward to it for weeks, and it lived up to our expectations. The room we reserved had a heart-shaped hot tub, and we indulged—in everything. And I must say that the sex was great. Spontaneity is wonderful, but planning can be delicious too.
Joan

Dear Joan,
My five-year-old daughter is getting in the way of sex with my husband. Most nights she sleeps in our bed. All night. If we try to get her to sleep in her own room she screams, and since we're both tired, we finally give in and there she is, between us in the queen-size bed. What can we do?
Babs

Dear Babs,
No one in your family is benefiting from your daughter's trips into your bed. She's learning to "manage" her parents, and both of you are totally stressed. She has to learn to sleep in her own bed.

How? Put her there and don't allow her into your room. Since you obviously can't lock her into her room, lock yourselves in instead. Get a hook and eye lock and put it at least five feet off the ground, on the inside of your bedroom door. Talk to her and tell her that Mommy and Daddy have their room and she has her room. Ask her what will make sleeping in her bed more attractive. Her very own flashlight? A sleeping bag? A new toy she can take to bed? Would she like you to leave the lights on?

Then do it. Lock your door, and when she knocks, tell her that Mommy and Daddy are sleeping in their room and she's expected to be in hers. If you want, once or twice, take her back into her room and settle her down. Once she understands that she's not going to be permitted into your bed, that's when the fireworks will begin. I warn you in advance, she'll scream. Loud. Maybe most of the night. Maybe two or three nights. You've already set the pattern—she screams and you give in—and she well knows it. So don't give in, even when it costs you a night's sleep, or two. Every time you give in it gets that much harder to make the point the next time. Eventually she'll get the message. I promise.
Joan

Dear Ms. Lloyd,
My husband is a very private person and doesn't like the children to see him naked. One morning our five-year-old son wandered into the bathroom as he got out of the shower and he nearly freaked. I want my kids not to be ashamed of their bodies. I think the human body is beautiful. What should I do?
Gerri

Dear Gerri,
In some households it is perfectly natural for children to see their parents without clothing. The kids wander into the bedroom when their parents are dressing and it's always been that way. That's the normal state for them and that's great. In other families, children seldom if ever see their parents unclothed, and that's fine too.

You two have to be the people you are. If you're totally comfortable with your children seeing you naked, fine. If your husband isn't, get a lock for the bathroom door so he can have his privacy. Put the lock really high on the door so the children can't accidentally lock themselves in.

I guess the only thing I would caution you about is that your husband shouldn't get angry at the children if they happen to walk in on him at an awkward moment. Suggest that he say, "Daddy's getting dressed, so you can come back in a little while. Now scoot!" Otherwise, just be what you are.
Joan

Dear Joan,
My six-year-old son loves to touch his penis while he watches TV. I find it embarrassing and I worry that he's masturbating. What should I do?
Pam

Dear Pam,
He is masturbating. Most, if not all, little boys do. Remember that his penis feels good when he touches it. And he touches it every time he goes to the bathroom. I don't see anything wrong with his touching himself. After all, it's his body.

IMHO, boys are going to masturbate, and the only control you should exert is to insist that masturbating is a private activity and he has to do it in his own private space, his room. If you find that he's touching himself while he's watching TV, ask him to go upstairs, or to stop. I think that controls the problem.
Joan

Dear Joan Elizabeth Lloyd,
This isn't really a question about sex, or maybe it is. How can I explain about touching to my five-year-old daughter? All this talk about good touches and bad touches, it feels too difficult to ask her to understand. Is there an easier way?
Paula

Dear Paula,
I'm not an expert in child psychology, but it seems to me that children need to understand only that no one touches them, especially

where their bathing suit goes, without their permission. Period. You can make exceptions for Mommy and Daddy if you feel you need to, but by five, your daughter should be bathing herself so parental touching should be unnecessary. You might have to explain about doctors too, but even the doctor should explain what s/he's doing and Mommy or Daddy should be in the room.

I hope that helps.

Joan

Age Differences

Hi Joan,

I'm a thirty-five-year-old woman and I have met a wonderful man who's fifty-one. Initially I was resistant to the thought of developing a relationship—not due to the age difference, but because I was being careful after two bad marriages. He was all for establishing a relationship. After several months of getting to know him and becoming closer, I have definitely changed my mind and would love nothing more than for this to progress into something more serious. We have similar values, likes, and a lot in common. We are both unattached, and both of us have been divorced for many years.

Here's the problem. Just when I have finally decided to relax and let things happen, he's become resistant to a possible relationship, explaining that the age difference is too large and would eventually pose a problem. I'm pretty sure that he's planning to end it.

We both have great careers and financial security and we seem very compatible. Love is hard enough to find, and I wouldn't want to give up this possibility without even attempting to see if it could work. The age thing is not an issue for me. What do you think?

MaryRose

Dear MaryRose,

I agree with you that, at your stage of life, the age difference isn't a major hurdle, and if you two want to, it can be overcome when everything else is wonderful. However, that's not really the problem now. Unfortunately, the person who's less interested in continuing the relationship is the one in control, and thus he's the one who's able to call the shots. Whether it's the age difference or something else entirely, he wants out, and that's that. I'm sorry to say it that harshly, but it's so.

You can discuss it with him, of course, but it's not going to do much good, I'm afraid. If you want some ammunition, here are a few letters from folks who've made such relationships work.

Dear Joan,

Older men, from my experience, are more giving and much less selfish than younger men. I am a thirty-year-old woman who is married to a fifty-three-year-old man. We met when I was twenty-four and we were married a year later. I can honestly say that I have never had a more fulfilling relationship in my entire life.

I was married the first time right out of high school to a guy just my age and that one lasted only a few years. So, as you can see, I have some experience with men my own age. When I met my current husband I was recently separated and not looking for another long-term commitment. But meeting him was the best thing that could have happened to me. He has been my encourager, my confidant, my best friend, and the most wonderful lover I have ever known. While making love he is giving and so tuned in to my desires.

He has encouraged my fantasies and even made some of them reality. Most important, he has fulfilled my need to feel loved for exactly who I am. Completely and totally loved. I have no doubts that I did the right thing at age twenty-five when I said "I do." Despite what everyone may think, romances like ours really DO work.

Cindy

Dear Joan,

I am a fifty-six-year-old man and I'm currently dating a woman who's not quite thirty. I was married for many years, but for various reasons the marriage ended about five years ago. It was difficult to get back into the dating life, but I wanted female companionship, so I eventually started seeing women. You'd be amazed at how difficult it was for me to establish a relationship with someone close to my age. In my searching I could not find a mature woman who was looking for the same things I was.

Anyway, I eventually found a younger woman, and became very friendly with her. Almost immediately we became really close. We talked on the phone for hours just about ourselves and how our lives would be affected by our age difference.

At the time, age was no problem. We dated, went to dinners, movies, etc. It was difficult for both of us because people thought she was my daughter instead of my date, but we got used to it. It took us quite a while to get past the age thing, at least in long-term planning, but eventually we did. Just let me say that we're getting married in two months and we can't wait. Yes, it can work.

I know my story is probably unusual. Some things work for some people and not others. I guess what I'm trying to say is that a relationship will work, or it won't, but don't put artificial barriers in the way. There are enough problems without that.
Vick

MaryRose, I think Vick put it as well as I could. Take care and do what feels right.
Joan

Dear Joan,

When I was thirty-three years old, I fell in love with a wonderful man who was then fifty-five. We married soon after and all went great and we had lots of fun together. As I approached forty, however, I realized that I wanted a child. I had never had children, but my husband had been divorced and had a grown son and a daughter in college. He didn't want to start a family all over again. We discussed and argued, but he prevailed and we didn't have any children.

During the following years of our marriage, the age-difference problems increased. Bob slowed down, both physically and sexually, while I was still growing and doing more. Sexually, I wanted more and more, whereas he wanted less and less.

Now, at the age of sixty-one, I still feel young, alive, and sexual. I want to do things and go places. My husband, however, although he is relatively healthy at the age of eighty-three, feels old and acts old. All he wants to do is sit by the fireplace and do nothing. He has little interest in sex. Although I still love him, I am more of a nurse to him than a wife. Mostly I regret that we never had a chance to grow, explore, learn, and develop together the way same-age couples do.

I am sure that some couples can overcome large age differences, but if they think it will be easy they are just kidding themselves. No matter how much they love each other, the odds are stacked heavily against them.

Lisa

Dear Lisa,

You've had almost thirty years together, most of the time loving and enjoying each other. I know that the age difference has contributed to some of your current problems, but you seem to spend a great deal of time focusing on the negative, rather than on the wonderful years you've shared. Are relationships that involve large age differences difficult? Of course. Those disparate years provide a hurdle to be overcome, and the bar is raised when other problems appear. However, relationships in which religious, racial, or background differences are large face similar problems. Some work, others don't. Isn't that true of all relationships these days?

You might want to go places with friends, rather than resenting your husband for not wanting to go out. I never advise anyone to

depend on their partner for all social activities. When two people marry they still should maintain their own interests, hobbies, and talents. Invite a girlfriend to the museum, the theater, or to a movie. Take a vacation with a tour group and let your husband stay home. It's not necessary or even desirable to count on him for all your activities. You two can still share quiet evenings at home, and you'll treasure them even more for their singular and special nature.
Joan

Dear Joan,
Why is it that when an older man dates and forms an attachment for a younger woman, no one bats an eyelash, but when an older woman hooks up with a younger man, everyone makes a big fuss. I'm a forty-year-old woman who's interested in a man who's only twenty-six. We enjoy each other's company and have so much in common it's spooky. All my friends snicker behind my back, saying I'm just keeping him around as a stud, my boy-toy. I don't see the age difference as a problem. Am I just fooling myself?
Frannie

Dear Frannie,
No, you aren't fooling yourself. It's an amazing society we live in, where, as you point out, people make value judgments in situations about which they know nothing. Do what you feel is right, and if your friends don't like it, maybe they aren't really your friends. Relationships like yours can and do work. Like any other relationship, there are no guarantees. That's life, after all.

For example:

Dear Joan,
I'm a thirty-two-year-old guy and my girlfriend just turned forty-four. We've got the most amazing love affair going. In addition to all the other things we share, she is the only woman I have found who has the same interest in sex as I do. So, if anyone asks about age differences in dating and even marriage, I highly

recommend it. There are many girls in the world, but once you have been with a woman, you'll never look back! The passion and intensity of the sex is amazing. So is the rest of the relationship. If you get a chance . . . GO FOR IT!
Noel

Dear Joan,
I know you're interested in older woman/younger man relationships. I guess I'm one of the strongest advocates for saying "To hell with age." My husband is twenty-eight and I'm forty-three. We met six years ago and were married four months later. I don't mean to say we haven't had our share of differences, like everyone else I'm sure, but we manage to do okay and it has never been the age thing that has caused any of our minor problems. There are few men to whom a woman can relate, and it would be a shame to eliminate large segments of the population just because of their birthdate.
Dawn

Frannie, I know anecdotal information isn't necessarily the best way to analyze a problem, but I thought you'd like to know that others have made it work. Good luck to you, and I wish you all the happiness in the world.
Joan

Sex in Later Years

Dear Joan Lloyd,
Just for starters, let me say that I am an active, healthy, eighty-two-year-old male, who is having an exotic, erotic relationship with a young lady of fifty-nine! It might come as a surprise to many, but we have a very active sex life together, she being multiorgasmic and my being able to satisfy her fully through oral and genital sex. Her climaxes build from one event to the next, until she becomes semi-

conscious and her eyes roll back in her head. I have to stop and allow her to recover!

We met on the Internet. I was looking for a relationship, because my wife had passed away two years earlier. My new lady had been in a sexless marriage until her divorce four years before we met.

We both advertised on the same website, filled out questionnaires, exchanged information, and began e-mail conversations since we lived on opposite sides of the country. That was in mid-February of 2000, bless the millennium. Our relationship quickly grew closer, and in mid-April, she came to visit me for a week. It was fantastic to be able to share, in person, all the things we had in common, not to mention great sex. The week flew by, and we parted, with my arranging to spend ten days with her in late May.

To make a long story short, we're visiting back and forth, alternating staying on her side of the country and on mine, for a month or more at a time. Life couldn't be any better for either of us. We've been talking about selling one of our houses and moving in together permanently.

So don't tell us that "old" men can't "get it up." My penis wakes up most mornings at around six o'clock, ready and willing to venture forth into uncharted territory! We are sure that he will continue his forays for much enjoyment to come!
Zack

Dear Zack,
All I can say is bravo!!! Long may you continue to enjoy everything life has to offer. I think I'll make you my poster child for great sex at any age.
Joan

Dear Joan,
At what age should a person stop having sex? I'm seventy-three and I was just wondering.
Nick

Dear Nick,

As long as your doctor hasn't limited your activity due to a medical problem, sex is great at any age. I intend to keep loving Ed until we die having mutual orgasm in our room at the home for rowdy centigenerians.

Let me get slightly more serious for a moment. Since I guess I'm now a senior citizen, or rapidly approaching my "golden years," I am able to talk about sex and aging. In case you can't hear my growling, I hate the term "golden years" about as much as I hate the idea that I'll soon be sixty "years young." As you point out, us old folks (evil grin) enjoy sex just as much as younger people and we're proud of it. So there! I have better sex now than I ever did, and much of that is due to all the things I've learned in all those previous years. I experimented, as I still do, and learned the joys of all forms of great (and not so great) sex.

Okay, I'll climb off my soap box now.

There's so much good news about sex for those of us over forty or fifty or seventy. The kids are gone!!! Those of us who are fortunate have space and privacy, neither of which have we had since our dating years—and maybe not even then. If we want to turn that extra bedroom into a soundproof playroom, we can, and no one will be the wiser unless we want them to be. And perhaps we have a bit of extra money with which to put a hot tub in that refurbished bedroom.

However, there are problems associated with aging, and the first is perception. Our children often treat us as though our sex lives are over, or at least dwindling. The fire's pretty much out, they think. And frequently we begin to believe it. Well, hogwash to that. Recently a major senior residence just outside of New York City issued a Residents' Bill of Rights, which included a clause that permits (and even encourages) dating and consensual nocturnal visits between members of opposite sexes—or the same sex if desired.

I guess this attitude is typified by this letter I received.

Dear Joan,

Whoa, I could not believe the number of men and women over forty who sent you their remarks or opinions on oral sex and other sexual issues. I guess that as a twenty-something, married several years, I assumed that when you hit forty you only had plain old intercourse. I never really thought about it, and the picture in my mind was my grandparents. I almost laughed. But seriously though, you opened my eyes, and I hope I am still doing it then when I am a few decades older!!

Jenny

I wrote back,

Dear Jenny,

Over forty? I get wonderful letters from folks who enjoy my stories, books, and opinions who are in their seventies and eighties. They are still going strong, and I plan to be too when I'm several decades older.

Joan

So, Nick, as long as you're in reasonable health, go for it!!

Joan

Age and Lubrication

Dear Joan,

I'm a woman in my late fifties and I'm having trouble with intercourse. I don't seem to lubricate as I once did, and sometimes intercourse with my husband is painful. Is this normal, and what can I do about it?

Harriet

Dear Harriet,

If you're like me you associate feeling slippery with being excited.

When I first noticed the problem, at about fifty, I felt that I wasn't getting as excited as I used to. Actually, that wasn't true. It was just my body responding to the natural changes taking place, but it took me quite a while to get my sexual cues back in sync.

Changes in lubrication are normal. As a woman progresses through menopause, her hormone levels decrease and some of the things she used to take for granted slow down. Lubrication is only one. Many visit their doctor and decide to go on hormone replacement therapy and the lubrication problem usually disappears. You might discuss this with your gynecologist.

If you choose not to ask, or not to go on hormone replacement therapy, an external lubricant will solve the problem easily. Try K-Y Jelly or Astroglide, both available at your local drug or discount store, or find something from an adult catalog or website.

If you can't find a water-based lubricant, don't use baby oil, Vaseline, or another petroleum-based product. As I mention in the section on lubrication, they will eat through condoms and allow disease organisms to pass. In addition, when they get into the vaginal canal, they adhere to the walls and make a delightful breeding ground for nasty bacteria. So check the label.

Once you've found a product you like, use it generously. You can even incorporate it into your sex play as Ed and I do. A good lubricant feels wonderful, smooth, cool, and really sexy, on both of you.
Joan

Sex, Age, and Erections

Dear Joan,

My husband is sixty-seven and recently he has begun having trouble in bed. He can't seem to get an erection, so we don't have intercourse anymore. He's very affectionate and tries to help me toward orgasm as best as he can, but I feel we're losing an important part of our relationship. We've been married for almost forty

years and maybe it's time to give up sex, but I don't really want to. Can you help?
Marie

Dear Marie,
Don't give up on sex. It's the best thing going—nonfattening, legal, and moral. And it's just plain fun. There's no reason to do without a good sexual relationship just because of age. Folks of any age have a right to great sex.

Okay, so what to do to improve things. First, ask your husband to get a thorough medical checkup. There are dozens of conditions and lots of medications that have the side effect of reducing either the desire or the ability to have intercourse. Diabetes, blood pressure medication, prostate problems, and many more can result in bedroom difficulties. So rule these out first. If your internist can't help you, find either a urologist or a geriatrician and keep at it until you get satisfactory answers.

If your husband is taking blood pressure medication, your doctor might be able to adjust the dosage or switch medications entirely so that erections are possible. Don't be ashamed to make this a priority. Doctors are finally understanding that fixing the blood pressure problem only to cause a sexual one isn't necessarily the best answer for overall good health.

Another step is trying sex in the morning. Testosterone levels are higher then and many men find early-morning erections more possible than late-night ones. See how that works. If it doesn't, there are more possibilities.

Let me speak about one I don't necessarily recommend. There are dozens of herbal supplements "guaranteed" to increase sexual desire and improve sexual function. They advertise in magazines, on infomercials, and on late-night radio. Being a bit of an insomniac, I hear them night after night, touting their ability to turn a man into a horny teenager again. Let's understand these claims. The FDA must test and approve all medications, both over-the-counter ones and those available by prescription. However, and this is a big however, they have no jurisdiction over herbs. Therefore, all these claims are unsubstantiated, untested, and unproven.

Okay, we've all heard the testimonials. "I had sexual problems and I took Brand X for three weeks and now my wife and I are happier than we've been in years." Fine. Brand X worked for him. Is that proof? Not at all. It's an anecdote. And of course Brand X isn't going to broadcast testimonials from folks who've had no results from the product at all and especially form those who had problems.

So what do the testimonials and claims prove? Not much. Might it work? Sure. It might help your body, and, more importantly, it might help your mind. Much of our sexual function is between the ears, not between the legs. If you and/or your husband believe it will work, it just might, and hooray for that. Who cares why anything works, as long as it does?

If you decide to try one of these products, check carefully to be sure that any herb taken doesn't interfere with any other medications your husband is using. Read the label and any accompanying literature, do a bit of research, and ask your doctor and your pharmacist. Then, if you want to give something a try, go for it.

There are many physical devices that can help with this problem too. There are appliances that can be implanted to artificially, yet deliciously, enable the penis to simulate an erection. Pumps and mechanical contraptions can make lovemaking possible, even wonderful again. If this is something that sounds like it would work for you, again, consult a physician.

Of course, now there's Viagra. Although this book doesn't pretend to be a scientific treatise on sexuality, let me take a moment to get serious about Viagra. First, sildenafil (the technical name for Viagra) is a medication that is designed for men with erectile dysfunction—sexual impotence. It is NOT an aphrodisiac. It doesn't change the libido, it merely makes sex possible by helping to maintain the erection that occurs when the penis is stroked.

Viagra is available only with a doctor's prescription. Okay, I hear you now. "I can get it on the Web without seeing a doctor." Not a good idea. There are several medical problems that make taking Viagra unwise. There are also other risks associated with Viagra, including interactions with other medications (specifically, but not limited to, many heart medications), possible allergic reactions, and side effects, all of which need to be considered. All these factors need to be evaluated by a physician before deciding that Viagra may help you. Dosages must be decided on, and a follow-up visit is recommended to evaluate the success of the medication.

There are also scam artists on the Web who will take your money and send you diluted doses or sugar pills, hoping that you notice a change just due to the fact that you believe it will help. Some will take your money and send nothing. So sit on your wallet, send nothing, and see your physician.

Does Viagra work? You bet.

Dear Ms. Lloyd,

I have been on various blood pressure medications for many years and have had all the problems with related impotence. Now Viagra has liberated my wife and me. We've been married for forty years, and until several years ago we had lots of good, fulfilling sex. Three years ago, when the need for blood pressure medications started to interfere with our sex life, things got so tense that I finally discussed the problem with my doctor. He told me that the problem was permanent and that was that. Well, my beautiful, understanding wife accepted it and we adjusted. We tried lots of things, but finally we resorted to lots of oral sex for her and some frustration for me.

Then came Viagra! I heard all the hype, so on my next doctor visit, we talked and he recommended that I give it a try. I'm not erect like a teenager, but we're getting the job done and she's experiencing multiple orgasms just like old times. By the way, she's sixty-seven and I'm seventy!!

VIVA VIAGRA!!!!

Milt

Dear Joan,

I'm nearly sixty-five. About three years ago, I had some repair work done on my prostate, and shortly thereafter began to have trouble maintaining an erection. When Viagra first came out my doctor was not quick to prescribe it. She was worried about adverse reactions, but when nothing surfaced in the literature, she finally gave me a trial prescription of seven 25 mg pills, so I could try 25, 50, and 100 mg doses. I recommend this step. No point taking more of any drug than you need.

I found that 50 mg was right for me. At 100 mg, the erection was prolonged for an uncomfortable period. Anyone who thinks this drug will "put lead in your pencil" is mistaken. It does exactly what the technical reports say: it prevents the collapse of a normal but short-lived erection. That's no small matter. It makes the difference between intercourse and mutual frustration.

With all the jokes about Viagra, someone needs to say the obvious. Marriage is filled with tensions. They diminish in importance when you can express your love through sex. Talk goes only so far.

Jake

Dear Joan,

I am in my mid-seventies and had erection problems for about five years. My wife sort of gave up on sex and so we stopped trying. Sometimes I could get an erection and it would last for a long time if I stroked myself slowly. However, when I wanted to ejaculate, my penis would go limp. Very frustrating.

Last month I went to my doctor and he prescribed Viagra. Two days later, when I was alone at home, I played with myself for a wonderful hour before I finally let go. Well, last week I finally attempted to get my wife interested. We were both surprised, she by the fact that I could, me by the fact that she would. Well, we did. Life is great. Thank you, Viagra.

Mark

Dear Joan,

I thought I'd write and hopefully help some of your visitors who might want to try Viagra. I find it appalling to see the depth of ignorance one must deal with when talking to doctors these days. They just don't seem to have the time or the commitment to do their homework. One doctor told a friend of mine to be sure to wait four hours after taking Viagra before initiating intercourse. My friend was really upset because it seemed that the Viagra wasn't working for him.

We did some research together, visiting the Pfizer website at www.pfizer.com and at www.viagra.com. We also read some magazine and newspaper articles, as well as articles on many websites. We discovered that, actually, the drug should be wearing off after four hours, though I read that some people find that they benefit from Viagra much longer. Pfizer recommends waiting one hour, but says anywhere from half an hour to four hours will work. My friend was really saddened at the time he had wasted, not to mention the money. Now, with the proper waiting period, Viagra works well for him.

Patrick

So, Marie, there's so much more you can do now than there was ten years ago that it's a shame to let your situation continue. Remember, it's just as much your problem as it is your husband's, so bring the subject up and have a serious discussion, first with your husband, then with his doctor.

Joan

Dear Joan,

I read that I can't take Viagra if I'm taking blood pressure medication. Is that true? Does that mean no more sex for me?

Walt

Dear Walt,

Check with your doctor. From what I've read, there are cardiac medications that don't go well with Viagra, but others are all right. Only your doctor can properly prescribe for the particular combination of other medications you are taking. Please don't take any layperson's word for any prescription medicine. Consult your doctor! He or she may well be able to prescribe Viagra without adjusting your current regimen, or change your other medications to make Viagra possible. You might be denying yourself good sex for nothing.

Joan

Dear Joan,

My doctor has recommended a 50 mg dose of Viagra for me. He suggested that I get the 100 mg pills and split them. I worry. It would be much cheaper if I did this, of course, but is it okay?

Manny

Dear Manny,

If your doctor advises it, sure. Why not? I know that many insurance companies are, if not actually recommending it, turning a blind eye to pill splitting. Half of a 100 mg tablet is, in fact, 50 mg, and can cost quite a bit less.

Joan

Women and Viagra

Dear Joan,

I thought I would give you some information about Viagra from a woman's side.

I have been married to a wonderful man for thirty years. The last several years have been extremely emotionally difficult to me. I really enjoy sex, but felt that my husband had lost interest in me that way. He would get an erection and then lose it upon insertion. It made me feel like I was a turnoff to him. I felt that his impotence problem was somehow my fault. I thought of divorce several times during those years because I felt that I must be unattractive to him.

Other men would notice me and flirt with me, making it difficult for me to understand why the only man I really wanted to touch me, my husband, did not want to have any sex with me.

Anyway, several months ago my husband got Viagra. When he first told me about the magic pill I was excited about the possibility of again having sex with him. I was even more excited because he *wanted* to have sex with me. That was so very important to me.

Well, the magic pill worked, and now things are tremendously better at our house. My husband has more confidence and is much more comfortable about lovemaking. And what a treat for me. It's done wonders for my feelings about myself. I know the way I felt was wrong, but I felt what I felt. Now things are wonderful.
Loreen

Dear Joan,
First, let me tell you that I'm a sixty-four-year-old woman and I have been taking an antidepressant for about two and a half years. Sadly, it has had a really depressing effect on my sex life. Over the last eighteen months I have been having more and more trouble reaching an orgasm.

Women will know what I mean when I say I would get right to the edge and then not come. This is more than frustrating, and it left me physically shaking and crying. It was so terrible. Obviously this made me less than eager for sex. My wonderful husband tried everything we could think of but nothing helped.

Then came my semiannual visit to my doctor. It was difficult discussing my sex life with a man, especially at my age, but I was miserable enough to try. He told me that there had been some success treating women with sexual dysfunction that results from antidepressants with Viagra. I wasn't terribly thrilled to join the latest drug fad, but I did agree to give it a try.

Well, let me assure you that IT WORKS! I tried it the first time without a lot of hope, but it was just like having normal arousal again, except a lot faster and easier. I had always taken a long time to warm up and come, but with the Viagra it was easy. Physically it made me much more swollen and wet, more like I was when I was younger.

So women, talk to your doctors. There is no reason not to enjoy sex again.

My insurance denied my coverage on the basis of my sex. According to them, Viagra is only for men. I'm going to have a lot of fun fighting with them about this. I will let you know how it turns out. I hope this helps some women out there.
MaryLou

Dear MaryLou,
Keep fighting and I'm delighted that you've had such wonderful effects from Viagra. I didn't know it worked with women but I will be sure to share the information.
Joan

Dear Joan,
I just wanted to put in a word for consideration when a man uses Viagra.

Viagra does wonders for men who have health problems causing erectile dysfunction (ED). It can bring a marriage back to life. However, there has been no discussion of the effects on women when a man's ED is treated with Viagra.

The sensitive timing that long-time partners are used to can be disrupted because the drug doesn't care whether there is a partner at all. It just produces an erection, now, whether or not the partner is ready. The woman can be unprepared, unlubricated, not thoroughly aroused. So no matter how much she loves her partner there can be a physical sense of pain, burning, assault. My husband and I had this problem until we had a long, serious talk.

So men, please be sure you're not so wrapped up in the joy of "getting it up" that you forget about your partner. Remember how,

in your youth, women needed time to get ready even though junior was pushing out the front of your pants? Remember how you took the time to warm her up? Don't forget that!!
Kelly

Dear Kelly,
I've not heard this issue put in such straightforward terms. Thanks so much for setting us all straight.
Joan

Before
Doing It

Chapter
3

On Kissing

Dear Joan,

I'm a guy in my early twenties and I guess I'm not a good kisser. The women I date don't seem too impressed with my ability in that area. This is really difficult for me to admit, but maybe I could use some help. Can you tell me what makes a guy a good kisser? What should I do?

Tom from West Virginia

Dear Tom,

If a man's a good kisser, he's well on his way to being a superior lover. Many men view kissing as just a way to get further, a minor stopover on the path to bed. Nothing could be further from a woman's mind. Kissing is lovemaking. It's a joining of spirits, a beginning. So if while you're kissing you're only thinking about where to fondle next or how to get her into the bedroom, you're on the wrong track.

There are lots of different aspects to kissing, but here are a few suggestions that might help. Most important, you need to concentrate on your partner. Make her warmth and softness your entire focus. Touch her face, look deeply into her eyes. That may sound corny, but it's really what most women are looking, hungering for. Take time with kissing. Savor. Taste. Don't just aim for her mouth; kiss her eyes, her cheeks, her neck. Whisper sexy words while you kiss. Tell her she's sexy, that she has great eyes or a wonderfully kissable mouth. Tell her that she makes you hungry. Hold her, caress her back, thread your fingers through her hair.

I've gotten lots of letters from people on what they believe makes a good kisser, so I thought I'd copy a few here for you. The first two are from women.

Dear Joan,
I've been thinking a lot about kissing, and I thought I'd write to you. I'm a twenty-eighty-year-old woman and I think that a kiss reveals more about a man than anything that he says to you. I've had many kisses from many men, of all different sizes, shapes, and colors, and I know what I like, and what I don't like.

For me, a kiss begins well before his mouth even touches mine. It begins in his eyes, when he looks into mine. My lover has way of looking at me when he wants to kiss me that makes me feel like I'm the most desirable woman in the world. He has a way of holding my gaze that makes me know he's thinking only of me.

When he touches his lips to mine, he is gentle, sometimes just barely brushing my mouth at first. A really dynamite kiss from him can curl my toes. He explores my mouth in a way that is so sensual, so soft, as though kissing me is the only thing that matters. His kisses are not too wet and he doesn't drive his tongue into my mouth. So many men think that a French kiss means "Let's see how far down your throat I can push my tongue."

My lover uses his tongue more subtly, a gentle teasing to

part my lips; then he gives lingering little nibbles with his lips all over my open mouth. He slowly slips his tongue just far enough into my mouth to taste my tongue, then he withdraws so that he keeps working his magic on my lips. His kisses leave me dizzy and weak in the knees, as a lover's kiss should.

I've been kissed by many men, men who left my mouth feeling like I'd been kissed by the family dog and needed to go find a towel to dry my face, men who did their level best to re-arrange my dental work, and men who had mouths like vacuum cleaners, trying to pull my teeth out of my mouth. A kiss should be a slow heating, like building a fire; you start with small kin-dling, and add to it, blowing gently to make the coals glow bright. Before you know it, it bursts into a crackling-hot blaze.

I know I sound like a romance novel, and until I met my lover I thought that type of sensual kissing existed only in the minds of writers. I'm so happy I was wrong.
Mary Ellen

Dear Joan,
I'm a forty-seven-year-old female and I thought I'd write regard-ing the question of how a woman likes to be kissed. I don't think there is one specific way to kiss. I really love to kiss and be kissed, and I know how a bad kiss can totally ruin any mood.

I think the secret to being a good kisser is to adjust to what the person you are kissing seems to respond to. Some people like deep, wet kisses, and others find it more appealing to have lots and lots of soft sensuous kisses. Personally, I am a fan of both and adjust to my partner accordingly. Every kiss and kisser seems to have its own distinct "personality." It just depends on the mood.

So, I guess I don't feel one style of kiss has anything over another, they can all be good at one time or another, with one woman or another. That doesn't mean, however, that good, re-sponsive kissing isn't HUGELY important. Overall, a good sensu-ous kiss is underrated as far as I am concerned. If the kiss doesn't click with someone in a short time, I'd bet that nothing else will either.

Cherrie

And, Tom, here are two from men on the same subject.

Dear Joan Elizabeth Lloyd,

I'm writing about kissing from a man's point of view, although I don't think that there is that much difference in what the two sexes would find sensual.

I can remember the first time I kissed a girl, so many years ago. I sucked her lips like a vacuum cleaner. No wonder I never got a second chance with her. Eventually I came to regard kissing as one of the most intimate experiences: the scent of the woman, the soft sounds from deep in her throat, the warmth of her breath shared through our nostrils, the feel of her lips parting against mine. As the kiss deepens and her mouth merges with mine, our tongues touch, and our saliva mingles. It really is oral sex, and kisses like that don't happen on the first date (not in my life, anyway). Rather, they take time and trust.

First-date kisses, for me, involve bringing her fingers up to my lips for a lingering touch, perhaps followed by a close-in hug and soft lip to lip contact. I usually let the woman decide when she is ready to move on to openmouthed kissing, and deep tongue-in-mouth kissing, which I have found associated with readiness for, or during engagement in, intercourse.

Being a good kisser is so important, and I believe, in all modesty, that this is why I never seem to have any trouble getting more dates.

Barry

Dear Ms. Lloyd,

Re: kissing. I'm a fifty-eight-year-old man, and a few years ago I reentered the dating game. It's really been a whole new experience for me, and I've met a lot of wonderful, sexy ladies. Many of them tell me I'm a fabulous kisser.

There are many techniques, but to me the most important ingredient is the mood. What are you trying to convey? To create? If you want her to know that you have a searing, primal need to fuck her like an animal, press hard, be demanding (but remember: teeth knocking against teeth is painful, not sexy). Devour her entire mouth and taste it forcefully with your tongue. Insinuate your tongue into her mouth, along the inside of her lips, lap at her tongue, draw it into your mouth and suck it. Simulating copulation with your tongue can be good, if it's not too fast and mechanical.

If your passion is more of a slow burn, hold back a bit, draw it out. Taste every part of the mouth you are kissing: each lip and the corners. Draw each lip slowly into your mouth and suck on it, as you would her clit. Use your tongue to make slow, tantalizing licks along the outside of her closed lips. Kisses along the jaw line, especially near the ear, usually give her delightful shivers, as does suckling the earlobes and behind them. The nape of the neck, and the spot where the neck joins the shoulder, are also very sensitive.

When tongues touch, slow down and pay attention to technique. A wet tongue simply pistoning in and out of her mouth at breakneck speed is not inherently sexy. Circle each other, play along one side, then the other. Overall, let the mood of your encounter be your guide. Remember, people often kiss you the way they want to be kissed, so pay close attention and reciprocate. Too much spit, speed, or clumsiness can be a turnoff.
Gabe

Tom, I think you've got the idea. Go slowly and concentrate on your partner. One last idea. Most romance novels are written by women, for women. The kisses in them are pretty good models. Pick up a paperback at your local bookstore or library and open to any page from about seventy onward. You'll learn even more about how a woman wants to be kissed.
Joan

Dear Joan,

My boyfriend is a pretty good kisser, but he's got an enormous moustache that gets in the way. I often get a mouthful of fur rather than a taste of him. Can I tell him?

Peggy

Dear Peggy,

Most certainly you can, and should, tell him, but as with any other serious comment about sex in any form, be sure to couch your comments in a positive way. For example, "I love the way you kiss me and I love the way you taste. It would make it even nicer if you could trim just a little of your moustache so I could better enjoy you." You might ask him, at the same time, whether there's anything you can do to make kissing better for him.

And if he's not receptive, maybe he's not the kind of guy who cares as much for you as for himself.

Joan

Music to Make Love To

Dear Joan,

I want to play some romantic music while my wife and I make love. I have a few of my own ideas, but I'd like to know what you think. Also, is there a particular collection of music guaranteed to get her really hot? I've heard that there is one that ends with Ravel's *Bolero*. Is that true?

Thanks for helping.

Mark

Dear Mark,

I too have heard about particular music "guaranteed" to seduce but I've never met anyone who actually knows anything. Of course, if you listen to Ravel's *Bolero*, you can certainly understand why that would have been the culmination. The increasing rhythm seems to get into the bloodstream and heat everything up.

Remember that I'm fifty-nine now, so my personal choices are from my era. For me "Could It Be Magic" by Barry Manilow is an orgasm set to music. The repeated "'Come, Come, Come into my arms" is more than suggestive. It's an invitation to climax. I also love anything by Barry Manilow, Johnny Mathis, or Frank Sinatra, and the great songs of the fifties and sixties.

There's another way to answer this question. The sexiest music is the music that speaks to you, maybe the music you were listening to when you first met, first danced together, or, of course, first made love. Ed and I still enjoy listening to Grieg's first piano concerto, the music that was playing the first time we made love. Like most other things having to do with lovemaking, it's really personal.

I posted this question on my website and got lots of suggestions of songs or albums from my visitors. Here are a few, in no particular order. I'm sure you'll see how diverse music selections can be.

Chambers Brothers, "In the Midnight Hour," an orgasm in sound
Bob Seger, "We've Got Tonight"
Sting, "Fields of Gold"
Sarah McLachlan, "Possession" (the piano version) and "Touch"
Pretenders, "Love Me from the Heart Down"
Peter Gabriel, "In Your Eyes," "Passion"
Lisa Gerrard and Pieter Bourke, "Duality." It is AWESOME.
Prince, "When Doves Cry"
Miles Davis, *Tutu* and *In a Silent Way*
Yo-Yo Ma, *Soul of the Tango*
Enigma
The Church—anything by the moody pre-Goth Aussie band will do, especially their recent CD, *Hologram of Baal*
Loreena McKennitt's *The Mask and the Mirror* helps me get in the mood

Metallica, *Ride the Lightning*
Slayer, *Reign in Blood*
Iron Maiden, *Powerslave*

And here are a few letters with more details.

Dear Joan,
I'm writing about the music to make love to. One of my favorite CDs is *Deep Woods Deepwaters* by Douglas Wood. It's sounds of water and animals, like a night under the stars. It has the sounds of nature, including the sound of the lake waves, loons, thunder, rain, and birds. It's relaxing and wonderful at the end of a stressful day. My husband and I also like *Healing Waters* by Dean Evenson. It has the sounds of flutes, a dreamy guitar, flowing rivers, and ocean waves. It's wonderful. Check them out.
Kerry from California

Joan,
Some personal favorites to get and stay in the mood are: Enigma, *MCMXC* CD, Massive Attack, *Blue Lines* CD (LOVE it), Annie Lennox's *Medusa* CD, particularly "Downtown Lights" and her super sexy version of Al Green's "Take Me to the River." By the way, Joan, in the brilliant film *American Beauty*, the director had the great taste to include one of the songs from the *Medusa* CD during the scene near the end with Lester and the teenage girl.
Carla

Dear Joan,
My wife and I love to make love to Dire Straits, or Pink Floyd, *Dark Side of the Moon*. We also have several CDs of the sounds of nature, such as waves breaking on a beach, thunderstorms, birdsong in the woods, etc. These are especially good as background to a massage and lovemaking. Last but not least is Pachelbel's *Canon*, maybe not for the rhythm, but to me it is

easily one of the most beautiful pieces of music ever written. Include it in a sensuous compilation.

Derreck

Hello Joan,

The *Visions of Love* album by Jim Brickman. Our song is "The Gift." My lover and I live in different states, and on our anniversary each year I try to get a local radio station to dedicate the song to him. If you want a CD of love songs, this is the one to get!

Diana

Hi there,

I've found a variety of songs that work great during lovemaking. Believe it or not, *Pure Moods* and *Instrumental Moods* (you know, the ones that are "not sold in stores" but you can find them at any K-mart) are really good. I'm also a fan of Kitaro. His *An Enchanted Evening* CD is excellent. The best tracks are three and four, "The Dance of Sarasvati" and "Silk Road." I also like *Learning to Fly* by Pink Floyd.

Frank

Joan,

Concerning music for lovemaking, my wife and I enjoy an oldie called "Never on Sunday" from a movie by the same name about a prostitute who abstained on Sundays. It's great music for mutual masturbation or coitus. It has the bump and grind beat of striptease, the steady beat to stroke to, and a crescendo every fourth bar to cum to. My wife and I play games to the beat, wondering whether we can time our lovemaking to the rhythm. Now when I hear "Never on Sunday" on the radio, I get an erection and think, We need to do that tonight!

Lou

Joan,

By far Bryan Ferry's *Avalon* album is the absolute best music to make love to. I also suggest Gal Costa, the amazing Brazilian songstress. I think the Portuguese language is the sexiest. I can't understand a word of it, but my clothes just seem to want to fall when I hear it.

Jayne

Hi Joan,

I have always thought that Portuguese in general and Brazilian music in particular is very sensual. My favorite is Antonio Carlos Jobim's original album with Stan Getz on Sax and Astrud Gilberto on vocals.

Otto

So you see, Mark, it's all so subjective. Find out what she enjoys and you've got it.

Joan

Dear Joan,

I know you talk a lot about music to make love to, but don't forget that it can be really sexy to read erotica aloud to get in the mood. It all started when my wife read me a section from your erotic novel *Midnight Butterfly*. It really got me hot and the sex we had was fantastic. Now sometimes she reads to me, and sometimes I read to her, and it's great. We've branched out into short stories, some from books like *Bedtime Stories for Lovers* and some from websites. I'll admit it, I love your writing. Anyway, now I preread a story and that's good for one night's fun, then I read to her on another evening. It's really hot!!!

Davy

Dear Davy,

Bravo for finding something so delicious. There is so much good erotica out there of all styles and types. Many large bookstores have

now set aside a section for erotica and you can let your fingers and pocketbook do the walking. Also check the short story section for more collections.
Joan

Dear Joan,
I've always been curious about X-rated films. I've rented a few and they were terrible, just lots of come shots and no story. Is there anything good out there?
Helaine

Dear Helaine,
Yes, there are a few good films you might try. I love the softness and realism of the movies produced by Candida Royalle's Femme Productions; try *Three Daughters, Urban Heat,* or *Christine's Secret.* I also enjoy Marilyn Chambers's films, including *Up and Coming, Insatiable,* and *New York Nights. Playboy* has a huge selection of videos that are slightly softer core and feature lots of naked women. Their Fantasies series is particularly good. So just rent and click the stop button whenever you like. And when you find something good, try others by the same company.
Joan

Foreplay and Breasts

Dear Joan,
Okay, I'll admit it. I'm a twenty-three-year-old guy and I'm not too good at the buildup before sex. Sure, I put on some soft music, I even light candles and pour wine. I've seen that in movies. But when it comes right down to it, it's the next step I'm not really too good at. I don't know where to put my hands when I'm kissing her. I don't know when to touch her breasts or go further.

Can you help?
Joey

Dear Joey,

You're talking about foreplay, and like so many other aspects of love-making, it varies from man to man and woman to woman. Here is the best advice I can give you. Guide yourself by her needs and desires. Almost everyone has radar, that instinct that lets you know when things are going well and when you're on the wrong track. You've honed this instinct since you were two and knew when to push your mother and when to leave her alone. Well, use those skills.

Where to put your hands? Put them on her body, softly at first. Begin with areas that are uncovered when her clothes are on. Touch her neck, her face, her hands. Stroke her arms. Smooth your hands over what's covered by her blouse, leaving her breasts for last. Stroke her shoulders, slide your hands up and down her back and over her sides. Guide yourself by whether she's moving closer or pulling back. When she purrs or moans, do more of that. When she draws away, move your hands somewhere else, but most of all be gentle. Caress, don't grab.

Blowing in her ear has gotten to be such a cliché, but that's because it works. Don't blow as if you were blowing bubbles, but softly, letting the heat of your breath heat her. While you're there, don't overlook the erotic potential of a few hot words. "You make me so hungry," or "God, you're sexy," can work wonders.

Running your fingers through her hair is a tricky business. If she's got her hair done and organized, you might just want to smooth your palms over the surface. If it's short, or long and loose, and you want to thread your fingers through it, go for it. Begin slowly and see whether she guides your hands away. Personally, I love a man to drive his fingers into my hair, but mine's short and easy.

When you finally touch her breasts, be gentle, and remember that breasts aren't just nipples and other stuff. The pale flesh is soft and smooth, so enjoy that. Tease. Don't just "Go for the gold." Swirl your fingers over her skin, avoiding her nipples until they are fully erect and reaching for your hands.

Let me share some letters from women who enjoy breast play.

Dear Joan,

I'm a thirty-eight-year-old woman and I just love having my breasts played with. Oh God, sometimes if it's done right, I love it more than sexual intercourse.

First, start out by rubbing them, just to get them congested and heated up. My breasts seem to grow as much as another cup size when I'm really excited. Then I like a guy to run his fingers repeatedly over my nipples and areolae until they get hard and puffy. Then I'm ready for his mouth.

I particularly like him to squeeze them while licking them, but by far the most important is he has to suck on them! I go really crazy once a guy starts sucking on my breasts. I love it to death and I'll let a guy suck on them as long as he wants to. I get the best feeling when he doesn't just suck the nipple itself, but tugs a good portion of my breast into his mouth. It's doubly good if he's also touching me.

Breast play is one of God's most gracious gifts to us women, and there's no feeling like it.

Patsy from North Dakota

Dear Joan,

I love having my breasts played with, the longer the better. I love to have them sucked, squeezed, and, yes, the nipples even bitten gently, or not so gently—but not so hard that it causes more pain than pleasure. I read that a woman's nipples are super sensitive, but mine aren't, so I need something a bit firmer if I'm to feel anything at all. Biting is wonderful. I like a man to begin somewhat gently, then get firmer and firmer until I ask him to ease up. Oh, the feelings . . .

Lauri

Joan,

Just a quick note on breast play. What's sexiest for me is to have my husband come up behind me when I'm naked in the bathroom, reach around, and play with my breasts from behind. It's particularly

wonderful when I can watch his hands in the mirror. The sight of his darker fingers on my white skin is like a personal porno flick.
Freda

Dear Joan,
I'm a seventy-one-year-old man and even at my age I love breast play. I especially like it when the lady offers encouragement and directions. Believe me, the enjoyment of long, slow lovemaking doesn't disappear. I intend to love it for many years to come.
Patrick

Now that you've caressed her breasts, Joey, you might want to softly caress then rub her genitals more firmly through her slacks or panties. That muffled touch should be just what she needs to drive her still higher. Once she's really squirming, a sure sign of arousal, undress her slowly. Make each button count. Open her blouse and kiss everything as it's revealed. Open her jeans, and lick only what you can reach with your tongue before you remove them. Nibble on her inner thigh, her sides, her belly. Turn her on her stomach and tease her by caressing her buttocks and the small of her back. Stroke her upper thighs from the back, not quite to her wet tissues.

That should give you quite a bit to practice with, Joey.
Joan

Dear Joan,
Let me start off by saying that I'm a nineteen-year-old male and I've been with my girlfriend for over a year now. We have the most unbelievable sex, but there's a little problem. During any type of sexual act that involves rubbing the clitoris (and even sometimes during sex), my girlfriend becomes very ticklish, and she usually asks me to stop. She describes it as feeling really good, but just unbearably tickly. Do you have any clue what this might be, or what causes it? I understand you're busy, but please respond back as soon as possible.

Thank you.

JJ

Dear JJ,

The clitoris is a very sensitive organ and must be touched very delicately. It's possible that you're pressing a bit too hard and that she's telling you sweetly, trying not to hurt your feelings, that she wants something more gentle. It is also important to realize the strength of pleasant touching will differ as she gets more excited. At first she'll probably want teasing, soft touching, stroking, then later something stronger might be better. As the clitoris becomes erect, again, you have to be gentle, since it will become extrasensitive.

The best way to find out what she's feeling is to ask her to show you what she wants. Let her touch herself so you can see what she likes, or ask her to touch the back of your hand while you're touching her. That way she can show you exactly how she wants to be touched.

If she won't, or can't, show you what she wants, ask her to moan or purr when it's good. That way you'll have a good clue as to what she's enjoying. If neither of those suggestions works, be aware of her movements and you'll discover that she's telling you anyway. Watch the way her body reacts. Is it toward your hand or away slightly? Is she getting more excited or less? Wetter? Are her nipples more erect? All those signs are ways to tell whether she's responding to what you're doing.

I hope this helps—it's all up to you.

Joan

Aphrodisiacs

Dear Joan,

I have a very simple question. Do aphrodisiacs work? What can I try that will get her in the mood?

Jeffrey

Dear Jeffrey,

Here's the aphrodisiac men (and probably women, too) envision. Slip a bit of some chemical into her coffee and she's your sex slave, slavering, ripping your clothes off, ready to do anything and everything you've ever wanted. No hesitation, no inhibitions, and no repercussions.

Hogwash. Nothing like that exists, and if it did, the result would be chemical rape. Remember that the sexual activities I advocate occur between consenting adults, and if either one is under the effect of any mind-altering drug, it's not consensual.

So let's get real here. There are some things that can smooth out the bumps along the sexual road. Alcohol does relax some of a person's natural inhibitions, but too much can inhibit the ability to perform. Pot, technically illegal but in small quantities only a minor offense, seems to do the same thing, although many folks I've talked to state that they continue to have the desire but are unable to focus sufficiently to consummate the act. Other illegal drugs are just that— illegal. And they have serious side effects. So don't even consider any of those! I must reiterate here: Lovemaking when your partner is drunk, drugged, or stoned isn't lovemaking. It's rape!

There are many other products that purport to create desire. Spanish fly is just an irritant of the urinary tract. Yohimbine is a derivative of a South American tree bark and is under study, but no benefits have been proven and side effects have not been ruled out. Herbals or combinations of supposed herbs come with risks and no scientifically documented rewards. Evaluate with care any statements in any advertisements you read.

The best aphrodisiac is a well-told erotic tale, a hot kiss, or a deliciously lewd suggestion whispered into her ear. Remember, the most effective erogenous zone is between the ears, not between the legs.

Joan

Getting into the Mood

Dear Joan,
What can I do to put her in the mood? You know, before getting to it.
Erik

Dear Erik,
Before I answer your question, I'm afraid you've got the wrong idea about foreplay. Foreplay is a pleasure for its own sake. You seem to be viewing "getting her into the mood" as just a prelude to sex. That's costing you, and your lady, so much pleasure. Remember, it's the journey, not just the destination, that's the joy of lovemaking. Stop worrying about intercourse and enjoy touching, kissing, stroking, and all the accouterments to great sex.

Okay, to answer your question, candlelight, incense, soft music, whispers, and soft kisses all work wonderfully well.

How about some slow dancing? Select some romantic music and invite her to dance. After all, what is dancing but vertical body rubbing?

How about a long walk after dark, holding hands and talking about loving and sharing?

How about a drive in the country? Stop in some secluded spot and just neck.

How about a dip in the pool together, then see whether she'd be interested in taking off your bathing suits?

How about a picnic in the middle of the living room floor, with sticky food you can lick off each other's fingers?

Read an erotic story together, either silently or, more arousing still, aloud.

Watch romantic movies and use their ideas too. Just, whatever you do, think soft, warm, and loving.
Joan

On Teasing

Dear Joan,
My boyfriend and I are going to a wedding this weekend. I want to get him really horny during that day, since he's in the wedding party and will be dressed in a tuxedo. I want to be able to look at him and see the bulge in his trousers and know it's just for me. I want to do something special. Please give me a suggestion.

Thanks.
Vicky

Dear Vicky,
Just before the ceremony begins, whisper into his ear that you're really hot for him and every time you look at him during the ceremony you'll be thinking about his big, hard cock. Then, every time he catches your eye during the festivities, wink at him, then lower your gaze to his crotch. If you're really brave, take off your panties right before the ceremony and tell him that you have.

If that doesn't appeal, try this. Make up a secret signal that tells him that you're hungry for him—touching your earlobe or stroking your cheek. I guarantee that he will get the message.
Joan

Talking Dirty

Dear Joan Elizabeth Lloyd,
I've been reading lots of women's magazines and many suggest that I talk dirty to my husband to increase the sexual tension. I'd like to try it, but I've no idea what to say. And I'm a pretty shy woman, so I can't see myself using vulgarity. Can you help me?
Abigail

Dear Abigail,
Using language you might not ordinarily use is a really hot way to ex-

cite your husband, but I also know that it's really difficult to do. I would advise you to begin small. You don't have to dive right into those Anglo-Saxon four-letter words to talk dirty. All you have to do is take a baby step. For example, "You make me really hot, you know." Or, "I'm getting really wet." Letting him know how excited you are is a great way to begin.

If you want to continue, how about, "I need you to touch my breasts," or "Rub me between my legs." Those forthright suggestions are guaranteed to heat up the moment, too.

Telling stories in the dark is a great way to talk dirty without getting too deeply into "dirty words." Set the scene. Like, "Let's pretend we're all alone on a desert island. We've been shipwrecked but we've salvaged lots of supplies and we know there will be another boat along in a few days. But for now, we're totally alone. I'd love to take off my shirt and sunbathe, feeling the warmth on my body. Would you like it if I did that?" Then let him continue the tale. Delicious? You bet!

Joan

Joan, Dear,

I wanted to tell you about the delicious thing my husband did to (or for) me recently. I'm a bit shy and have never used a four-letter word during sex in my life. I know that sounds difficult to believe, but it's true. Oh, I occasionally curse when I hurt myself or something, but I have never talked dirty in bed. Anyway, we have a great time in bed, and Doug, my husband, really knows how to get me excited.

A few weeks ago, I was really high. He had his fingers inside of me and he was teasing me with his mouth. When I was ready to come, he stopped touching me. I'll say I was frustrated. "Please," I said.

"Please what?" he asked. "Tell me exactly what you want."

Well, I beat around the bush because I couldn't say the words for exactly what I wanted. He wouldn't let up. He just insisted that I tell him, in detail, what I wanted him to do. Eventually, with lots of teasing and stopping, he "forced" me to tell him what I needed.

When I did and he touched me, I climaxed so hard I thought I'd died and gone to heaven.

Now "forcing" me to say bad words, and tell him what I want, has become part of our hot sessions. I hope others can learn to do that too. It's so fabulous.

Dana

Dear Dana,

How fantastic. I remember the first time I was "forced" to tell my lover what I wanted. It was difficult, but so great when I finally did it. Wow!!!

Joan

Chapter 4

Doing It

About Condoms

Dear Joan,
Like everyone else, I've heard all the horror stories about AIDS. I'm dating and having sex from time to time. How can I be safe? I'm really worried.
Daria

Dear Daria,
You're right to be worried. Right now, having sex with the wrong partner can lead to death. That's harsh, but it's the way things are in the twenty-first century. The best plan, of course, is abstinence. And that means no penis-vagina contact, no penis-anus contact, and no oral sex. All these activities involve risk.

Okay, you're not going to abstain from intercourse. You know that and I know that. So what's the next best thing? Using condoms and a spermicide containing nonoxynol-9. These together can

lessen (but not eliminate) the risk of contracting a sexually transmitted disease.
Joan

Dear Joan,
I don't really have to use a condom since I question my partners carefully to be sure they have no diseases. I'm safe, right?
Mary from Cleveland

Dear Mary,
I'm afraid you're not as safe as you think you are. Studies have shown that most people lie about their sexual history. Many prospective partners will tell you what you want to hear. After all, they think they're safe, so they won't necessarily be honest. Would you tell a partner that you were in bed with a one-night stand just last week?
Joan

Dear Joan Elizabeth Lloyd,
I'm a sexually active man and I really hate using condoms. I've read all the propaganda, but maybe it's just fear stuff and not really true. Can you give me the real deal? I trust your judgment.
Tony

Dear Tony,
It's not propaganda. In this era of disease transmission, sex has become a high-risk activity. Not only do couples have to worry about HIV, but there are several other very serious diseases, like chlamydia, herpes, and genital warts, that are transmitted by sexual contact. Other than total abstinence, wearing a condom and using a spermicide with nonoxynol-9 is the only way to lessen the risk of infection. Condoms do not make sexual contact truly safe. The best they can do is lessen the possibility, but only if they are used correctly and consistently. I understand a man's desire to "feel" intercourse, but it's just something you have to get used to.

Of course, once you've been with a monogamous partner for at least six months, and each of you has had two AIDS tests, six months apart, you can feel relatively safe.

Buying condoms is your first task, and it's not a difficult one. Go into any drug or variety store and you'll find one-packs, three-packs, twelve-packs, and more. Don't get too many at one time, since if they get too old they dry out and can crack during intercourse. And, for that reason, don't use one that's more than a few months old, and, of course, don't even consider one that's been in the back of your wallet since high school.

Condoms now come in flavors and colors to match any type of sexual desire. They have pictures on them that only become visible when you're erect. They come in flavors like chocolate and mint to make your lady smile. Some even glow in the dark. You can order a variety pack from many of the online or catalog companies and have fun deciding which feels best or is the most outrageous.

Condoms come one-size-fits-all, and that's probably fine for most men. If you're unusually large, there are companies that advertise and sell super-size condoms. Don't, however, get the larger ones if you don't need them. A condom that doesn't fit properly is worse than not using one at all. You think you're safe, and you're not. A condom that's too big will allow fluids to leak out around the sides, and one that's too small will feel restrictive and uncomfortable. Oh, and don't get the natural skin ones if you're interested in stopping disease transmission. Those have tiny openings, too small to see, that will allow organisms to pass through.

Most men think they know how to use condoms, but here are a few lessons. First, you must put it on before any genital contact. Precome, that small drop of lubricating fluid that leaks from the tip of your penis when you become excited, is filled with sperm and, possibly, disease organisms. Enough said. You need to unroll the condom completely, all the way down, leaving a pocket at the tip for your ejaculate. You need to leave it on during intercourse, then hold the base when you withdraw, to prevent any fluid from leaking out around the sides.

I know it seems like an odious task, but it's really, really necessary.
Joan

Dear Joan,
On the subject of condoms, do those ribs and ridges make any difference? I'm a sexually active woman and I've been with lots of men, and they all have to use condoms if they are to have relations with me. Some have bragged that they use ones with ribs or ridges or with ticklers on the end. I have never felt the difference. Should I have? Is there something wrong with me?
Elaine

Dear Elaine,
I haven't felt any difference either. Only the first two inches of a woman's vaginal canal have sensitive nerve endings anyway, so the ticklers and such are not too useful, IMHO. And when I'm involved in good sex, I'm not really paying attention to the texture of a man's condom. Maybe there are women who feel that stuff, but I've never met one.

Have any of your partners ever used one of the prelubricated ones? I love the sensation of a cool, slippery erection sliding inside of me. And here's a cute trick that I gather feels really sensational. Have your date put a new ribbed or studded one on inside out. That way he feels the sensations, and I'm told it's pretty wild.
Joan

Dear Joan,
Okay, I know I have to use a condom, but it's really pretty awful. It means I have to stop what I'm doing and all. Yuck. What can I do to make it less of a pain?
Larry

Dear Larry,
If you make the condom a natural and consistent part of your love-

making, it does become less of a chore. And since it's absolutely necessary, you might as well get used to it. I've gotten several letters from folks who've made condoms part of their sexual routine. Maybe a few of them will help.

Dear Joan,
I like having my wife put a condom on me, and during our time together she has taught me different ways to wrap some latex over my erection. Sometimes she plays with me while I'm standing, and puts it on that way, either with her hands or with her mouth. It can be very stimulating. Sometimes she even "lubricates" my shaft with her mouth first. Actually, there was an evening I particularly remember when she was "having her way with me" for quite a while and during that time I didn't even realize that she had put one on my penis. It was fabulous.
Igor

Dear Joan,
My husband and I have to use condoms since I can't take the pill. It seemed sort of a shame, but we've found several ways to make it less of a chore. I keep a variety of condoms, colored (I love BLACK), ribbed, studded, even glow-in-the-dark ones, in my bed table drawer. There's also a stash in my hubby's nightstand. Usually we make love in the bedroom, so they're readily available.

When we make love, one of the things I loooovvvveeee to do is tease him, then once he's erect, I ask him to find a condom. He grabs a handful and we'll pick one together, really slowly. We giggle while we discuss the virtues of each type. Sometimes he gets really hot while we talk about it in exciting detail. Then I put it on him, and just doing that makes me even hotter. I won't go into the rest, but you get the idea.
Sally

Dear Joan,
I guess I don't understand all the negative comments about condoms. My significant other and I love sex, but we don't want any children right now, so condoms are a way of life for us. I have to tell you that we even keep a supply in the glove compartment of his car so we can fool around late at night in some quiet parking spots. It's really just part of our loving and neither of us minds at all. Something silly? We have a few that glow in the dark. In the blackness of the car, it's really kinky to see his penis glowing, just inviting me to . . .
Amanda

So, Larry, since using condoms is mandatory, you might as well make them part of your lovemaking. Both you and your partner will benefit, in more ways than one.
Joan

Dear Joan Elizabeth Lloyd,
I have read all about how you can incorporate condoms into foreplay and how they do not necessarily detract from a man's enjoyment of sex, but for me the bottom line is that they do. A lot. For me, wearing a latex condom during sex not only decreases the physical sensation, but it also decreases the feeling of intimacy. How would you enjoy kissing if you had to wear a rubber dental dam over your lips and tongue? Perhaps you may agree that it would feel somewhat less intimate than a "naked" kiss.

I agree with you, of course, that if you have multiple sex partners, you must use condoms. After all, in the era of AIDS your life is at stake. But if you limit your sexual activity to one partner at a time, there is no need to wait years before dispensing with condoms. There are a number of alternative ways to prevent conception, and as for disease, well, even waiting a year is no guarantee of safety. People can carry infections without showing symptoms for their entire life and no one really knows how long HIV can remain dormant and symptomless. The only way to be reasonably safe is to

be tested for HIV and other STDs. If you and your partner test negative for everything after being monogamous for a couple of months, that's about as safe as you are going to be, no matter how long you wait. Is that not so, or am I missing something?
Les

Dear Les,
You're right. The CDC is recommending that both partners have an AIDS test, then another six months later. It is claimed that if all tests are negative, then the danger of contracting AIDS from each other is pretty near zero. However, some studies show that a person can be infected with chlamydia without symptoms for five to fifteen years.

Once you have a monogamous partner, only you can decide the degree of risk you're willing to take.
Joan

Dear Joan,
My wife sometimes has difficulty with lubrication. We sometimes use Vaseline, but I've heard that it's not the best thing. What can we use and why is Vaseline bad?
Davy

Dear Davy,
What you've heard is correct. Vaseline is not good to use for vaginal lubrication for several reasons. First, any petroleum product, including Vaseline, baby oil, and products that use mineral oil, will break down the latex in a condom, causing tiny holes that can allow both disease organisms and sperm to sneak through. Second, Vaseline is difficult to remove from the vaginal canal. It coats the tissues and makes a wonderful environment for bacteria to live and breed in, eventually causing nasty infections. Buy a water-based product designed for vaginal lubrication and for use with condoms. You can get K-Y Jelly or Astroglide in any drugstore and there are lots more products available through adult products catalogs and websites.
Joan

Dear Joan,

I'm a woman in her early thirties, and I know the dangers of unprotected sex. I insist that my lovers use a condom all the time. But I was wondering about the dangers of mouth to genital contact. I love both giving and receiving oral sex. Should I be worried?

Liza

Dear Liza,

Oral sex has associated risks and you should be aware of them. It is currently rated as a low-risk activity, although ejaculation makes it more risky. There are only a handful of reported AIDS transmissions through oral-genital contact, but herpes is particularly easily transmitted this way. Here are a few tips to make it safer.

Never have unprotected oral-genital contact when either of you has an oral or genital herpes outbreak, or for that matter, an open mouth sore of any kind. There are commercially available latex and plastic barriers, but a condom, plastic sheet, or even Saran Wrap can be used to protect both parties. Dental dams, particularly larger ones specially designed for oral-genital contact, are available through catalogs and on the Web, and they even come in flavors. To enhance the sensations, put some lubricant on the non-mouth side.

With a few precautions, oral-genital contact can remain a delightful part of a sexual evening.

Joan

First Times

Dear Joan,

My name is Betsy and I'm nineteen. I had sex for the first time about a week ago, and I can't tell you how disappointed I was. I had been waiting for this to be with someone special and it was. He and I had been going out for almost three months. He'd been wanting to do it, but I had stopped him. He was good about it so we necked. He touched me and really got me hot.

Anyway, finally I got so hot that I agreed to let him. He knew I had never done it before and he was pretty patient with me. Well, I had pictured something quite different. We were in his car and it was uncomfortable just getting into a position where he could . . . Finally we got my panties off and he did it. It hurt. Bad. I'm still sore down there. There was some blood and it messed up our clothes. I didn't come or anything and it was just frustrating and painful. Did I do something wrong? Is there something wrong with me?

Betsy

Dear Betsy,

You did nothing wrong, nor is there anything wrong with you. Romance novels, while really enjoyable, give women this glorious picture of making love for the first time. In the story he takes his time and makes sure that she is ready. He enters slowly, and then, at that moment when the hymen is broached, he "swallows her groan of pain with his passionate kisses," and soon she's hot and enjoying intercourse like she's done it dozens of times.

Does it happen that way sometimes? Sure. Should virgin women expect that? No! Intercourse is a messy, awkward process and can be painful the first time. And for you, if you're still experiencing any discomfort, make an appointment with a good gynecologist just to be on the safe side. There might be small tears that some medication might soothe or other difficulties that your doctor needs to tend to.

I can, however, guarantee you that the next time, as long as it's with someone who cares for you and for whom you have strong feelings, it will be better. Take your time and learn. Teach each other what feels good and what doesn't. Oh, and try to do it somewhere where you can both be comfortable. The backseats of cars don't work. Been there, done that, have the bruises from the window crank. I enjoyed it because I was really excited and we had no other place to go. But it wasn't my first time, and we knew what and how.

I might point out one thing you might have done wrong that

wasn't clear from your letter. Be sure that with every encounter he uses a condom. Carry them yourself and don't be afraid to insist. Neither of you wants to transmit disease, and you certainly don't want to become pregnant. Please take care and be strong about this. It will save you from future misery.
Joan

Dear Joan,

Hi. My name is Brandy and I just turned eighteen. I don't want to be a virgin anymore, so I've decided to let my current boyfriend go all the way. He says he'll love me even more afterward, and that letting him do it will show him how much I care for him. And after all, I'm of age now and most of my friends have already done it.

I'm a little nervous about all this and I don't know who else to ask. Can you tell me what I can expect? What will it feel like? Will there be a lot of pain?
Brandy

Dear Brandy,

Let me sound like your mother for a moment. Sex is a wonderful thing when shared by two people who care about each other. Making love should happen when it's the best way to express the feelings you have for each other. Love? I'm not sure what that word means to you, but deep caring and consideration should be a part of it. He should care enough about you not to be pressuring you into it.

Be sure you make love for the first time, and every time, for the right reasons. Respect yourself enough to make love because you want to and for no other reason. Don't let him blackmail you into it by saying that he'll love you more afterward or that everyone else does it. It's your body, and only you should decide when the time is right.

Okay, enough from the mother in me. Let me answer your question. Will there be pain? Maybe, and maybe not. In this age of tampons, motorcycles, and girls playing as roughly as boys, the hymen—the membrane that protects a woman's vaginal passage—is often ruptured long before some women have their first sexual experience. In other women, the thin bit of skin just atrophies, wastes away in youth. I wonder how many marriages in the "olden days" were destroyed on the wedding night when the husband discovered no "important" evidence of his new wife's chastity. Oh well . . .

So for some women there will be the minor pain of the breaking of that membrane, and for others there will be nothing but a stretching of internal passages that haven't yet become accustomed to invasion. If you've used internal sanitary protection, the passage might be stretched enough to feel no discomfort at all.

I knew a woman lots of years ago who went to her doctor before her marriage and her first sexual experience, just for a checkup. The doctor discovered that her hymen, instead of being only a few layers of cells thick, was the texture of a callus. Fortunately it was a small matter for him to use a sharp instrument and cut away the tissue. However, if she had waited until her wedding night, it would have been fraught with frustration for both her and her husband.

There might also be a small amount of bleeding, only a few drops or so. One of the other things I'm involved in besides writing is emergency medicine. I've been riding ambulances for more than fifteen years. Once, several years ago, we were called to the home of a teenage girl with severe bleeding. She was embarrassed and had delayed calling to her family for help because the bleeding was a result of her first sexual experience. Suffice it to say we comforted her and took her to the emergency room, where she was treated. That, of course, was a very rare occurrence. The reason I repeat it here is just to suggest that if anything unusual happens, anything that causes you more than immediate pain and very light bleeding, don't hesitate to ask for help.

I thought you might benefit from reading some letters I've received about first times. I hope they answer any additional questions you might have.

Dear Joan,

My first time having sex happened when I was younger . . . too young, now that I look back on it. Actually, we were both virgins, and both wanted to experience sex very badly. He took me to a motel by bus, as I recall, and got a room. He made some lame joke about not being able to believe he used his real name.

Anyway, most of it wasn't much worth remembering, but there were a couple things that stick out, and that I think you'll find, at the very least, amusing. Probably because he was so excited about his first time, frequently he would accidently "slip out" and keep going . . . against my thigh! Another "memorable" part of the evening was him grabbing the phone in the middle of the event to call his friends to tell them exactly what he was (finally) doing. There was little discomfort—bleeding, pain, etc. All in all, it was a memorable event only in that it amuses people when I tell them.

Suzanne

Dear Joan,

I want to share my first time with you because it wasn't anything like others I've heard. I was in my early twenties and I was waiting for the right moment. My boyfriend and I had been friends for many years before we began dating. We had kissed and done lots of heavy petting. When we finally did it, at my house when my parents were away, he was so nervous he had problems keeping his erection. I was so scared, I was afraid to touch him. He took out a condom and put it on, but entering me was really difficult. We just couldn't get it comfortable. I never bled or tore or anything like other women do. We loved each other and for that reason the problems didn't seem to matter, but our first time was less than romantic.

Lana

Dear Joan,

Hi. My name is Josie and I thought I'd write you about my first time having sex. I was seventeen and I felt very pressured by the guy I was with. He kept telling me how beautiful I was and how it would feel so good. I didn't want to, but I went along. I guess, as I look back on it now, it was really sort of rape, except I didn't insist that he stop. I was too scared.

For me that time was very painful, the whole way, I guess because it wasn't the guy's first time and I didn't want to anyway. Afterward, I looked for bloodstains. I wanted to get rid of the evidence, and couldn't find any on the sheet. There was some in my underwear, though, after a while. It was dark, like the last few hours of my period. I was very sore for a day or so afterward, can't imagine how in those romance novels they keep doing it all night after the first time.

I was several years older the second time, and it hurt at first, just like the first time, but that only lasted a few seconds, then all was fine. Luckily, I didn't let those first times rule my life, and now enjoy sex with my husband to the fullest.
Josie

Hi Joan,
About first times, mine was as wonderful as I could have wanted and dreamed, with a man I loved and the way I had read in romance novels. It might sound a bit corny to some people, but that is the way it happened to me.

I was twenty-two at the time. Yeah I know, I was old to lose it, but I think one of the reasons I waited so long was because I was waiting for the right guy to do it with. At that time, he was the right one for me. We ended up in a hotel room.

Needless to say I was as nervous as I could be, very tense, so he gave me a glass of wine to relax me. Actually, I ended up drinking half the bottle. We kissed, and before I knew, he had undressed me and was kissing me all over. I was as aroused and excited as I had ever been. I will always remember the look on his face when the time came for him to enter me. It was a mix of desire and concern—wanting me really bad but not wanting to hurt me either. I remember how awkward the feeling of being entered for the first time was for me, but it was a pleasurable one too.

He pushed into me until he was all the way in, and the pain that I felt, well, it was much more intense than I ever thought it would be, and he could tell. He held me and comforted me. When I got up off the bed and I looked at the white sheets, there was this huge stain of blood there. I began to think that maybe there was something wrong with me, and I ran into the bathroom. As I washed myself he came into the bathroom and kept apologizing over and over.

That night we didn't have sex again because he was afraid of hurting me. I guess that when you look at it from just a sexual point of view, it was a pretty lousy experience, but from our emotional point of view, it was the most precious it could be. That's what I remember most, his caring and love for me. After that night we made love lots of times, and those were really good. I started this letter with how great it was, and that loving was the biggest thing I remember about that night.

By the way, that guy is now my husband. I just thought you'd like to know that.
DeeDee

Dear Joan,
The first time I had intercourse was not only unlike the romance novels, it was downright frustrating. My hymen was so tight that no amount of his thrusting would penetrate it, so, on my first night out, I had to take the initiative, get on top, and do it myself. Then, yes, there was a surprising amount of pain and bleeding that eliminated any further desire I had to have sex at all, and my date and I both went home frustrated!
Margo

Dear Joan,
I know a lot of women have written to you about their first time,

and I'm a bit embarrassed to say that my first time was really a nothing. There was no pain, no bleeding, and no real fun. We just sort of graduated from breast play to genital play to intercourse. It just sort of happened. I guess I didn't have my membrane, but I didn't think about it at the time.

Since then sex has been good sometimes, great at others, and not so good from time to time too. But that first time didn't live up to the fanfare.
Molly

Dear Joan,
About first times for women. I know this will be hard to believe, but in 1977 I was twenty and still a virgin. I became deflowered for all the wrong reasons and have always regretted it. In fact, I hated it so much that sex to me was disgusting, until I met the right man, who taught me what true lovemaking was. My first experience was totally unlike in the romance novels—there was lots of pain and bleeding.

About that first night, the only reason I decided to give up my virginity was simply because my younger sister had been doing it for years. The truth of the matter is, when I finally decided to do it and had all of my clothes off, I chickened out and told my boyfriend I had changed my mind. He wouldn't hear of it, and all the crying and begging in the world could not get me out of the most painful experience of my life. I always thought no meant no, but I guess he didn't value me enough to stop.

My advice to all women who are considering giving up their virginity is just this: Make sure you love the person you're with and make sure he has a gentle heart. You'll know when the moment is right. Oh yes, make sure the man understands that no means no, but don't tease him either.
Margaret

I hope all this advice helps. I know it's a bit one-sided, but

there's a lesson here. Do it for the right reasons and it will all work out wonderfully.
Joan

Dear Joan,
I'm a nineteen-year-old man named Wes and I've never done it. Oh, I've told my friends I have, but I haven't. I was wondering whether there are older women who might be interested in teaching someone like me about sex. I've read lots of erotic stories about older ladies teaching younger guys, but I don't know how to go about finding someone. Any suggestions? I know you're an older woman . . .
Wes

Dear Wes,
Thank you so much for your compliment, but I'm not the person you're looking for. I understand your dilemma, but although it's the story line for lots of erotic tales, I'm afraid finding a Mrs. Robinson isn't all that easy. You can learn a lot without needing a tutor, however delicious that might seem to be. Read. Erotic stories are often written by women, and are good indications of what they want. When with a woman, be tuned in to what she's feeling. Usually they make their needs quite clear. And let your first time be with someone you care about. That way all the fumbling and such will become part of a wonderful memory.

Just remember, everyone in the world had to have a first time, and as awkward and silly as it might become, if you and she keep your senses of humor, it will be wonderful.

Other men have written about their first times. Maybe these letters will help.

Dear Ms. Lloyd,
I've heard a lot about women's first times, but let me say that not every man knows what to do either. I'm now happily married, and my wife and I have a great sex life together. However,

my first time was a disaster. Actually, maybe it wasn't really my first time, because I shot my load before I could ever get inside. She had the nerve to giggle and I was totally humiliated. Needless to say, my next experience was much better and I've learned a lot since. I guess the lesson to be learned from this was it was the wrong woman that first time. I don't think anyone who really cared about me would have done anything like that. It still hurts.

Carl

Dear Joan,

My name is Dan, and I thought I'd write and tell you about my first time. It was more than twenty years ago, but I still remember it as though it was yesterday.

She and I had been dating and fooling around for several months, and I guess we had both decided to lose our virginity that afternoon. We were both seventeen, it was summer, and we were both feeling like hot shit seniors about to return to school.

Well, we snuck up to my bedroom one hot afternoon while my folks were off at a wedding, and I asked her if she wanted to do it. That was the moment of truth. I wouldn't have started anything if she hadn't been willing, but she said yes, rather hesitantly. I asked again and pulled out my package of Trojans to reassure her, and she shyly said that she really wanted to.

We gently embraced and kissed, but I was getting kind of worried and didn't want to blow it by getting too anxious. We moved toward my bed and I pulled out one of the condoms. I'd practiced with them before, so I knew what to do. I rolled it on and then rubbed some K-Y on. The next few moments get kind of blurry.

It was over pretty quickly, and I remember making sure to withdraw as soon as possible so I wouldn't mess it up. There wasn't much blood, which was a surprise to both of us. What I remember as much as the actual thing was lying together afterwards listening to the sounds of summer outside the window. We heard kids playing ball and the guy next door mowing his lawn. Although we were different, nothing in the rest of the world had changed.

After that we dated and made love when we got the chance all through our senior year, but after that we went different ways. I hope she remembers that afternoon with as much nostalgia as I do.
Dan

You're not alone, Wes, so just be patient and it will all happen in its own good time.
Joan

Sexual Positions

Dear Joan,
I'd like a suggestion on a new sexual position that my husband and I can try. I guess the ones we've been using have gotten a bit dull, and I'm looking for something new. Thanks for helping.
Margaret

Dear Margaret,
For me, sexual positions flow from one to another without much thought. Ed and I do whatever seems natural and comfortable at the time, with no prior planning. On the other side of the coin, *Cosmopolitan* magazine has an article almost every month on new positions for lovemaking. So, for what it's worth, let me copy some letters for you from others who've found particular positions wonderful.

Dear Joan,
My lover and I have been experimenting with new sexual positions and we've found that having the room filled with lots of pil-

lows of various sizes and thicknesses really gives us toys to play with. Sometimes he stacks several thick ones on the floor beside the bed and kneels, allowing him to penetrate me from below, sort of. Sometimes he puts one beneath my hips while we make love so he can penetrate me from a different angle, and at other times I lie on my stomach with a thick one beneath my belly and he does it that way. It's always nice to have whatever props you need handy.

Just one thing. We also keep several big towels around so the pillows don't get messy. Just a thought.
Jessica

Dear Joan,
I would like to share our favorite sexual position. In this position I sit on top of him while he is lying on the bed and slowly slide my body down along his hard shaft. Then I slowly roll my upper body forward so I can rub against his chest, then I sit back up. That movement seems to drive us both higher and higher each time I do it. We've begun calling it Doing our Fuck-Ups.
Sadie

Dear Joan,
Okay, this sounds really strange, but it works, for us at least. Let me first tell you that my wife and I have been happily married for almost twenty years. Recently she began taking yoga classes, and that has resulted in the odd position we've come to love. Here's how it goes.

We position two rolled-up pillows on the floor, about six inches apart, against a wall. My wife then puts her head between the pillows so they support her shoulders and stands on her head with her back to the wall. I know you're probably laughing, but it's amazing how different it feels and how many unusual ways I can stimulate her and myself. I won't go into details; rather, I'll let you use your imagination. Suffice it to say, it works for us.
Howard

Dear Joan,
As a fifty-four-year-old man married for almost thirty years to the same woman, who happens to have back problems, we have had to improvise in the choice of positions. Our favorite, and least harmful for her back, is where she lies on her back, missionary style, and I lie on my right side, perpendicular to her, with my groin at her crotch level. She raises one of her legs, and I slide under it and into her warm, moist body.
Quinn

Dear Joan,
I am a male, aged forty-three, and delightfully married for almost twenty years. We have always found it best for my wife to assume the superior position, I guess sort of reverse missionary. This allows her to control the depth of the penetration, the thrusting, and the motion. I can reach and touch all her sensitive spots—her breasts, her rear—and stroke her between her legs, all of which serves to turn her on even more. I find that in this position I can better control my response and time my orgasm so that I can come when she climaxes.
Roger

Dear Joan,
My personal favorite position for intercourse has to be when I lie on my stomach with my legs slightly apart. My boyfriend enters me from behind and then I close my legs and hold them together tightly. He then sort of straddles me, like riding a horse. He and I have found that if we do it on his weight bench, it's really fabulous, since he can have his feet on the floor and still be inside of me.
Polly

Dear Joan,
This might sound kind of amusing, but I had an idea and it worked. My girlfriend has an artificial hip, and finding a comfort-

able position has always been difficult for us. Amazingly enough, doggy fashion, with me behind while she's on her knees, seems to work best for us, but getting the right height gave us a problem. Whatever we tried, either her on the bed with me kneeling behind or me standing on the floor, nothing worked exactly right.

Well, I'm an amateur carpenter, so I made a platform to put beside the bed for me to stand on. Then I kept adding stacks of newspapers until it was the right height to enter her. You talk about fun? It's just perfect, and so comfortable for her, too. And I love being behind, where I can use my hands on her to my heart's content. For anyone having a similar handicap, I recommend something like this.

Have fun.

Josh

Margaret, that ought to give you a few ideas.

Joan

Dear Joan,

Are there positions that work better for a man who's not really hard? My husband and I have been married for almost forty years, and now he's soft a lot of the time. Sometimes while we're making love, he falls out. I'm a bit embarrassed to discuss this with him, and it doesn't seem to bother him, but sometimes it leaves me hanging to have him fall out at the strategic moment. What can we try?

Vanessa

Dear Vanessa,

Man on top or side-by-side positions seem to work best, since they use gravity to assist his erection. Missionary position, the simplest of these, might do well for you two. However, if age and medications are affecting his ability in bed, you might suggest that he visit his doctor and discuss Viagra. It really works and can put the spark back in your love life really quickly.

Joan

Dear Joan,

I'm a twenty-two-year-old guy and I've got a question for you. My lover and I are doing well and we have been going together for just over a year now. We make love on occasion and it's usually pretty good. I was wondering if you could help me out with something, however. I have brought her to orgasm, which was thrilling, but why does she like it lots when I go really deep and touch the back of her channel? And what is it that I touch when I press far inside—is it the cervix? I just want to know so I can make it better for her.
Bret

Dear Bret,

If you feel a hard projection at the back of her channel it might be her cervix, the entry to her uterus. However, what she's probably enjoying isn't the depth of your penetration but the pressure of your pubic bone against her clitoris and vaginal tissues. Since only the first two inches of a woman's channel have any nerve endings, there's nothing for her to feel any deeper. If you want to increase her pleasure, try to locate her clitoris with your fingers and gently stroke it during intercourse. Check to see what she likes, hard strokes or light strokes, long ones or short, quick pressure. I'm sure she'll enjoy that immensely. Write and let me know how it all works out.
Joan

Dear Joan,

I don't know whether you'll remember, but I wrote to you several weeks ago about what my lady was feeling when I penetrated her really deeply. Well, you were certainly right about touching her clitoris. It took me some time to know what to do, and that was really stressful for a while. At first I couldn't find her clit, but later on I realized that when she's not excited it's really small. Well, one evening I touched her when she was really hot, and wow, she nearly went through the roof when I stroked her. When she was really excited, her clit was really easy to find, sticking out like a tiny penis.

Now I touch her a lot, especially while I'm inside of her. Sometimes she even comes from that alone, and I can actually feel her do it.

Thanks so much for your help.

Bret

All about orgasms

Dear Joan,
I'm a thirty-one-year-old woman and I've never had an orgasm. I've tried with several different men, and it just doesn't seem to happen. What's wrong with me? What can I do?
Patty

Dear Patty,
Are you sure you've never climaxed? I find that many women don't know an orgasm when they have one. For some women it's not dramatic fireworks, the earth-moving, mind-shattering experience that's portrayed in romance novels. Rather it's a quiet trip to a summit of pleasure, then a slow, smooth downward slide. It's possible that you were so intent on looking for the explosion that you missed the small spasms.

Exactly what is the cycle toward orgasm for a woman? During arousal, a woman's body changes in several ways. The vaginal canal lubricates and enlarges, and the labia or lips that usually cover the vaginal opening become engorged with blood and swell to allow easier access for the penis. The clitoris swells and emerges from beneath the fatty pad that usually covers it. Breathing and heartbeat quicken, and sometimes the face or genital tissues flush. As the tension builds toward orgasm, the vaginal canal tightens, squeezing the penis in an attempt to keep the eventual ejaculated fluid inside. Finally, orgasm occurs with contractions of the lower vagina, the uterus, and the anal area.

Phew. When viewed clinically, it doesn't sound like fun—yet it is. I won't go into the details of the hormones released, but suffice it to say that orgasm is wonderful. It is not, however, all there is, but it is something that can happen during some (not necessarily all) love-making sessions.

Patty, if you truly haven't climaxed, it's necessary for you to learn about your body. We women think that men are all born with some cosmic knowledge that permeates their being and teaches them all about a woman's pleasures. Hogwash. Men have to learn about pleasing women just as we have to learn how to please men. How do they learn? From listening to other men talk, from reading, from other women, but most important, they learn from us, their partners. We have to help them understand what we need to achieve climax, just as they have to help us to understand the same things. And how can we teach them unless we know the answers ourselves? If we don't know how to reach orgasm, how can we show them?

How do we learn? Masturbation. It's really the only way to learn what pushes us closer to the orgasmic edge, what maintains the pleasure level and what actually diminishes the experience. How hard should he press and for how long? Exactly where? What first, nipples or inner thigh? Exactly how sensitive is your navel, or your nipples? If you can't answer those questions, you won't be able to help him. And, since the answers to those and all the other questions about your body are so personal, even the most experienced man in the world can't know about your individual needs and desires.

Joan

Dear Joan,

Okay, I know you're going to tell me that I should masturbate, but I don't know how to begin. It's really scary. I remember my mother telling me that if I touched myself I'd never get pleasure from my husband, that it's dirty and BAD, with capital letters. How can I get past that and where do I start?

Please help me.

Connie

Dear Connie,

First, and most important, it's your body and you have a right, and a responsibility, to touch it wherever you choose. Period. Why do I say responsibility? Because you need to know yourself to become a better and more responsive lover.

So where do you start? First, with privacy. In today's world it can be really difficult to find time and quiet, away from your kids and your husband, but without privacy you won't feel comfortable touching yourself. Put a hook on the bedroom door or cuddle under the covers where what you're doing can't be seen. Soak in a warm bath (the place where I first learned about my body) beneath a thick layer of bubbles. Set the mood if you can, with soft music, candles, wine, whatever will enhance the atmosphere and lessen your natural inhibitions. Get your mind in the mood by reading a sexy section of a novel, an erotic story from a book, magazine, or an erotic story website. Let the tension build.

Then begin to touch where it feels good. It's really just as simple as that. Experiment. There's a section of this book devoted to masturbation, so use the information there to help you and just go for it. It might not happen your first time, or even your fifth, but it will happen. IMHO, every woman is capable of climax, and you're no different, so just make the time and do it. And even if you never climax, the experimentation is such fun.
Joan

Hi again, Joan,

I asked you for advice once before and it helped, so I'm coming to you again. Recently my husband hasn't been able to last as long during sex. This doesn't bother me as much as it bothers him. It just doesn't seem to take much at all anymore for me to make him cum, and once that's happened he goes soft and loses the mood completely. This is a problem because he knows it takes longer for me to orgasm and he doesn't feel like he's satisfying me in bed very well anymore. We've heard of using rubber bands to maintain his erection, but that sounds dangerous. A few months ago he bought a cock ring, thinking that might help, but it didn't. He's very well endowed, and the ring was very uncomfortable for him. What else can we try? Any advice? Neither of us feels that it's a medical problem.

I'd appreciate your advice.

Marsha from California

Dear Joan,

I'm not sure how to ask you this—it's very embarrassing. I have a problem—I come too fast. I know that my wife is frequently unsatisfied, and I want to be a good lover for her. What can I do so I don't shoot so fast?

Andy

Dear Andy,

I guess the first question I should ask you is "too fast" for what? The usual answer is that I come before I'm ready and, more important, before she's ready. Let's tackle one thing at a time. If you find a sudden change in your "performance" it's wise to check with your doctor to rule out any physical problems like diabetes, prostate, or urinary disease. Most of the time, however, the problem is none of these.

A most important part of my answer is this: women don't need an erect penis to get pleasure. It's not prolonged thrusting that builds a woman to orgasm, it's foreplay. Like many women, I can't come from just intercourse alone. It takes stimulation of many kinds.

Learn how to use your hands, your mouth, toys, and your imagination to give your partner pleasure, with or without penetration. If you climax and she's not satisfied, don't roll over and go to sleep. It's important to join forces and make sure she gets the additional stimulation she needs. Just because you achieved orgasm doesn't mean the lovemaking is over!

The second part of my answer involves the physical aspects of ejaculation and how to slow yourself down. Contrary to popular wisdom, distracting yourself by doing the times tables or thinking about something else usually doesn't work. Actually, many men find that it just makes them more anxious and makes the problem worse.

There are products to prolong erections advertised on adult websites and in magazines, and they do work. The cream usually contains a small amount of benzocaine or lydocaine, an anesthetic similar to what a dentist uses on your gums before he or she gives you a shot of novocaine. The cream numbs the entire penile area, and the lessening of sensation mutes the stimulation. You can accomplish the same thing by wearing a condom, if you don't now, or, if you already use one, use two.

Another method involves restricting the return blood flow to the penis. You can use a cock ring, which fits around the base of the penis and is usually adjustable so that it's snug but not too tight. Thus, blood can get in, but not back out. They comes in sizes, so experiment with several different ones. And no rubber bands! Something narrow like that will cut off the blood flow too completely and can cause serious damage.

You or your partner can accomplish the same thing by using a thumb and forefinger. When ejaculation seems inevitable, either one of you can grasp the shaft of the penis just below the head, one finger on the top surface, one on the bottom (not the sides). Squeeze for about four seconds, or until the urge diminishes, then play some more, repeating until climax is desired. This, of course, requires withdrawal if it happens during intercourse, but it's worth it. As this technique succeeds in lengthening the period before ejaculation, you can move your hand lower, to the base of the shaft, again top and bottom only. Once you've moved to the base, this can then be done by either party, while the penis is still in the vagina. I've also heard that pulling down on the scrotum just before climax can delay male orgasm. I don't know whether it's true or not, but it's certainly worth a try.

A while ago I read an article that made a lot of sense. The author maintained that one reason for a man's rapid ejaculation is that he's trained himself that way. In childhood, when he masturbated, it was important to get it done fast to avoid detection. Also, those couples who practice withdrawal as a form of birth control trained the men to be satisfied with short periods of penetration.

You can reverse that training, either during lovemaking or masturbation. Try getting to the edge, then stopping until the urge subsides. If you succeed, try again. If not, try again the next time by not getting as close to climax. Do this whenever you head toward climax, with or without a partner. Train yourself to enjoy the stimulation. It really can be done. Make it part of sex play. I know, I can hear you now. I don't want my partner to know about this. Well, she already does, so why not let her be part of the solution?
Joan

Dear Joan,

I'm ashamed to say that I take a very long time to ejaculate. I know it shouldn't bother me, but it does. I have gotten really good at foreplay, so my partner is really hot. Then I enter and do lots of thrusting, but by the time I'm ready to come, she's done and maybe a bit bored with it all. I usually warn my partners, but what else can I do? Is it that I'm not good enough? Is there something wrong with me?
TJ

Dear TJ,

Everyone is different in bed, and out of it, too, for that matter. I know you've probably heard that many times, but it's true. Just as some women heat very quickly, some men take quite a while. Have you considered that maybe your unselfish attitude is part of your problem? You need to take a bit more lovemaking time for yourself, rather than concentrating on getting your partner worked up. Find the things that raise your heat level and suggest that she help. You needn't tell her why, just share your knowledge about your body, as she should share her understanding of her body with you.

And remember that it's not good or bad, it's not that you're a better or worse lover, it just is.
Joan

Dear Joan,

I've read about premature ejaculation, but my husband's problem is a bit different. He used to masturbate a lot before we were married, and now he can't seem to come from intercourse. He says that it just doesn't feel the same as masturbation, and that intercourse doesn't give him the same sensations. It used to be frustrating for me, but we deal with the problem by mutual masturbation. Is there any way we can fix the problem? Is this mutual masturbation normal?

Shelly

Dear Shelly,

First, whatever you've found that works for you two and gives you both sexual pleasure is fine and quite normal. Mutual masturbation is a delicious part of lovemaking, and if it satisfies you both, bravo.

As for his difficulty, first, of course, rule out any physical problem with a visit to a health care professional, especially if this started suddenly. With physical problems ruled out, there are several things you can do to help. Try having him masturbate until he's just about ready to climax, then have him penetrate. As he learns what it takes to climax, gradually reduce the amount of masturbation. It's also important that he learn that it's important to focus on his own pleasures, not just yours. Be his slave for an evening and let him tell you what pleasures him. Let him indulge himself completely. Wait for intercourse until he's really ready, begging for the opportunity to come. Prolong the process—and enjoy it too. Or just set a timer and play, with no genital stimulation for him for, say, half an hour or longer.

Let me know how this works for you.

Joan

Dear Joan,

It's Shelly again, and I just thought I'd let you know that we've started to allow him to come only when he's inside of me. It's become a game. He masturbates while I watch, but I won't let him come. If he climaxes suddenly, without being inside, I "punish" him by making him my sexual slave. It's really become fun again.

(It's Shelly's husband here, and I thought I'd tell you that sometimes I come quickly just so she'll punish me. What a great time we have. I can't thank you enough.)

Thanks from me, too.

Shelly

Hi, Joan,

My husband and I have heard how great it is to climax together, but we never seem to be able to do it. Usually he comes first. He's always wonderful, using his fingers or his mouth to help me climax, but I can't seem to come exactly when he does.

What can I do?

Sally

Dear Sally,

My advice is to forget it. I've never mastered the art—or skill—of coming at the same moment as any man I've ever been with, and I've given it some thought. It seems to me that if simultaneous orgasm happens, great. But if both of you have this as a goal, someone's always rushing and someone's always holding back. That seems to be a distraction, and for me it would spoil the joy of what's happening. In your letter you say that you and your husband have a great time together, so relax and just enjoy that, and forget the stress of trying to come together.

Joan

Dear Joan,

I think this may be a stupid question, but are men capable of multiple orgasms like women are? I guess I've always envied women in that, and I'm just hoping I'm wrong, that men can really come more than once. Please don't disappoint me.

Lenny

Dear Lenny,

No man I've been with has ever experienced multiple male orgasm, nor has anyone I know ever really tried. However, from all I've read it is possible.

Clinically, men have what is called a refractory period, the rest period after ejaculation during which it's difficult, if not impossible, for a man to achieve another erection. For some men it's a very short time, for others it can be hours. Like so many other things, multiple orgasm isn't something to strive for. Working toward some illusory goal can ruin the pleasures to be had with one climax. However, if the idea tickles your brain and you want to see whether you can make it happen, read on. And, of course, you can have a great time practicing (evil grin).

One of the ways to achieve multiple male orgasm is for the man to climax without ejaculation. That seems to many like a contradiction in terms, but orgasm and ejaculation aren't necessarily the same thing. If you can train your body to climax without the draining effects of ejaculation, it can be possible to climax again, and again. How? That's the tricky part.

Most men can sense when they are close to the inevitable edge, that point beyond which ejaculation is certain. If he can continually approach that edge, then back off, resting for a minute or so and consciously relaxing, or, as some men say, squeezing, the pelvic muscles, a man can train his body not to come. Squeezing or relaxing is up to the man in question—whichever works to lessen the sexual tension is fine.

Practicing this technique is probably best done, at least in the beginning, during masturbation. Later, when you have isolated the muscles necessary and have developed some rudimentary control, your partner can play along with you. Just remember not to leave her hanging while you're busy concentrating on your body.

Joan

Faking It

Dear Joan,
I think my girlfriend is faking orgasm some of the time. How can I tell?
Paul from England

Dear Paul,
You probably can't tell. If you hold really still at the moment she's achieving orgasm, you can feel the small spasms of her vagina. That's a fabulous feeling, by the way. At the moment of climax, she should be well lubricated and her nipples should be erect, but other than that, it's really difficult to know when a woman's reaching her peak.

The bigger question here, though, is why she'd be faking orgasm at all. Is it possible that you're pressuring her in order to be sure she's achieved climax? Sometimes a woman doesn't really care whether she's physically come or not. A woman can experience peaks of pleasure without the physical responses typical of actual orgasm, then relax into a period of afterglow. If she says she's climaxed, that's fine. Often, I find that I can achieve pleasure just from my partner's climax, and that's enough for me.

Maybe the better question for you to be asking is, "Do you want anything more?" Ask her, "Is there anything I can do to make it better?" That might get you the response you're looking for.
Joan

On Female Ejaculation

Dear Joan,
I have a question. I have been hearing and reading a lot on the topic of female ejaculation lately. Personally, this has only happened one time, but I'd like to know more. Are there any tips, things I could do to have this experience again? I know some women can do this

every time they have sex, and I am just curious to know how this happens.
Amy

Dear Amy,

I've never experienced this phenomenon, but I know from letters I've gotten that it happens to some women quite frequently. From what I gather, during a particularly violent orgasm, there's a sudden gush of fluid. For a long time experts thought it was just urine or a mix of urine and the natural lubricating fluid produced to ease intercourse. Now, however, it seems to be accepted by most scientists that it's a different process with a different fluid entirely. Some researchers report that as many as 40 percent of women say that they've experienced female ejaculation at least once.

Whatever the scientific opinion, it's normal. The only complaint seems to be that it's often messy, so take a towel to bed and enjoy! It seems from letters that once experienced, it's like a new sex toy, one that keeps you aroused waiting for the next occurrence.

One important thing. Don't forgo the other pleasures of sex to strive for female ejaculation. If it happens and it makes orgasm better for you, great. If it's just another part of the process, relax and don't concern yourself with it. I don't.

Here are several letters from people to whom this has happened. I think you'll find these anecdotal tales very enlightening.

Hi Joan,

I have recently been experiencing something new in my sex life—female ejaculation. I think that the first time it happened was several months ago, but it's really difficult to tell because my lover and I came at the same time and I didn't ejaculate a whole lot. About a week later I was masturbating using a small vibrator as well as my hands, and I was close to cuming when the vibrator slipped and hit my clit hard. All of a sudden, as I came really violently, there was this huge gush of fluid. I actually thought I had lost control of my bladder. I checked later and it didn't look or smell like urine, so I concluded that this was the same thing that had happened with my husband.

Since then, I have gotten into teaching myself the joys of ejaculation, both during masturbation and while making love with my lover. It seems that since I've learned to pleasure myself, my climaxes with him are getting bigger and wetter.
Flo

Joan,
I don't know whether I experience female ejaculation or not, but I do know that sometimes I have sex that is incredibly better and wetter than other times. When it's really good I will get soaking wet, so wet I will need a towel to wipe some liquid away prior to penetration. It does not come out forcefully and I can't feel it as it gets wetter, but my mate states it feels like fluids are dripping down as it occurs. I also know the fluid is clear and satiny-feeling, with no tinge of yellow. It does not have to occur with physical stimulation of my genitals. It can occur when I am in a highly aroused mental state, and no physical stimulation whatsoever to my genitals has to occur.
Helena

Dear Joan,
My wife and I have been together for almost twenty years. Though we have a good sex life, she's very timid and doesn't like trying many adventurous things. Recently, something happened that changed our lives. My wife rarely gets wet from manual stimulation; it's only after I put it in that she begins to lubricate. Well, on this night, I was inside of her and she was lubricating. About ten minutes in, her pussy seemed to open still wider. I'd never felt her so open and wet. But that was just the start. Soon, I felt something warm just below my tummy. My wife was coming, hard. She seemed to ejaculate three or four times, all the time wetting me and the bed. Now, whenever we have sus-

tained sex, she comes like crazy. It's great, and it's rejuvenated our sex lives.

I hope others can learn to enjoy this special treat.
Walter

Hello, Joan,
Over the last several years, my wife and I have honed our ability to make her ejaculate during orgasm. It seems several spurts of fluid come out. It only takes a bit of stimulation and she gets really aroused, very wet, then whammo. All of this works best in the missionary position, or with her sitting on the edge of the bed with her legs spread wide open. I'll leave the rest of what we do to your imagination.

In closing I would like to say, "Gentlemen, take the time to try some of my techniques, and BE PATIENT! Ladies, relax, breathe, and try to concentrate on the sensations your body is giving you. It will all COME out in the end. Happy Spurting Everyone."
Billy from Texas

Dear Joan,
I have been ejaculating during intercourse for as long as I can remember. I was always embarrassed about this in my younger days, and my ex-husband always thought I was peeing on him. He said it was disgusting, but, of course, he's now my EX-husband. After my divorce I was celibate for many years because of this uncontrollable reaction to intercourse. I was afraid of the way a man would react—I guess my ex had poisoned me to something that I eventually found out is so normal and natural.

Thankfully, I met a most wonderful man; he delights in my ejaculation and loves to keep me flowing. The big question is how many towels will we need. I cum from varied types of stimulation: his hands, his mouth, light clitoral spanking, and have also discovered that pinching or having my nipples nibbled on is a direct route to this phenomenon.

I'm convinced that if everyone would allow themselves this pleasure, stress levels, anxiety attacks, and the drugs folks take for such conditions would be reduced by half. And you'd be greeted on the street by smiling faces, too. I say, "Women, enjoy your body and find yourself a partner who can enjoy it too."
Betsy

Dear Joan,
I was pleasantly surprised to find out that there are so many other women who have this ability. I experienced it myself for the first time when I was in my twenties, and I thought I was a freak of nature. I can't make myself ejaculate through masturbation; it usually happens during oral sex or intercourse. My husband says he knows exactly which spot to stimulate to make me cum that way. I don't do it every time I have sex, but often.
Gloria

Amy, it's obvious that female ejaculation exists, but don't make questing for it the center of your love life. If it happens, great. If not, not.
Joan

The Elusive G-Spot

Dear Joan,
I'm a woman age thirty-eight and I've always been curious about the g-spot and g-spot orgasms. Does the g-spot really exist? How do I locate it in the first place and are g-spot orgasms better than others? I am extremely enthusiastic to learn more about it and maybe, if needed, practice it a bit on my own so that my sex life with my husband can improve.
Thank you so much for your help.
Brenda

Dear Brenda,

Yes, I think most experts now concede that the g-spot really exists. Men and women are convinced that it's the magic orgasm button and if they can just find it, they can immediately trigger explosive orgasms. They are disappointed when they "can't find it." Unfortunately, the g-spot isn't magic. Rather it's a pad of tissue wrapped around the urethra—the tube from the bladder to the urinary opening, that can be stimulated through the front wall of the vagina. Named for Ernst Grafenberg, the g-spot is felt as a spongy mass of tissue that varies in size from the size of a dime to a half-dollar, found on the belly side of the vaginal canal about as far in as you can reach with your finger.

What magic there is lies in the woman's reaction to that stimulation. Some women find it explosively pleasurable, some find it irritating, and most fall between. I have never found any particular pleasure in g-spot stimulation, and I have tried. Other women have written to tell me about the earth-shattering orgasms they have when their lover presses on or strokes their g-spot.

If you want to locate it, just insert a finger, crooked slightly, and explore the front wall of your vagina. You might find it a very awkward position and so you might need to ask your partner to try for you. There are also dildos, curved at the right angle, so that you can try to stimulate your g-spot with that. Just relax, lower your expectations, and see what happens. Don't expect to rock the earth, just see what feels good.
Joan

Sex and a Woman's Period

Dear Joan,

I don't know whether I'm crazy or not but I just don't like making love while I have my period. My new husband says I'm nuts, that menstruation is a normal process and he doesn't mind a bit of mess. You see, he's a horny guy and wants to make love almost every day.

Since I have my period for about a week, by the time I'm done he's positively crazed. Am I nuts like he says?
Beverly

Dear Beverly,
No, you're not nuts. Women vary as to whether they are comfortable, physically or mentally, having intercourse while they have their period. Personally, I'm in your camp. I didn't enjoy it, although at my age it's no longer a problem. I did discover, however, that using a diaphragm during the last few days allowed me to feel clean and permitted intercourse without the mess.

Making love at this time of the month is a very personal decision, and if you're not comfortable then you won't enjoy sex. If you don't enjoy sex his pleasure will be diminished as well. So do whatever you need and your husband will just have to understand. Of course, it makes that first time after the enforced abstinence really great.
Joan

Chapter 5

After Doing It

His Reaction

Dear Joan,
I think this must be a common complaint, because I hear it kidded about on sitcoms and such. But for me it's a real problem. After we make love my husband just rolls over and falls asleep. It's really frustrating for me, since I want some cuddling and loving time. I say I *want*, but it's really a *need* for me. What can I do? I've tried asking him for some consideration, but he just doesn't get it. Help!
Carol from Ohio

Dear Carol,
Sleeping after sex is a natural part of nature's plan. Leaving your body horizontal is mother nature's way of helping sperm make their way toward your egg. After all, fertilization is nature's plan, and who needs to fight gravity? It's a difficult enough trip for the sperm without swimming uphill. So feeling drowsy is hormonal, and men feel that way too.

Okay, that said, I understand that you want some loving time afterwards. I know it's frustrating, but I would guess it's just as frustrating for him. Here he is, in bed, warm, cozy, and delightfully satisfied, and you are asking him for something he's not sure how to give.

So help him. Be very specific about what you want. Say, "Come over here and hug me. I want to feel your arms around me." Or, "Tell me how good that was." Or, "Tell me how much you love me." That gives him something concrete to do to make you happy. It's not that he's insensitive, just puzzled. He's content and can't quite understand that you aren't.

You can also focus on his face and tell him how wonderful he was. No one was ever quick to pass up a compliment. This can be a learning and teaching time, too. Tell him, chapter and verse, if you can bring yourself to be a bit graphic, exactly what you most enjoyed about your lovemaking. Then ask him to return the favor. You can gather a lot of information about what he most enjoys, and transmit the same to him, in this wonderful afterward time.

I hope this helps, and let me know how it all works out.
Joan

Dear Joan,

I know you get so many letters that I don't think you'll remember me. I wrote about my husband, who used to just roll over after sex. Well, I tried your suggestions. I asked very specifically for what I wanted. The first night, I whispered, "How about giving me a big hug before you fall asleep." To my surprise, he did, and we fell asleep holding each other. It was wonderful. I'm slowly learning to convey my needs to him in a very gentle way, and now it's really so much better.

Now don't get me wrong, he's not one to volunteer lots of kissing and stuff after sex, and he still falls asleep within a few minutes, but we're usually holding hands or hugging, and we've done some good-night kissing before he conks out.

Thanks for all the help.
Carol from Ohio

Dear Joan,

I don't smoke, but my boyfriend does, and he always has a cigarette after we make love. Is there something chemical? I'd really rather he didn't. Can I ask him not to?

Angie

Dear Angie,

Smoking a cigarette after sex is a bit of a cliché, but when I smoked (about thirty years ago), I did enjoy a relaxing puff or two after orgasm. I don't think there was anything chemical, just a feeling of well-being during that wonderful afterglow. I will say that it also gave me something to do with my hands and a way to make conversation with someone who wasn't very talkative after sex.

I see no reason why you can't ask your boyfriend not to light up or to take his cigarette into the bathroom. These days it's not an insult, just a matter of taste. Maybe suggest that he substitute a sip of soda or water, a hard candy or a stick of gum. Be sure to have a few things handy for him. Let me know how that works.

Joan

Dear Joan,

It's me, Angie. I wrote to you a few weeks ago about my boyfriend, who smokes after sex. I took your suggestion and mentioned it to him. He was great. He had never realized that it bothered me. Now we keep a roll of Pep-O-Mint LifeSavers beside the bed and he sucks one after sex. An added benefit is that his good-night kiss tastes delicious. Thanks for helping.

Angie

The Dreaded Wet Spot

Dear Joan,

I hate sleeping in that awful wet spot that happens after my husband and I make love. It's cold and icky. It always seems to end up

on my side of the bed, too. What can I do? Jeff, that's my husband, just laughs when I complain.
Janice

Dear Janice,

In the romance novels I'm so fond of, no one ever talks about the mess afterwards. I've always wondered how the heroine can make love on the sofa in front of the fire, then calmly waltz out and rejoin the party. Not I, at least not without several tissues and the inevitable damp panties. And, of course, making love in a bed usually results in fluids on the sheets and the dreaded wet spot.

There are a number of ways to combat this. First, be aggressive and make love on his side of the bed. Then he has to sleep in the wet spot. Or, after he falls asleep, go around to his side of the bed and slide in. He'll slide over to make room, and, again, he'll end up in the cold ickies.

Okay, all kidding (or was I kidding?) aside, there are a few specific things you can do to deal with the problem. First, keep a large bath towel under the bed, and after making love, spread it on the bed over the area in question. Or put the towel on the bed before making love so that it gets wet, not the bed. You can even be decadent and take the towel out of the dryer just before bed, fold it tightly to keep in the heat, and spread it out, warm and cozy, just before or just after.

Another way to combat the wet spot is for him to wear a condom. I know that's not necessarily part of your lovemaking, and it shouldn't be viewed as a punishment, but if you make it a normal part of preparations, it can be a good way to control his semen.

Here's a letter from someone who solved your problem in a wonderfully loving way.

Joan,

I know a lot of folks wonder what to do about the mess after making love, but my husband and I have developed a routine that really works. After intercourse, I raise my knees and tilt my pelvis to control the outflow. My husband fills a basin with warm

water and then uses a face cloth to clean me up. It's such a loving gesture that I was blown away the first time he did it. Now it's an everytime thing, and after he cleans my genitals, I wash his. I have to admit that sometimes this leads to more lovemaking, and the need for still more washing. It's dynamite!!!
Cherise

Great idea, no?
Joan

Bidets

Dear Joan,
I read a novel that was set in Europe and the bathroom contained a bidet. I'll 'fess up that I have no clue exactly what a bidet is, what it's used for and how. I've asked a few of my friends, but they admit that they don't know either. Can you enlighten us?
Heidi

Dear Heidi,
Sure. A bidet is a very common bathroom fixture all over Europe. It looks like a low, oblong sink, narrow enough to straddle and sit on, usually placed beside the toilet in European bathrooms. There are faucets on one end and a drain that can be closed. Sometimes the faucet has an adjustable, pointable nozzle.

There are lots of folks who don't like to go to sleep all sticky after intercourse. What a man or woman can do is use the bidet. He or she, usually she, sits on it, facing the faucet end, adjusts the water to a comfortable temperature, and uses a washcloth or the nozzle and some gentle soap to wash the genitals. It's just that simple. It's a lot easier than using the bathroom sink and dripping down your thighs and onto the rug. For many it's as common as brushing teeth.

I hope you get the opportunity to use one. It's really a lovely way to feel clean.
Joan

Caring for Your Toys

Dear Joan,

My husband and I play with toys a lot, and naturally they get slimy. Is there anything special we should do to clean or store them?
Laural

Dear Laural,

The only thing I can recommend is lots of soap and water. It's important to "do the laundry," as Ed and I put it, so that nothing goes back into use dirty. You might choose to wash things at night or the next day, but do it carefully and thoroughly.

As for storage, you just need a private place that the kids won't find, prompting embarrassing questions. Nothing will mess up an evening with friends faster than Little Johnny holding up your favorite purple dildo and asking, in a loud voice, "What's this, Mommy?"
Joan

Dear Joan,

Is there a proper way to dispose of a used condom? I know that sounds silly, but it gets a bit messy to just wrap it in a tissue and drop it into the trash. Can I flush it down the toilet? Have you any other suggestions?
Cliff

Dear Cliff,

You might want to tie a knot in it to keep the fluids contained, then wrap it up and toss it into the garbage. Please don't flush it, as it can clog the plumbing. It would be really embarrassing for you and your lady to have to call Roto-Rooter and have them snake out a cute little bit of plastic—or several.
Joan

Dear Joan,

I'm really young and new to this sex stuff. I don't know who else to

ask, so here goes. I know I'm supposed to use a condom, and I've practiced putting one on so I won't fumble at the wrong moment. But those things are expensive. Can I wash one with lots of soap and water and use it again? I know my friends would laugh at me if I asked them, so I was hoping you could help me.
Frank from New Jersey

Dear Frank,
No, you can't reuse a condom. During cleaning there's a distinct risk of damage. You can cause holes so small you might not see them but which would ruin the condom's effectiveness for the next time. So despite the cost, use a new, recently purchased one each time.
Joan

Was It Okay for You?

Dear Joan,
I'm a fifty-three-year-old woman and my boyfriend and I have lived together for seven years. We don't have any reason to get married, so we aren't. Anyway, after making love, I find that occasionally I need some reassurance that sex was okay. Is that really childish?
Ruth

Dear Ruth,
Not in the least. I'm supposed to be an expert on the subject of sex, and I find that, from time to time, I need to hear those words, too, especially when we've tried something new. I've gotten quite forthright. I merely ask Ed, "Was it okay for you?" It's amazing how many times he laughs, wondering how I can *not* know. "Of course, it was just great. Was it okay for you?"

Actually, I am asking two separate questions: "Were you satisfied?" and "Did I do okay?" Sometimes you need that, and it's impossible for your partner to know exactly when that is, so ask. Just do it.
Joan

Dear Joan:

I know that many men are concerned about how they perform in bed. So many of your letters from men express anxiety about the size of their penis or their sexual technique. I guess I've been lucky. Somehow, that has never been an issue for me. I have never thought about sex in terms of "performance." However, it has always been very important to me that my partner be satisfied. And asking "Was it good for you, dear?" just doesn't work. What is she supposed to say? "No, I would have preferred to watch *ER*?"

When my wife has an orgasm during sex, it's easy for me to feel confident that she is satisfied. But she doesn't always come during sex. Although she has assured me time after time that, although she sometimes needs an orgasm to be satisfied, there are times when she feels perfectly satisfied from just our sex play and from my own satisfaction. As a man, it is very difficult for me to accept that. For a man, orgasm and satisfaction—or, rather, lack of orgasm and frustration—are so closely linked. Although there are rare times when my wife's satisfaction is enough for me, most of the time I feel unsatisfied and frustrated if I do not come.

The only thing that assures both of us that we are not leaving the other frustrated after sex is that we have a deal. Our agreement is that if either of us is not satisfied, he or she will tell the other exactly what he or she needs. When my wife comes and I don't, it's pretty obvious that I am feeling frustrated. She will ask me, "What would feel good?" My telling her inevitably leads to my total satisfaction. If I come first, her body usually tells me whether she wants more or is satisfied to just stop. Even if my penis is temporarily not functional, my hands and mouth are, and there are always dildos and vibrators that I can use. But the most important thing is that I know that if she does want more, she will tell me so. That assures me that I am not leaving her frustrated and unsatisfied.

As in all aspects of a relationship, trust and communication can solve many potential problems.

Ed

Dear Ed,
What a wonderful letter, and what a fantastic relationship you have. If more couples communicated as you two do, there would be so many fewer problems. Bravo!!!
Joan

One-Night Stands

Dear Joan,
I'm a sexually active woman and I enjoy frequent one-night stands or short-term relationships. Though it's not really sexual, I have one problem that I was hoping you could help me with. I invite the guy back to my place and the sex is great. Frequently, however, I don't want the guy to stay over. How can I politely tell him to leave? I've tried a few casual remarks, but sometimes he just won't take the hint. Any ideas?
Belinda

Dear Belinda,
Yours is a common problem, and maybe I can help. During my one-night-stand days in the early eighties, I had similar problems. I found that gentle honesty was the best solution. I used to say something like, "I really enjoyed the evening, and I hope you won't mind, but I'm really used to sleeping alone. I'm a bit of a bed hog, so for both our sakes, would you mind very much if we said good night?" Occasionally the guy was a bit put out, but I figured that if he didn't understand something so simple, maybe he wasn't the kind of guy I was interested in over the long haul anyway.

You, of course, will find your own verbiage, but I hope this idea helps.
Joan

Joan,
I'm having a problem I hope you can help me with. I'm never sure

whether I'm supposed to stay over with a girl after the first time we go to bed together. What's the proper etiquette?
Matt from Texas

Dear Matt,
I don't think there's a proper etiquette in such a situation. She's probably having the same problems, wondering how she should discuss it with you. My suggestion is to be honest. You might try, "I'd love to stay the night if you'd like, but if you'd prefer to be alone, I'll certainly understand." That let's everyone off the hook without insulting anyone. I always think that being tactfully honest is the best way to handle potentially awkward moments like this one.
Joan

Instead of Doing It

Masturbation

Dear Joan,
I know my husband masturbates when he's away on business. We have a great sex life, and I think we're both satisfied—I know I am. So I don't know why he feels he has to do this. Why can't he save it for me? I certainly don't touch myself when he's gone.
Cora

Dear Cora,
Masturbation is such a volatile topic. Men have been doing it since the caves, and enjoying it thoroughly, I might add. For thousands of years they probably felt free to touch themselves whenever they wanted. Eventually someone got the idea that masturbation might cut down on the frequency with which they had intercourse, and thus reduce the chances of fertilization, so they declared this delightful practice off-limits. Okay, it wasn't that simple, but something of the sort certainly did occur.

Cora, let me just say this. It seems obvious from your letter that his masturbating isn't detracting from your sex life, so why shouldn't he do it if it relieves some of his frustrations at being away from home? I'm sure you'll admit that it's better for him to solve the problem himself than pick up some woman in a bar.

As for you, if you don't masturbate, that's your choice, but it's not necessarily the good news. Knowing your body can help you to improve your sex life, and your reactions to stimulation. Let me give you some background that I hope will help you understand.

A man learns to masturbate early on in life. Here is this pleasurable penis that he touches every time he goes to the bathroom. It feels good to fondle it, and thus the touching moves from the bathroom to the rest of the house and beyond. But soon he begins to hear the most outrageous stories about what happens to "bad little boys" who touch themselves. "Your wee wee will fall off," they tell him. Or, "You know, it causes insanity." Or, "If you do that you won't be able to enjoy sex with your wife." Or, "You'll grow hair on the palms of your hands." Then comes the biggie, "You only have so many orgasms in you, so if you waste them now, you'll run out." Phew. It's a wonder boys ever find ways to enjoy sex, but they do, probably learning about the pleasures of their bodies from secret masturbation. While they fondle themselves, they probably worry about everything they have been told, all of which is hokum.

For women, it's worse. Their mothers tell them it's bad and dirty to touch themselves, so women don't. Ever. Oh, of course they do in the shower or bath, but that is quick, clean, and clinical. A woman's private parts aren't to be seen or touched by anyone. Until recently that included doctors. In olden days, doctors had anatomical models that a woman could point to to indicate "female problems." Even now the phrase "female complaint" exists to refer to those things that a woman isn't supposed to talk about or even think about.

So a woman wanders into marriage or into a sexual relationship unable to help her husband understand how to increase her excitement level. She has no clue. You might think that I'm talking autobiographically. You're right. I was born in 1941 and hadn't ever touched myself in a sexual way until I had been married for more than ten years and had two school-aged children. I began my experimentation after reading the wonderful book *Our Bodies, Ourselves: A Book by and for Women,* which came out in 1976. I read it with great interest, studying the anatomy and physiology of sex and giving myself permission to explore. So explore I did, in the bathtub, learning the feel of my own body and the way it reacted to various touches. I remember it very well, including the guilt I felt about doing something I thought was so forbidden. And I hadn't been fed all that guilt stuff from my mother, a very enlightened woman for her generation. We had never discussed it, but, of course, the propaganda was everywhere else.

Eventually I learned and slowly became able to indicate to my then husband how to increase the pleasure of sex.

When I wrote my first book, in 1989, I thought that this level of ignorance was a thing of the past. Most women, I thought, would have already learned about their own bodies, from books like *Our Bodies,* or *The Joy of Sex,* from TV talk shows, from X-rated films, books, and magazines, and from the most common source, other women. Alas, it wasn't entirely true. I still get questions from women who have never climaxed and men who are still caught by the old masturbational fears.

Cora, let me address your comment that you don't masturbate. The only way to help your lover learn how to best please you during sex is to know yourself. You wouldn't attempt to teach someone French if you didn't speak a word of the language, so naturally you can't show your partner about your body until and unless you learn about it first.

So do whatever you want, but don't fault him for doing something that is such an integral part of the male psyche.
Joan

Dear Joan,
I've read lots of books on sex, and many of them say that to help my

lover improve our sex life, I should masturbate in order to learn about my body. Phew—it's even difficult to write that. Anyway, I've no clue how to go about that. Can you help?

Maureen from Colorado

Dear Maureen,

I know that it is really difficult to get started, so let me see if I can help.

Begin in your mind. Repeat after me. "It's my body. Nothing bad will happen to me if I touch it." I promise. Relax and think sexy thoughts. Or, if that makes you uncomfortable, get clinical. Either way, begin with a small anatomy tour. The outer lips, or *labia majora,* are those fleshy pads on either side of the opening to your vagina. Those are the ones covered with pubic hair and which are usually closed over the vaginal and urinary openings when you're not aroused. Between them are thinner lips, the *labia minora,* also usually closed over the vagina. In older women they might extend through the outer lips as two petal-looking structures.

Between the inner lips is the opening to the vaginal canal, into which a penis can be inserted. Between the outer lips, forward of the inner lips (more toward the belly) is the clitoris, the only organ of the body devoted to pleasure alone. When not aroused, it's a tiny, BB-sized lump well hidden beneath layers of flesh. As a woman becomes aroused, it swells in that same way that a penis does. Eventually it becomes hard and an inch or more in length. In addition, as the arousal level increases, the tissues of the vaginal canal produce a lubricating fluid to ease insertion of the penis. If you want a more detailed anatomy lesson, try any one of the books in the sexuality section of your library or bookstore. You can also satisfy your curiosity by just looking at your genitals using a hand mirror. Check them out so you get familiar with the landmarks.

Okay, now that we've got the technical (or as technical as I need to get) anatomy lesson over with, let's get to your body. It's like other bodies, yet it's as unique as you are. So you need to learn about it and what arouses it. You can learn anywhere, at any time, but I would recommend a few things. First, you need privacy and time. Set aside some time when you know you won't be interrupted by the kids, your partner, the phone, whatever. Maybe in bed one evening when he's stayed late at work. Maybe in the bathtub beneath the bubbles. Maybe early in the morning after he's gone to work. Maybe in the shower. Carve out the time. It's important. You also need clean hands and smooth nails, so a bit of grooming might be a good idea.

Now you need the courage to touch. Okay, it's a bit scary and unfamiliar. Just do it. Slide your fingers over the folds and valleys. Learn how your body is constructed. If you want to keep the first session purely clinical, great. Slide your finger inside a bit and just see how it feels. Not sexy? That's okay, we're just getting acquainted this first time. Have you ever inserted a tampon or used a diaphragm? If so, you're at least familiar with your vaginal canal. If not, now's the time. Done? Okay, enough for today.

Soon you should become a bit more comfortable touching yourself. Okay, so far it's not sexy, so let's move on to sexy next. What gets you interested? Fantasy? Erotic scenes from books or movies? Get relaxed with a bit of alcohol if you like, then think sexy thoughts. Read a hot erotic story. Watch an X-rated film (if you can find one that's arousing and not just boring). Put on some sexy music, maybe lots of saxophone or a hot male vocal. Slowly begin to touch where it feels good. Do you want to touch your nipples? Go for it. Feel how they swell and tighten as you get excited. Stroke your belly, your thighs, whatever feels good. That's the most important part of this lesson—do what feels good. If you begin to get cold feet, stop for today and continue at another time.

Take your time. Slow down—speed up. It's your body! Do what feels best! Eventually you'll get the urge to touch "down there." And if you're still thinking of it as "down there," loosen up. Slide your fingers into that previously only clinical area. Has it changed? Arousal will do that. The lips should swell and open. You should be able to feel wet, slippery stuff. That's good. If not, take more time getting in the mood. Explore.

The rest of the lesson is easy. Do more of what feels good, less of what doesn't. Notice that different types of touches feel good at different stages of arousal. Soft, tickly touches feel good at one time, firmer pressure feels good at another. Learn. Take your time. Whenever you feel you've had enough, stop. Do it again another time.

If you proceed as I did, you might want to insert something into your vagina. I learned about my body in the bathtub and used the handle of my toothbrush the first time. I was really curious and just did it—and it felt great. Soon I found a well-shaped shampoo bottle and tried the neck of that. Take care. Your tissues are quite delicate, so be sure anything you insert is smooth and scrupulously clean. It must also be long enough that it won't slide inside and have to be retrieved. That's really embarrassing. If you want, try a candle or a conveniently shaped vegetable, a squash or carrot. Again, please, be sure it's clean, smooth, and large enough not to get lost.

Will you achieve orgasm? Eventually. That might mean three sessions, or thirty. Who knows? It probably took me six or eight times before I finally learned enough to drive myself over the edge, and I was surprised and delighted. I was like a kid with a new toy and kept trying to duplicate the feat. Once I had gotten in the habit of orgasm, I found it was easier to come with my then husband too. I also showed him a few things he could do (or not do) to increase the excitement level. But if you don't get to climax, so what? If you're giving yourself pleasure, that's the idea.

Try it and let me know what happens.

Joan

Dear Joan,

It's Maureen here again, and I did what you suggested about masturbation. It was really scary, but I did it. I can't thank you enough for your advice. It's taken me almost two months to get comfortable with all this, but last night I gently took my husband's hand and guided his fingers to just where I'd discovered I wanted to be touched. He was thrilled when, with just a little rubbing, I came. God, it was fabulous.

Again, thank you, thank you, thank you.
Maureen

Dear Ms. Lloyd,
I've been worrying recently about whether masturbation can dull the sensations in my penis and reduce the pleasures of intercourse. Can it?
Lester

Dear Lester,
The only harm it can do is if you rub really hard, and I mean really hard. I understand that you can eventually desensitize the skin of the penis. That is really rare, but if you are worried, use a bit of lubricant.
Joan

Dear Joan,
Can you tell me what I can do to make masturbation feel better? I'm a thirty-four-year-old man and I am "between women" right now, so I have to depend on my hands for satisfaction. I seem to do it the same way all the time. Maybe you know some tricks?
John

Dear John,
I've gotten quite a few letters from men who've found ways to make masturbation more pleasurable, so I've included some of them here.

Dear Joan,
I have found that it is very stimulating to play with myself while looking into a mirror. I have found that if I lie on my bed in just the right spot, I can watch myself in the mirror over my wife's dresser. What a sight.

If men are interested in spicing up masturbation, don't overlook the thrill of watching. Oh, and if you use your nondominant hand occasionally, I really think it feels like someone else.
Tim

Dear Joan,

Masturbation is such a great thing, I absolutely love it and do it at least once a day. I do a variety of different things to get myself off. Sometimes I will lie down on the bed and just rub myself against the mattress like I'm having sex until I explode all over the sheets. Other times I'll stand over the bed and just stroke until I come. If I have more time I really enjoy sitting at the computer looking at sexy pictures, reading stories, or reading about other people's experiences. When I do this I rub myself through my briefs until I'm just about ready to come, and then I stop or slow down. I repeat this several times until I just can't hold it anymore. Then when I come it is much stronger. Well, I'm getting excited, so it's time to end this letter and . . .
Charles

Dear Ms. Lloyd,

I know this is going to sound really bizarre, but I've built a masturbation box. I took a small plastic box and cut a hole in one end. That was the hard part, but I have a small portable saber saw that did the trick. Anyway, I filled the box with cotton, and then, with my finger, made a tube through the hole I cut. Then I rubbed Vaseline in the tunnel and stuck my penis inside. It's wonderful, just like doing it with a woman.

I hope you won't think me too weird, but it works for me and I know you always say that anything that gives you pleasure is okay.
Bernard

Dear Joan Elizabeth Lloyd,

I recently bought a masturbation toy. It's shaped like a hand and wraps around my penis and moves with the help of a battery. The fingers squeeze and release. It's dynamite.
Jay from Rhode Island

John, I'm sure you've gotten a few ideas, but the best way to in-

crease your pleasure during masturbation is not to succumb to the usual every time. Be creative and I know you'll enjoy.
Joan

Dear Joan,
I'm curious. Have any men written to you about how old they were when they masturbated for the first time? I'm curious because I can't remember a time when I didn't and I was wondering whether I'm normal.
Ricky

Dear Ricky,
You're normal. Period. Many men have been touching themselves since they were babies. Why? Because it feels good. As for letters? I have gotten a few.

Dear Joan,
How far back do I go and what is the definition of masturbation? As far back as I can remember, I enjoyed touching my penis. In private, of course; I didn't dare let the grown-up folks know. It puzzled me that my penis would get stiff when I touched it. Boy, was I ignorant. In my early teens (or maybe even earlier) I began to have these crazy dreams at night which featured all kinds of activities with almost everyone I had ever seen.

Eventually an older boy with hair around his root taught me and his brother how to get a super good feeling by various types of self-manipulation. It felt great! He also taught us what he knew, and borrowed some books about sex from his dad (without his knowledge, of course), which showed us what went where, etc.

I have practiced this art of self-contentment and pleasure ever since, most of the time alone and in private.
Franklin from Australia

And I got this letter from a man who describes what it was like the first time he masturbated.

Dear Joan,
The first time I actually remember masturbating was when I was twelve years old. I took a shower, then went into my bedroom with just a towel around my waist. I took the towel off and sat naked on the bed as I watched the small TV in my room. It felt good being nude and I noticed that my penis was stiff and sticking straight up in the air. I just reached down with my fingertips and began stroking the shaft very slowly. All of a sudden a wave of pleasure swept over my body and the manipulation of my penis felt better and better with each new stroke. Then I lay on my back and closed my eyes and could not help but be amazed at how good my erect penis felt under my own touch.

After this stroking for more than five minutes, I suddenly felt a new sensation. I let go of my penis and I watched in amazement as it began jerking back and forth and white creamy fluid came shooting out. What a wonderful experience to masturbate and get a surprise like this! I now play with myself in front of my girlfriend and she loves it!
BJ

Dear Ms. Lloyd,
I'm a sixty-three-year-old man and I remember that first masturbation experience like it was yesterday. I was thirteen years old. My parents had gone out for the evening and I was alone in the house, sitting in the living room, watching TV. I had homework to do but I had been feeling restless all evening and was unable to concentrate. I wanted something but I didn't know what it was that I wanted. I had found a magazine my father had hidden under his mattress, and I gazed at a picture showing Marilyn Monroe, nude, against a red satin background.

I decided to take a bath before going to bed. As I sat in the steamy water, I began to touch my penis. Each time I touched it, it jumped out of the water. It felt so great. After a while I tired of that game and began to wonder what else might make my penis feel good. I took the washcloth and made a sort of parachute out of it so that when I brought it under the water, it trapped a large air bubble. I brought the washcloth containing the trapped air bubble under my penis and squeezed it so that a thin line of bubbles rose from it. It tickled the entire length of my penis and made it rise up out of the water.

After the bath, when I had dried myself, the feeling of wanting something was stronger than ever. I looked at the bar of soap in the soap dish and wondered what it would feel like if I were to make my hand soapy and rub my penis with it. I soaped my hand and began to stroke my penis, which became bigger and harder than I had ever seen it. Now I began to feel a sense of urgency, a need to stroke harder and faster. It felt wonderful, and as I stroked, it felt like I was, somehow, closer to whatever it was that I wanted. Suddenly I stopped stroking, closed my eyes, and clutched my penis hard as wave after wave of the most exquisite pleasure that I had ever known swept over my entire body. This was what I had been wanting all evening, even though I had never experienced it before.

After a few minutes I opened my eyes and found my hand and belly covered with a milky fluid. I suddenly realized what had happened. So this was what an orgasm was. I had read about it but had never had any concept of how incredibly good it would feel. Unfortunately, because of the prudery and misinformation that were so prevalent in those times, it would be many more years before I would be able to give myself that pleasure without believing that I was, somehow, harming my body.

Lester

I hope that answers your question, Ricky.

Joan

Dear Joan,

My husband and I have recently been talking about masturbation and about making it part of our sex lives together. Is that too weird?
Jeanette

Dear Jeanette,

Masturbation is normal and natural, even with your lover. I remember the first time Ed asked me to show him how I touch myself when I am alone. Phew—I was a wreck. I was titillated, nervous, very excited, and scared. He asked again, and when I didn't comply, he let it drop. It was several lovemaking sessions later that he asked me again. This time, I took the risk. It was fantastic—not only pleasure for me, but a joy watching him watch me. I finally asked him to show me, and I discovered he had the same reaction. Now mutual masturbation is part of our lovemaking.

I've gotten many letters on the subject of mutual masturbation. Many couples enjoy stroking themselves during love play, either one at a time or simultaneously. Let's see what some folks wrote.

Dear Joan,

I am a forty-year-old female and I've been married for six months now. My husband enjoys watching me masturbate, and I him. I will admit that when he first asked me to touch myself while he watched, I was uncomfortable. But he was so encouraging and gentle that I finally did it. Well, after a couple of times, I found it to be quite a turn-on. Knowing he was watching, and being as turned on as I was, was a very horny thing. He will often stroke himself as he watches me. We find it to be a mutually satisfying activity.
Diana

Dear Joan,

My wife of almost forty years and I have always enjoyed masturbation. When we were first married, we were shy about it, but

I let her know that solo sex was okay for me if she was so inclined.

As we grew older and more sexually at ease with each other, we enjoyed jerking off while watching videos or just enjoying each other. Sometimes she puts on a show for me with her toys. Man, can she get hot! She has had a number of vibrators and enjoys large dildos from time to time.

Sometimes we masturbate alone. My wife is a morning person sexually, and sometimes she wakes up by enjoying a couple of orgasms before getting out of bed. She says it starts her day out right. For me, I've always enjoyed erotic literature, movies, or videos. Now with the Internet, I can surf and get off to my heart's content. None of our solo masturbation has any effect on our lovemaking, which is as frequent and enjoyable as ever.

Zachary

Dear Joan,
I will always remember the first time my wife masturbated while I watched. It was such a learning experience. It had taken quite a bit of persuading before she'd do it, and when she did, to my amazement, I discovered that I had been touching her all wrong. I watched her fingers, and where I had been gentle, she was forceful. Where I had quickly thrust fingers inside her, she came without any penetration.

We talked about all this later, and learned and taught. That evening marked a real turning point in our sex life. Not that it had been bad before, it was just much better after.

Toby

So, Jeanette, do it. It's a delightful addition to anyone's sex life, and I'm sure you and your husband will wander down many delicious pathways during your experiments.

Joan

Dear Joan,

How can I convince my husband to masturbate while I watch? I've always wanted to, but I don't know how to begin.

Can you help me?

Sue

Dear Sue,

I guess the answer is to encourage, not convince. Tell him how sexy you think it would be if he touched himself while you watched. If he doesn't, fine, try again next time. Put his hand on his penis with yours on top, or put your hand on him and let him place his hand over yours. Tell him you want him to teach you how best to touch him. Eventually you might be able to slip your hand from his and watch. If that happens, continue to tell him how great it is, how hot it makes you, and how great it is for him to show you.

Here's a letter that I think will answer your question as well as I ever could.

Dear Joan,

I had to comment about getting your partner to masturbate in front of you. I've had fantasies for years about this!!! I love to watch a man come. It's so intense, and nothing turns me on more. My husband and I had been married for almost two years and I kept dropping hints about wanting to watch, mostly when we were watching porno movies together.

One night we were taking a breather from some hot sex, and he was slowly stroking himself to get hard for another round. I gathered up my courage and said, "I love to watch you do that." He was a bit reluctant, but soon he started stroking faster. I kept telling him how much it turned me on to watch him, and how good it looked and so on. The more I encouraged, the more he got into it, and I was rewarded by watching him have an intense orgasm. Since then, I've also taken the initiative and begun masturbating in front of him. That sometimes ends

in wonderful mutual masturbation, and other times ends with some fantastic intercourse. I'm not complaining either way!
Mindy

So, Sue, give it a try.
Joan

Dear Joan,
Sometimes my wife just isn't in the mood. I'd love to ask her to touch me or watch while I masturbate, just so she's a part of it all, but I'm really nervous. Would I be asking for too much?
Benjamin

Dear Benjamin,
There are often times when I'm just not in the mood. In my younger days I didn't like making love while I had my period, and that often frustrated the men I was with as well. So I would frequently suggest that I touch them, or watch. Some men were surprised that I would be anxious to help, but why would I want to leave my partner frustrated when I could be part of something so rewarding?

So suggest it to your wife. "Darling, I understand you're not anxious for intercourse tonight, but would you just touch me?" You might also mention that this can all be part of lovemaking. Loving isn't just intercourse, after all.

Here are two letters that might help you.

Dear Joan,
When I need a little relief and my partner isn't interested in making love, she will sometimes "help me out" with masturbation. Sometimes she uses her hands, or breasts, or sometimes she just sucks or pinches my nipples while I do the stroking. I find that having both nipples stimulated while my penis is stimulated heightens all the sensations greatly!

I was really nervous the first time I asked her, but she was

so delighted to be able to help that she readily agreed. Now it's not even an issue. She usually asks *me.*
Harry from New Jersey

Dear Joan,

How to handle the situation when one partner wants sex and the other doesn't must be a big issue for me. In past relationships, when I was in the mood and my partner wasn't, her response would be a brusque or even angry "no," spoken either verbally or with body language, after which she would turn away and fall asleep. It still hurts to think about those nights. The worst thing about those times was not that I was being left sexually frustrated—masturbation solved that problem. No, the worst thing was that I would lie awake for hours feeling hurt—feeling that she didn't care that I was going to bed feeling "hungry" and frustrated. What I wanted and needed much more than sex was caring.

In my current relationship, caring about each other's feelings is such an important part of our relationship that it would never occur to me that she doesn't care about my sexual desire, even when she isn't in the mood. After all the years of believing that if my wife is not in the mood I didn't have the right to ask anything sexual of her, it is still difficult for me to ask for what I want under those circumstances. But with my current wife I know that it's okay for me to ask. She may still say no, but I know that she will not be angry that I asked. On the contrary, she loves it that I want her, even if she isn't in the mood for sex.

Most of the time, if I ask her to touch me, she is more than happy to help. And this may sound strange to you, but those times can be as exciting for me as when we are both turned on. Like most couples, she and I do not have exactly the same tastes in sex. While there are many things that turn us both on, there are some that she likes more than I do and vice versa. As far as I know there are no sexual activities either one of us likes that are repugnant to the other. When we are both in the mood for sex, we tend to play the games that both of us like. However, when she is not in the mood and I ask her to touch me, I feel free to ask for things that I like but that I know don't particularly turn her on. I think of it as a gift that she is giving to me—given not because it is expected or demanded, but out of caring. What often happens, however, is that even though those activities are not particularly "her thing," she gets so turned on by my excitement and enjoyment of what she is doing to me that the game changes to a more mutually enjoyable game in which we both become sex-crazed beasts.

It's a win-win situation for both of us. I end up falling asleep sexually satisfied and feeling very cared for, and she falls asleep feeling good because she has given me so much pleasure, and often because she is also herself physically satisfied at having had a great sexual encounter despite the fact that she had not initially been "in the mood." And we both fall asleep loving each other very much.
EH

So, Benjamin, just do it and see what happens. You will probably get what you want, something you certainly won't if you don't try.
Joan

Sexual Massage

Dear Joan,
I've always wanted a sexual massage, and recently my husband agreed to give me one. We got a book on the subject, but I wondered whether you had any tips on how to go about it. It sounds so wonderful, but we're both a bit stumped as to exactly what to do.
Polly

Dear Polly,
Sexual massage is whatever you want it to be. It's time spent touch-

ing and concentrating on your partner's pleasure. It starts pretty simply with long, slow strokes, graduates to fondling, and ends up wherever you two want it to, with his fingers or mouth bringing you to orgasm, or with intercourse, or all of that and more.

As with everything else, start slowly. Set the mood with incense, candles, and soft music. Turn the heat up high and use a towel or blanket to cover areas not being massaged at the moment to keep them warm. Get some massage oil at a local department store or use simple vegetable oil. Stay away from baby oil or mineral oil if there's a possibility that it will end up inside of you or if you use condoms. Petroleum products are no-nos. Warm the oil for a while in a larger container of warm water.

Begin with a nonthreatening area, like feet or hands. Then just slowly move from one part to another as seems appropriate. I'm sure you get the idea.

Here's a letter from a woman who seems to have it down to a delicious pattern.

Dear Joan,

I thought I'd tell you that my husband and I have developed sexual massage to a fine art. At first we used the bed, but soon it became obvious that it was too low for his back and much too wide. We found an advertisement for a used massage table in our local paper and jumped at the chance to own something so convenient. So here's what we do.

We put some towels in the dryer so that they are warm and yummy. Then I strip (or he does, but let's deal with me first—smile) and lie on my stomach on one warm towel while my husband drapes another over me. Although we turn the heat up, it's really nice to have that warm, soft towel to cuddle in. Anyway, he warms the oil for a moment in the microwave (we find about fifteen seconds for a small amount of oil works great), and then he goes to work.

He starts with my legs and arms, then my back and shoulders. An occasional erotic stroke up the insides of my thighs keeps me on a sensual edge. Finally I turn over and again he works on my legs and arms, staying away from the parts of me I want touched. He's such a tease!!

Finally, he plays with my breasts and rubs his fingers over my pubic area. It's wonderful and I think sensual massage can be a great addition to anyone's sex life.

Allison

So, Polly, I think you should have lots of ideas. Let me know how it goes.

Joan

Dear Joan,

I got your letter about sexual massage a few days ago, and I thought I'd write and tell you that my husband and I both read it and couldn't wait to try out some of the ideas. I won't go into all the details here, but just let me say it was fabulous. I think I came three times, and when my husband finally thrust into me, we both exploded. Wow!!!

Thanks to you and to Allison, who wrote that wonderful letter you sent.

Polly

Breast Play

Dear Joan,

Sometimes, especially when I have my period, I don't want to have intercourse, so my husband has started using my breasts instead. He smooths on a bit of lubricant, then presses my ample flesh together and rubs his penis in the valley between. Is this totally strange? He likes it, and actually, so do I. I see this stuff in the X-rated films my husband and I watch occasionally, and I'm afraid we're getting totally perverted.

Help us!

Heather

Dear Heather,

As with everything else involving consenting adults, whatever you do that gives you both pleasure is fine. Just fine. I think the question you're also asking is, Do real people enjoy this? and the answer here is a resounding yes!

Let's admit it, breasts are fun to play with. Men love to fondle, kiss, suck, knead, and otherwise play with breasts. Why? Psychologists and anthropologists will give you reasons, emotional and historic, but who really cares? Men enjoy doing it and women enjoy being fondled, kissed, sucked, and such. Sometimes a woman can actually climax from this sort of breast stimulation alone.

For those with larger breasts, pushing them together, creating a channel, and then letting a man rub his penis deep inside that warm cavern is a delicious part of love play, and why not? In your case, Heather, it means that you both can enjoy making love and he can ejaculate at times when you don't want to be penetrated. Great!

I have gotten several letters on the subject, and I'll add a few here to convince you that you and your husband aren't alone.

Dear Joan E. Lloyd,

I have loved breasts ever since I can remember, so my ideal companion is a woman who loves to have lots of attention paid to her tits and nipples.

I like all forms of lovemaking, but one of my favorite sexual activities centers around my wife's breasts. I just love using lots of oil and tit-fucking. Maybe I shouldn't use that term—I don't usually use such graphic four-letter words, but that's what it is, really. I hope you will excuse my language.

One of my favorite positions involves me lying on my back, legs around her waist, with her bending over me. In this position, I can use both my hands, and so can she. Another good position is for her to be lying down, with me lying right beside her, on my side. Again using oil, I stroke myself on her breasts and nipples while she and I both watch what's happening. Provides a great visual for both of us!

My wife and I love intercourse, but this is the next best thing for both of us.
Tyler

Dear Joan,
I have always been well endowed (38E), so I am well aware of how men like to, to put it bluntly, tit-fuck. I have done it in many positions, but I like the "on my back" position the best. I spread oil on my chest, then squeeze my breasts together and pinch my nipples while my husband rubs himself between them. I prop my head up on some pillows so I can intermittently lick the head of his penis. This is a great way to please my husband when I am otherwise "out of commission," but that is not the only time we do it. (It does a lot for me, too!)
Debra

Dear Joan Lloyd,
I am a thirty-eight-year-old female, married for fourteen years. One of the most exciting sexual positions that I have enjoyed does not even involve my vagina!! Breast-fucking is very arousing to me and I come with just the enjoyment that my husband gets. I lay on my back with my head slightly raised against the headboard of the bed, using a pillow. My husband straddles my chest just below my breasts. As he or I squeeze my breasts together, he lodges his penis in that warm cavity and has at it!!

With my head slightly raised I can lick the end of his penis as it peeks out between my breasts with each thrust! And I am able to enjoy his very powerful explosion! I must admit to you that I'm getting wet just at the thought of it! Ladies, try this and I am sure your husband will enjoy it as much as you do!
Joyce

Dear Joan,
I am a thirty-six-year-old mother of five and I think my husband using my breasts is great. I am not really big-chested, but that is

a very, very sensitive area for me and I enjoy being played with. My husband can make me come simply by playing/pinching/biting my nipples and making love between them. Since I'm small up there, I can't really hold him between my breasts, but I use a combination of what flesh I have along with my hands and we make do. :) We both love it.
Faye

Dear Ms. Lloyd,
About breasts and penises. One of the best positions I know is when I am crouched over my wife, with my knees behind her shoulders and my head toward her belly. That way I can touch her with my free hand (I need one to balance on, of course). I find it highly erotic that I can thrust between her breasts and she can play with me while I do.

The feeling can be exquisite when she wraps her breasts tightly around my erection. I enjoy this position more than just straddling her chest.
Ray

I hope this will convince you, Heather, that you are not alone. As a matter of fact, if the letters I receive are any indication, a substantial percentage of the population enjoys breast-thrusting.
Joan

Chapter 7

Sex in the Modern World

On Phone Sex

Dear Joan,

My husband is out of town for several weeks at a time. Recently we have been experimenting with more, let's just say, "adventurous" sex than previously in our marriage, and it has definitely brought us closer. The thing is, I want to try phone sex while he's out of town this time. I've never done it and I'm not quite sure how to go about it. Any suggestions?

Amy

Dear Amy,

Phone sex is a delightful way to keep the fires burning while you're apart, whether that's for long periods, the way you and your husband are, or only for the day while you and he are at work. Where to begin? How about this?

"Hi, honey," you say as he answers the phone.

"Hi, what's new?"

"I've been thinking of you and missing you."

"Me too."

"I've been thinking about the night before you left and how great the sex was."

"It was wonderful, wasn't it?"

"I particularly loved it when you . . ."

Remember that you don't have to use four-letter words if that makes you uncomfortable. You can use those words and phrases that the romance novels use if the more direct verbiage makes you uneasy. Of course, the bit of sexy discomfort might be just the thing to keep those juices flowing.

Another way to go is to write an erotic story together on the phone. Set the scene, and then say, "What do you think happens next?" You can adjust the scenarios I've written as you like, changing the looks of the characters to suit your mood. They are just guides for you, if you want to use them.

For example:

"I was reading a story this afternoon. It was about a couple who gets snowed in at a ski cabin in the mountains. There's a blizzard but they find that the cabin has lots of wood for the fire, food, and wine. They get comfortable, grill steaks in the kitchen, and then bring their dinner and glasses of wine into the living room and eat on the soft rug in front of a big fire.

"She cuts a piece of meat and offers it to him and he bites it off the fork with his strong white teeth. Then he offers her a piece with his fingers. They feed each other bits of potato and hot rolls dripping with butter. Butter gets all over her fingers and he licks it off, sucking each fingertip into his mouth.

"Soon they have put their plates aside and stretch out, sipping wine. They kick off their shoes, and, as the room gets warmer, he suggest that she remove her heavy ski sweater."

Now you can ask him to continue the story. Maybe you can each do a paragraph at a time. You might keep your senses turned up and listen to the direction he takes the story. You might get some clues as to what other sexual activities he's interested in trying.

If skiing doesn't do it for you, here's another scenario you can use, along a different line.

"A man is sitting in his hotel room, lonely and bored. He's a traveling salesman and he's on the road almost every week. It's his birthday and no one has remembered. There's a knock at his door, and curious, since he can't imagine who could be there, he crosses the room and opens the door. To his amazement, there's a beautiful woman standing there.

" 'Jack?' she says. 'Jack Jones?'

" 'Yes?'

" 'I'm Melanie,' she says, then she takes out a slip of paper and reads. I'm your birthday present from the guys at the office. We were going to get you tickets to a basketball game, but we thought this would be more fun to play with. And it's signed, from Tom, Greg, and Andy.'

"As he stands stupefied, she walks into the room, and closes the door behind her. She removes her long coat and he sees that she's dressed in a short miniskirt, long black stockings, and very high heels. Her shiny silver blouse doesn't cover much. 'I'm yours for the evening,' she says, then walks to him and gently presses her mouth against his. Slowly, as the kiss deepens, she rubs the length of her luscious body against his."

Again, Amy, you can then ask him what he thinks happens next. Want one more idea?

"She's in the bathtub, thinking that her boyfriend won't be back from his business trip for three more days. She's taken some of her adult toys and arrayed them on the floor beside the tub and she's reading an erotic story. The room is lit with a dozen candles, and she's sipping a glass of wine. Suddenly the bathroom door opens and he's there. 'My meetings got canceled and I thought I'd surprise you. Looks like you're ready for some fun.' He picks up a toy and leers at her. 'Maybe I'll just watch.' "

I think you get the idea. You don't have to sound like a porn star, just be yourself and expand on those wonderful activities you do together when he's home.

And here's a letter from a woman who's expanded still more on phone sex.

Dear Joan,

I wanted to suggest something for those who are interested in phone sex, and that's to use a vibrator while you're talking to him. I myself am a woman in my forties and I'm in a relationship with a sweet, loving man, also in his forties. Sadly, his business requires him to travel much of the time. Since I also work, I can't travel with him, so we do what we can online and by phone. At first I was a bit intimidated when the phone conversations got too sexy, but slowly I got used to using the explicit language he likes.

Well, recently, I got still braver. I went online and bought a vibrator to use while on the phone. The first few times when I got hot while we were talking, I just used it to, let's just say, lessen the tension. One evening he asked me what the sound was. I guess he heard the buzzing of my little friend. After a lot of ers and ums, I told him. I was really amazed at his reaction. He asked me to tell him exactly what I was doing, in detail.

Now toys are an integral part of our phone conversations. We both lie in bed and describe everything for the other, the lighting, our position, what music is playing, like that. I tell him what I would be doing to him if he were here (step-by-step, of course), and he tells me exactly how and where to use the vibrator. It's very erotic, and my orgasms are pretty intense while using the vibrator and hearing his soft, sensuous voice in my ear. Somehow, the use of that vibrator seems to make our time "together" on the phone much more intimate. We love it.

Thanks for listening.
Tammy

Amy, sounds like fun, no?
Joan

On Internet Dating

Dear Joan,

My name is Christine and I'm twenty-seven. I've met a wonderful thirty-year-old guy through an Internet chat room. We were both in a room chatting about global warming and we got to talking. We met there each night for a week, then found a private room and kept talking. It was wonderful. We share so many interests. Well, eventually the talk got sexual, and again we share so much. I wasn't embarrassed to tell him all my secret thoughts and dreams, and he told me his. We're right in every way.

We exchanged phone numbers and my phone bill is getting enormous from calling halfway across country. He's in the Midwest and I'm in the Northeast. He calls me on alternate nights and it's so much better than writing. I guess you could say we have phone sex. Anyway, he's finally arranged a business trip near to where I live, and I can't wait to meet him in person. I've seen his picture and he looks great. I love him very much and he says he loves me too.

I've heard horror stories about this kind of thing, so I thought I'd ask you. Even though I'm sure everything's going to be okay, I'm a bit nervous about it all. What's your opinion and what should I do to calm my nervousness?

Christine

Dear Christine,

I think it's wonderful that you and your guy hit it off so well. I do have a few caveats for you, however. First, you really can't love this guy yet. It might grow into it, but true love comes from knowledge and understanding, and you don't know him really at all. You only know the person he's projecting. And the same thing goes for him. I certainly don't mean that you're lying to each other, you're just being a bit selective in what you share. You've never barked at him because you had a lousy day. He's never snapped at you because he has a bad head cold. You've never farted in his presence nor has he in yours. Somehow, IMHO, it's the bad stuff that helps us understand about love. It's the evening that he comes home from work all excited by some project and you've stepped into a deep puddle in your best shoes. I think you understand what I'm getting at. Let love grow.

About meeting him when he comes to town, take care. Meet in a public place, maybe a nice restaurant for dinner. Bring your own car so that if you two end up not hitting it off, you can escape easily. Don't share your home address yet. I'm not insinuating that he's a weirdo or anything, but why take chances when there's really no need? Make sure he gets his own hotel room while he's visiting—again, just in case. You certainly don't want to find out you two aren't working out when he's staying at your house for another few days.

We hear so many horror stories about things that went bad. Here are some letters I've received, on both sides, so you can make your own decisions about your meeting.

Dear Joan,

I met my wife in a chat room on the Internet. We hit it off immediately and began speaking of almost everything, including sex. We began chatting every day, exchanged e-mail addresses and then photographs. Finally, we began using a popular videophone Internet program so we could interact even more intimately.

She was half a country away, so we weren't sure where it might lead, but we became very close and fantasized about meeting. Finally we split the cost of a ticket so she could visit my area. The second she walked off that plane and into my arms, it was like magic! After a wonderful long weekend, she reluctantly returned home, and we traveled back and forth several times before we decided we had to be together always.

Eventually we decided she would move here. We lived together for about a year, and were married seven months ago. Never before have I been happier. She is my perfect partner, my other half and my soul mate. My advice is to exchange pictures early. Be honest and get to know the person VERY WELL before you ever meet. But the opportunity is out there!

Ain't modern technology the best?

Ryan

Dear Joan,

I struck up a "cyber-relationship" with a woman about three years ago. We chatted online for several months before actually engaging in cybersex. A few months later we started having phone sex.

Business travel took me through the city in which she lived occasionally, and when it was possible, we would meet for dinner. No sex, just nice visits. We were friends and I never really expected anything to come of it other than just friendship.

About a year after we first met online, I was once again traveling through her city. She had started to see another guy on a regular basis, and I figured that our relationship would likely end soon, but we both had expected that. She met my plane, and as we walked through the airport late that night, we ended up in a dark concourse. We kissed and hugged, increasing in passion until we were groping and grinding. We hurried to my hotel and spent the night having great sex. The next morning I went to my meetings, then dashed to the airport for my flight back home. She met me at the airport and we said a passionate good-bye.

I wish this story had a happy ending, but it doesn't. About a month after my visit, I got an e-mail saying that she was moving in with the other guy and that she had fond memories of our time together. I must say that although I said I realized that it was not going to last, I was really bummed out and it took quite a while for me to get over it.

Now I'm married and I have shared the story of that evening with my wife. We've actually had great sex thinking about it. Oh well . . . Things don't always go the way you might want them to, but I'm really happy with my life now.

Chuck

Dear Joan,

I've got an Internet romance story for you, and it's not too good. I guess I was a fool, but I've learned quite a lesson.

Let me tell you first that I'm a single woman of almost thirty. Should I have known better? You bet. Anyway, I met a guy in a chat room and one thing led to another. Eventually, after lots of chatting, e-mails, phone calls, and long-distance sex, we arranged to meet. He drove almost five hours to be with me. We met for dinner and we clicked right away. He was just what I wanted, and I was in heaven. I was in love. Really in love, for the first time. We went to my house and the sex was fantastic.

Sounds nice, no? No! I found out several months and several visits later that he was married and cheating on his wife with me. Needless to say, I dropped him like a hot potato. Ladies, you can't ever be sure about the people you meet on the Net. My advice after having my heart broken? Play it safe and don't lie. And try to be sure that he's on the up-and-up too. How? Damned if I know.
Kristin

Dear Joan,

I am a twenty-eight-year-old woman, divorced, with a four-year-old child, and I met the most wonderful man in the world about nine months ago online. He's a bit older than I am, and lives on the West Coast, about as far away from where I am as he could be and still be in the States. When I first met him, I thought about everything I'd heard about meeting someone online, but I was determined to prove that they were wrong.

We met in a chat room in January and talked via Internet and telephone every day. Within a few months, I knew that I was in love. When I finally met him in person, it didn't matter what he looked like. I had gotten to know the person that he was and was totally gone on him. We had the most romantic, passionate, and erotic first night together, and it will always be a cherished memory for me.

I flew down to meet him again a few months later, and I brought my daughter with me. If there was any hope of making this a real relationship, all three of us had to agree. Hooray, we did. He not only loved me, but he loved my little girl as well, and she was crazy about him. Well, I am moving down there in a few weeks and we have discussed wedding plans for the near future.

I strongly believe that I have finally met my soul mate in this man, and could not be happier. This is not saying that there aren't some weirdos out there using the Net as a dating service or what have you, but follow your instincts. There are some lonely guys out there, and this might just be the way you can meet one too.

Marlene

Dear Joan,

I'm a thirty-eight-year-old guy and I guess this is somewhat of a confession. I was a real louse and I did something really bad to a really nice lady. I'm writing not only to get it off my chest, but to warn other women about what can happen out there in cyberland.

I met a woman online who was really unsophisticated, shy, and reticent. She seemed like a challenge. I wanted to get her to open up, to enjoy what the world had to offer. Then, when I found out she was married, I wondered whether I could actually cyber-seduce a woman who was determined to stay forever faithful to her loving husband.

We started as just chat friends. We talked about family, friends, life in general, but whenever sex was mentioned, she stopped talking. I was determined though, and continued to pursue her by saying "the right thing," etc. Eventually, she actually said something of a sexual nature, and I seized the chance and started cybering with her. The cybersex was great for her, because her sex life was rather ordinary, to say the least.

As time passed, her desire for me became too much, and

we arranged to meet. We had physical sex, and it was great. She decided that once was enough, so she went on her way without any thought of seeing me again. We continued e-mailing from time to time, and eventually she told me that her husband had found out about that night we spent together. Although they agreed to stay together, things weren't the same afterward. Actually, I'm glad they stayed together, because I wasn't interested in an ongoing relationship with her.

Now, looking back on it, I am really sorry for all the misery I caused. But I also want to say that no matter how much you think you can withstand the constant pressures placed upon you, one day someone (maybe a guy like me) will lead you down the path to a full sexual partnership. If you aren't looking for that kind of relationship, then I implore you not to play. It's really dangerous.

Joey

So, Christine, be wise, protect yourself, and let nature takes it course. I wish you all the luck with this man you're meeting, and I hope it turns out even better than your best fantasy.

Joan

Cybersex and Cheating

Joan,

I need some advice, please. My wife is involved in playing a very popular online game. It's a fantasy game that allows role-playing. You have a character and you interact with others. I have no problem with that. The role-playing does lead to love stories, which can get pretty hot, not XXX-rated, however. Again, no problem.

However, now my wife is into writing to the characters and other players, two in particular, by regular mail, sending them things like CDs of music she has recorded and love letters. The letters are all in character, not signed with her real name, but the other

stuff is signed. She says she is just having fun, but some of the letters are, well, pretty spicy. Like, "I want to feel you in my mouth . . ." etc. We share the same computer and she has just recently passworded her e-mail account so I can't get into it. Are my fears or jealousy warranted? Is this normal behavior on her part? She originally said this is just an online game, but now it seems to have gone offline.
Mike

Dear Mike,
It's not cheating unless there's lying involved or she's breaking an agreement that you have made with each other. If she's just getting hot with her friends and then making love to you, so much the better. If her online playing is cutting into your time together, then you might ask her to limit her time on the computer to an hour or two—or whatever seems reasonable—but in general, I'd prefer she spend her energy online than in a singles bar. That's my take. Of course, if you think she's lying to you, that's another story, and in that case, you need to decide what you want out of your relationship, then have a serious heart-to-heart talk about it.

A while ago I asked my visitors for their opinions about whether cybersex was cheating. Few questions have created the furor that this one did, and I thought I'd include some of the responses here so you can read both sides of this ongoing argument. After you've read what people think, consider and make up your own mind.

Dear Joan,
Is cybersex cheating? I don't believe so. My husband and I have been married for more than five years, and we both feel that if there isn't anything physical, then it can't be cheating. On the other hand, if a person gets too wrapped up in it, then he or she should move away from it for a while. I have been cyber-chatting for a long time, and occasionally it gets pretty hot, and when it does, it gives me a lot of pleasure. Maybe it is the unknown person behind the screen, maybe it is the fantasy of him.

Sometimes it's just the mystery of it. My husband knows about it and he's fine with it.

As long as people can keep it on the Net, then I believe it is safe and fun. There's an old saying, "It does not really matter where you get your appetite from, as long as you eat at home." If there were more "safe" sexual outlets that couples could enjoy together or separately, maybe fewer people would stray into destructive behavior.

One warning about cybersex. If you're going to do it, you need to constantly remind yourself that fantasy is almost always WAY better than reality.

Darlene

Dear Joan,

I agree with you that as long as cybersex does not involve lying or breaking an agreement you have with your mate, it is not cheating. But the whole discussion about whether cybersex is or is not cheating is not the only issue that cybersex raises.

Of course, lying and violating trust is death to any relationship, but equally important is caring. Even if a couple decides that cybersex is not cheating, neither one has the right to ignore the feelings of the other. Cheating or not, if something that I do results in my wife feeling jealous, hurt, insecure, or angry, whether her feelings are reasonable or not, it is my responsibility to deal with those feelings and to help her do the same. If I'm not willing to do that, it means that I don't really care very much about her, and without caring, our relationship is in big trouble.

That doesn't mean that I will always avoid doing anything that makes her uncomfortable, or, on the other hand, that I will always do as I please. It does mean that I will communicate with her, be honest with her, and consider her feelings before acting on something that I know may cause her distress, just as I know she will always consider my feelings. Maybe I will decide that cybersex is not important enough for me to cause her to deal with negative feelings, or maybe she will decide that her negative feelings are not so bad that she wants to prevent my enjoyment of cybersex. But we will always work it out together.

Love cannot exist without both trust and caring, so maybe we shouldn't focus on the narrow issue of whether or not cybersex is cheating.

Lester

Dear Joan,

Yes, cybersex is cheating. I just found out that my husband of more than thirty years is doing this, and it has destroyed me. I plan on filing for divorce. Your heart does not belong to your mate if you are looking elsewhere. I don't do chat rooms for this reason, and I am no damn prude, but in my opinion, "God made sex to be between a man and his wife."

Janice

Hello, Joan,

I'm a forty-two-year-old married woman and I wanted to comment on cybersex and cheating. I don't think cybersex is cheating if you can keep it on the computer and not let it move into real life. I have no problem with my husband cybering, and I even told him so. To me it's not any worse than calling a phone sex line. If it's kept strictly to the computer, then there's no physical touching and it's a good way to play out fantasies of being with someone new, being with a stranger, etc., without actually doing it.

Sometimes there are things you like to fantasize about that you can share online but don't feel comfortable sharing with your partner. You just have to be very careful, because it can be very tempting to turn the online relationship into something more real. Remember that there are always people throwing the temptation at you. Don't be tempted to act on it.

Melissa

Dear Joan,

I am writing about my cyber experiences. Originally I thought talking online was really silly and not something an adult would do. Maybe kids enjoy it, but not real grown-ups. Well, I found a chat room. First I just watched as people exchanged words, then I became involved. I have been happily married for almost fifteen years, but this was something quite different, apart from my marriage. It was amazing. I was really bonding with complete strangers. Who would have thought? I got really caught up in it and I found that the men always seemed to say just the right things, things I wanted to hear.

I have made some great friends of both sexes and we have exchanged e-mail and snail-mail letters. I have a newfound sexuality. I use some of my online ideas as foreplay when my husband and I make love, and it doesn't seem wrong. After all, my husband has *Playboy* magazines and other things he can use, but words do it for me. It is seduction at its best, safe from disease, with no risk to losing my family life. It is the wave of the future, and I'm riding it in.

Thanks for listening.
Maureen

Dear Joan,

Hi. I'm a forty-two-year-old wife and mother and I feel that having any type of relationship with a person of the opposite sex just leads to sin, either a real-life affair or an affair of the mind. My husband has been hooked on playing cards on the Internet, and many times he plays with other women. They flirt back and forth and I feel this is a form of cheating. Once you agree to spend the rest of your life with a person, you should not have friends of the opposite sex or be flirting. My husband says I'm just being silly and jealous, but it is more than that. It really hurts me, and if he truly loves me and respects me and our relationship, he would stop.
Tammy

Dear Joan,

I was discussing this very topic with some officemates recently, and one of the women said that cybersex was cheating and that her husband shouldn't talk to or have friends of the opposite sex because he's a married man now. My husband has several female friends, and I have absolutely no problem with it. I've met them and I trust him. Why should it be that we can enjoy the company only of members of our own sex? That's so limiting. Men and women are so different and have such different things to share. In my opinion, people who can't deal with partners having friendships with members of the opposite sex either have a trust issue or are really insecure.

Anne Marie

Dear Joan,

In response to whether cybersex is cheating, I say no, not any more than reading an erotic story, watching an X-rated movie, or even thinking of another person. I engage in it, and my husband knows and has no problem. I have been with my husband for more than fifteen years, and our sex life is great. However, he works long hours, and sometimes we have to go without good sex because he's tired. That's when I play and it takes nothing at all away from him.

I know that a lot of people who play online have a new partner each night. I would rather not have different partners all of the time. Sex of any kind is important to me, and I prefer not to be promiscuous. I would rather find someone online who I can get to know and develop a sincere and caring friendship with. From there we can share a mutual, harmless yet very fulfilling interest.

Nancy

Dear Joan,

As a woman in her forties who really enjoys cybersex, I feel very strongly that it is not cheating. Some men love their wives dearly

and use this as a means not to cheat. Sometimes a person's sexual needs are not being met by their partner, so rather than resort to real physical cheating, they get online and explore things in the fantasy realm. Some wives of my cyber-lovers even say it actually enhances their performance and they love it when I cyber with their husbands just before sex. In my opinion it's no worse than watching a porn flick or reading an erotic magazine.
Judith

Dear Joan,
I visited a sexy chat room once and I won't do it ever again. I find a keyboard an impersonal tool. As for the right or wrongs of it, if you get a sexual high by cybersexing, and it is done as a part of foreplay, then sharing the whole experience with your partner can be fun. If you do it on a one-on-one basis, without your partner knowing, well, I consider that cheating. So if you have to lie or withhold information from your partner, it is cheating.
Petra

Dear Joan,
In general I agree that cybersex isn't cheating. However, there is the hidden issue of the possibility of one falling in love with one's cybersex partner. Everyone seems to dismiss the issue with, "Well, if we just have great long-distance sex, what's the problem?" The problem to me is that any kink in one's real relationship may result in a deepening in the relationship with one's cybersex partner(s).

In my opinion, passive fantasies or pornography are less risky because there isn't another real human involved. Acting out one's fantasies increases the risk of damaging the relationship with that one special person.

So for me, cybersex with shared knowledge and acceptance is not cheating, but it is asking for trouble.
Alissa

Dear Joan,
Is cybersex cheating? I think it's a very easy question to answer. Somewhere in the Bible, I don't remember the exact verse, Jesus is talking about divorce. He says something to the effect of "It doesn't matter if you physically commit adultery, all you have to do is think about it and God views it as the same thing." This is why in the past people used to dress in a more reserved fashion.

Of course, we are all guilty of mentally sinning. Who hasn't been looking at some beautiful person and had a wish for an instant? But we aren't acting on it, so I have to believe that God factors that in when deciding guilt. If we continue and indulge in cybersex, however, we have gone far beyond a momentary urge. We have acted on it.
Billie

Dear Joan,
I think cybersex is quite simple, and wonderful. After all, a cyberpartner isn't going to get pregnant, spread any germs, or smoke my dope. Have a ball.
Mathew

So you see, Mike, there are as many views on cybersex and cheating as there are people who've given it some thought. Make up your own mind.
Joan

Dear Joan,
I'm a man in his fifties, with a wife to match. We've been married for almost thirty years, and wow—we've just found the joys of cybersex. We play one or twice a week. Sometimes we sign on individually, sometimes as a couple, and I must say we have had a ball!

It took some convincing to get my wife to do it the first time, but we have found that she is the one in demand! Women ask her how we have stayed together so long, and men are constantly hitting on her and inviting her into private rooms!

There's another very interesting aspect to this online stuff. Together we've discovered some fantasies that we've both had but never shared, not in all these years.

Cheating? Definitely NOT! This is the greatest thing since sliced bread! And the sex we have AFTER cybering is fantastic!
Dave

Dear Dave,
How wonderful that you and your wife have explored cybersex together. And to have found new adventures to share is doubly wonderful. Bravo!!!
Joan

Dear Joan,
Several months ago my live-in boyfriend of eight years began to spend more and more time on the Internet, so I asked him if it was because he was having cybersex. When he answered, no, I was relieved and I made it quite clear to him that I considered it cheating.

Well, last weekend I discovered dozens of files on the computer that turned out to be logs of him having cybersex over the past few months, and I was crushed! I started looking through more files, and found naked pictures of the women he's been cybering with. When he came home from work I confronted him, and he told me it was meaningless. "It's nothing more real than a computer game," he said, but to me it was very real!

After our talk, he promised to never do it again, but tonight I found a new file, and now I know that I have to leave him. Not so much for the cybersex itself, but for lying about it and doing it after he knew how I felt about it.
Katy

Dear Katy,
IMHO, you're right that it isn't the cybersex that's the problem here;

it's that he lied to you, especially since he knew how you felt. If a person lies about one thing, there's no trust left in the relationship. Period.
Joan

Dear Joan,
I know you have had tons of letters regarding cybersex, but let me inject one thought.

I was married for almost thirty years. I wasn't really happy, but I had no plans to leave the marriage. Then I met this married man online and we became good friends. Eventually we began having cybersex. It quickly moved from the Net to the phone and it went on for a year and a half. Boy, was I a dope. Finally, I asked myself, "What the heck am I doing?"

After much thought and soul-searching, I realized this cyber thing was simply a wake-up call. I was truly miserable in my marriage and this was a safe way out. I now have been separated from my husband for three months, and I have never regretted that decision. And have cut all ties with my cyber "lover."

For me cybering caused numerous sleepless nights and tons of tears. Day after day I agonized—"Will he be online" . . . etc., etc. But in the end, it made me realize just how unhappy I was in my marriage. It's really strange what will finally make you see and accept the truth about yourself.

Thank you for listening.
Phyllis

Dear Phyllis,
What a wonderful letter that really expresses my point of view—that if you're unhappy in your marriage, take care of that without the outside distractions of an online relationship. Decide whether to stay or go without any "noise." Bravo on discovering such wisdom.
Joan

Piercing

Dear Joan,

I'm twenty-two and female. I've been considering having my nipple pierced, and I was wondering whether you've ever had it done. How does it feel?

Candace

Dear Candace,

The only part of me that's pierced are my ears, so I'll copy you on several letters I've received. Like so many other things, opinions vary.

Dear Joan,

I had my nipples pierced last January. My husband came with me and watched as it was done. I have to tell you that just having it done was a turn-on; having breasts bared for another man to touch while my husband watched was wonderful for my imagination. Anyway, the sensitivity of my nipples has increased enormously, and now just looking at them turns my husband on.

Sandy

Dear Joan,

I don't personally have my nipples pierced, but my boyfriend does and I think they are very sexy. He says that his nipples weren't particularly sensitive before the piercings, but now he loves to have the rings played with, and it really gets him excited when I do.

He and I have discussed having one of mine done, too. I know it hurts, but I also know that in the long run it feels fabulous! If it could turn a guy on to have his done, then with my sensitive nipples, I am going to have a field day.

Clara

Dear Joan,

Pierce my nipples? No, no, a thousand times no. No one is going

to disfigure my body with holes. I have no problem with changing my hair or my makeup. I even tried shaving my genitals. But all those things are reversible. Piercing isn't, so *not a chance.*
LisaMarie

Dear Joan,
I had a lover recently who got her nipples pierced while we were dating. I was not really sure about it, but it's her body, and I figured anything that increased her pleasure was a thing to be enjoyed. Her nipples were already quite sensitive, and the piercing did wonders for her. She never wanted me to stop when I played with them. Obviously, I came around on the whole piercing issue, and they added quite a bit of spice to our lovemaking.
Matt

Dear Joan,
Ugh! I HATE piercings. Nothing gets me out of the room faster than a woman with anything but her ears pierced. Please note that I am in no way condemning the practice, but I just think it's horribly unattractive. If someone thinks pierced nipples (or anything) looks good, that's their business. I just want people who are considering it to realize that there are a lot of people who are revolted by bodies that are pierced.
Chad

Dear Joan,
I had my nipple pierced about two years ago, and it was extremely painful! On a scale of one to ten, it ranked about an eight. However, I just had the hood to my clit pierced, and it only ranked about a three!

My husband loved the nipple ring and said it was very sexy. It did heighten my sensitivity somewhat, but it was more aesthetic than anything else. The clit ring is a different matter. It really does have a function! The ball of the ring lays right on my clit and definitely physically turns me on.

If you're going to have a body part pierced, you need some-one who really knows what's what. A good piercer will know how to position the ring or ball or whatever, and whether the style you choose would be right for your anatomy! So take care and do it right the first time.
Elise

So, Candace, like so many things in life, I guess you'll have to make your own decision.
Joan

Dear Joan,
I'm a twenty-three-year-old man and I want to get my penis pierced. I will admit that I'm a little squeamish. Does it really drive women wild?
Billy

Dear Billy,
Having your penis pierced has to be something you are completely committed to, not something to do on a whim because the women will like it. Let's see what others think.

Dear Joan,
Don't know about nipple piercing since I've never had it done, but during lovemaking my wife will sometimes suck and gently bite my nipples, and that can sting, in a good sort of way. I have even gone as far as letting her put nipple clamps on me. When they come off it can really smart, and it's really kinky. So maybe nipple piercing is okay.

Now let's get to the penile area, which is more sensitive than the nipples. I don't think I would let anyone with a needle anywhere near my penis. No one would ever do that to me. No, ouch, no.
Arnie

Dear Joan,

I had my foreskin pierced several months ago and my lady friend seems to love it. She says she can feel the little barbell bouncing around inside of her, and it drives her crazy. She used to have a difficult time reaching orgasm, but now, as soon as I penetrate her labia, she contracts and has a massive climax.

So, personally, I don't know how it feels, but by the look on her face, I can imagine just how pleasurable it is.

Van

Billy, if you eventually decide to do it, let me just advise you to find someone really reliable, clean, and careful. A minor mistake can have really serious consequences.

Joan

Dear Joan,

I am a thirty-one-year-old gay man and I was wondering about having my tongue pierced. Does it really make oral sex better? Can another guy feel it?

Terry

Dear Terry,

I've never been with anyone who had a pierced tongue, so I asked a few folks, and yes, it can be felt, and it's really exciting. As a male friend of mine said, "I was once with a partner who had his tongue pierced, and . . . wow!" Enough said. Oh, and I gather a pierced tongue is just as much of a thrill on a woman's genitals.

Joan

Chapter 8

Going Further

Fantasies

Dear Joan,

I'm a twenty-seven-year-old man and I'm really troubled. I have these sexual fantasies and they're really kinky. I won't go into detail, but when I think about them I'm really embarrassed. I fantasize about things I'd never dream of really doing. What's wrong with me?

Clay

Dear Clay,

Nothing is wrong with you. You're a perfectly normal male. Most if not all men, and most women too, have sexual fantasies. They might be really romantic: making love in a cabin in the woods or on a sun-splashed beach. Or they might be quite bizarre, involving forcing some woman to do really outlandish things. No matter. What goes on in your mind is your business and only yours. Period!

Joan

Dear Joan,

I recently met my best friend's fiancé and he's really adorable. I'm thirty-three and happily married. I would never consider doing anything outside of my marriage, but this guy has begun to creep into my fantasy life. I even think of him while I'm making love with my husband. What should I do?

Livy

Dear Livy,

Do? Nothing. It's always delicious to fantasize about a sexy guy who curls your toes. He's new, uncharted territory, so you can imagine anything you like about him. He's gorgeous, with a great, well-developed body, and, of course, he's a perfect lover. He knows all the right moves and his timing is impeccable. Your husband, on the other hand, is the same guy you've been in bed with for years. Sometimes he has bad breath, he often needs a shave, and he's comfortable.

So you fantasize. We all do. Whether it's Sean Penn or Sean Connery, we love to think about what it would be like if some great guy was in bed with us rather than our long-term partner. Don't worry about it. There are many fantasies I recommend that folks share with their partners. I don't think, however, that this is one of those. Keep it to yourself and enjoy.

And consider this. Someone out there may have just met your husband at the office and may be fantasizing about him. Or someone may be thinking and dreaming about you.

Joan

Dear Joan,

I'm a normal, totally heterosexual woman, but I've had an occasional fantasy about making it with another woman. Does this mean I'm a lesbian? It terrifies me. Please help.

Michelle from Iowa

Dear Michelle,

It doesn't mean you're a lesbian at all. It means you're curious, as most women are, and that you're acting out your curiosity in your mind. Let me give you my take on being gay.

Sexuality is a continuum that goes from totally, devotedly heterosexual to completely, unalterably homosexual, and includes everyone and everything in between. I think that a large percentage of the population has acted on their natural curiosity about homosexuality, has contemplated it or fantasized about it. And what's wrong with that? You don't have to be totally anything!

One last thing. From all I've learned, it's much more common for a woman to fantasize about, or even act on, a same-sex relationship than it is for a man. For men, it's really scary, and thus a homosexual fantasy is rejected out of hand. It causes so much pain, I'm afraid, and that's really sad.

Joan

Dear Joan,

My husband and I have recently gotten into fantasy games. I mean we really get into it, with props and story lines and everything. It's really hot for us, but recently I mentioned it, only in brief, to my sister-in-law, and she was shocked. She said it was abnormal to play fantasy games. She said, "If you can't get excited by your husband so that you have to resort to sick games, you should get counseling." Now I'm beginning to worry. I haven't mentioned it to my husband, but I thought I could ask you. Is she right?

Jeanne

Dear Jeanne,

Nonsense. Playing games the way you and your husband do is perfectly normal and delightful. Many couples do the same thing, including Ed and me, from time to time. Of course, some, like your sister-in-law, aren't interested, and that's okay too. But if you and your husband want to play, enjoy.

Joan

Dear Joan,

I've read stories about people who like to play fantasy games in the bedroom. I'm a thirty-year-old woman who's interested in doing something like that with my husband of seven years. Our sex life has become a little stale, and I thought this might juice it up a bit. My problem is that I don't know where to start. What are some of a man's favorite fantasies and how can I go about setting something like this up? I'm tempted by fantasies where I'm in control. Can I do something like that?

Vy

Dear Vy,

What a wonderful way to add a bit of spice to your relationship. Let me propose a few scenarios and you can see which one tickles your fancy. Remember, it has to excite you as well as your husband.

Playing Doctor

The props: A lab coat for the "doctor" and a paper gown for the "patient." If you can't get a lab coat, try a plain white dress shirt worn with the tails out. You might be able to get the gown from your doctor at your next visit. You'll also need a bottle of alcohol, several towels or a clean white sheet, and a pair of latex gloves, which you can get at your local pharmacy.

The setup: After you put on the lab coat, soak a piece of cotton in alcohol and place it beside the bed for that doctor's office smell. Direct a strong light onto the bed so you can perform your exam. Spread the towels or sheet on the bed beneath the strong light so the room begins to have the feel of the doctor's office.

The scenario: Tell your husband that it's time for his annual checkup, and that you've got everything ready. Hand him his exam gown and direct him to the bathroom so he can put it on. When he's ready, have him lie on the bed, and slowly, while he watches you, pull the gloves on your hands. Then perform the exam in whatever way you two enjoy playing. Begin with something small, his ears and mouth, his fingers and toes. Eventually, when you think you're both ready, you can move on and clinically "examine" his genitals, or his anus. Use your imagination here and just improvise.

The Female Pirate

The props: You'll need a pirate outfit: some black slacks, high boots, a flowing white shirt, and a colored scarf for your head. Add some really big junky jewelry and, if you can manage it, a toy gun and/or a sword. You'll also need some soft rope and a wide scarf for his blindfold.

The setup: After you put on your pirate outfit, add some very different perfume from what you usually wear. You might also overdo your makeup a bit: bright red lipstick and heavy mascara.

The scenario: "Order" your husband into the bedroom and quickly grab his hands. Tell him that he has been captured by Vy the Bold, the most feared pirate of the Caribbean. To help him follow along, you might say something like, "I know you're very frightened by what's happening, but if you behave, it will go much easier for you." Keep your voice pitched lower than usual and snap out the orders. Instruct him to strip, then tie his hands loosely in front of him. Don't tie them behind him since it's very uncomfortable for him to lie on his back that way. Then blindfold him and have your way with him.

The Prison Guard

The props: You'll need a uniform of some kind. Think about what a prison guard might wear and see what you have in your closet that might do the trick. It can be as simple as a black shirt, black jeans, a wide leather belt, and heavy boots. If you can, add a slender club of some sort and maybe even a toy pistol. Comb your hair into the most severe style you can manage, maybe with lots of slick mousse. No jewelry except possibly small studs in your ears. For him, maybe a soft denim shirt and pants, no shoes, socks, or underwear.

The setup: Turn your bedroom into a prison cell. Remove whatever knickknacks you can from surfaces and pull off the bedclothes to the bare mattress. Turn all the lights up as bright as you can.

The scenario: Tell him that he's been discovered smuggling cigarettes into the prison and that's a serious offense. You've been sent to see that it doesn't happen again. Snap out your words and smack the club against your palm while you're speaking. Grab his crotch, showing that you have all the power and he has none. Then go with it. You can order him to strip and do what you will from then on.

I hope these work for you. Please drop me a line and let me know what happens.
Joan

Dear Joan,
It's me, Vy, again. I have to tell you that we've now tried all your ideas. It was a bit awkward at first. I was really terrified, but I wanted to play so much that I just did it. We began with the doctor one and it was fabulous. My husband played along from the beginning, and it was everything I imagined it could be and so much more. Wow and wow!!!!

Now he wants some ideas for his "revenge." We've turned each of the ones you originally sent me around so he's the boss, but do you have any more that he can try? I hope I'm not being pushy, but could you think of something?
Vy

Dear Vy,
How terrific. I'm so glad you've had some great sex playing with my scenarios. Let me see what additional ones I can come up with.

Male Teacher and Female Student

The props: He'll need to wear a jacket and slacks and you need to find something as close to a school uniform as you can. Maybe a navy sweater, white blouse, navy skirt, white socks, and loafers. If you have plain white cotton undies, that would be great. You'll also need a ruler and a straight-backed chair.

The setup: If you've got privacy, this one might play better in the dining room. You can stand quietly while he's reading or writing on a sheet of paper. He should call you by your first name but you should call him Mr. Jones.

The scenario: He might say something like, "You've failed all your subjects this semester, and I really don't want to have to call your parents. You know how angry they will be if we have to expel you." Then you say, "Oh, no, Mr. Jones. Don't call them, please. I'll do anything." Now he's got you and you must do whatever he decides is the proper punishment for your failures. He can sit you down in the straight-backed chair and, if you're willing, try some light corporal punishment with the ruler.

The Dentist

This one's a bit heavier into the realm of power games. Remember the rules of power games. If you can't trust him to stop when you say stop, don't play. If you can't trust yourself to say stop if things get unpleasant, don't play. And establish a code word that means stop, and use it. Maybe something like "marigold," or the more common "red."

The props: You need a lounge chair, a long scarf or strip of cloth, and a roll of adhesive tape. He should wear a lab coat or white shirt. Like the doctor's office, you should have some alcohol for smell and bright lights, preferably pointed at the head of the chair.

The setup: You can sit in the chair and recline it to a dental-chair angle. He stands over you.

The scenario: "You know, Miss Jones, the procedure will be a bit painful, and it's important that you remain perfectly still. I think I'll need to control your hands so you don't grab for me at the wrong moment." Then he should use long strips of tape to fasten your hands to the arms of the chair. He can tape your ankles, too, if you like. Then he should use the strip of cloth to tie your head to the top of the chair, over your forehead. Now you're helpless and he can do as he wishes.

The Hypnotist

The props: You'll need only a sugar pill or vitamin and a chain with something to dangle.

The setup: Find a comfortable place, outside of the bedroom if possible. You can sit on the sofa, perhaps, while he sits in a chair. You've come to him because you just can't seem to give up smoking, and he's guaranteed to help you.

The scenario: He says something like, "I will help you, but you have to cooperate. I'm going to give you something to help you relax." He hands you the "medicine" and a glass of water. You take it and it makes you a bit sleepy. Then he can play with the hypnosis verbiage and the "shiny object," or not, as you two choose. Either the pill or the spell he casts puts you totally in his power.

I hope you have as much fun with these as you did with the previous ones. Maybe you can come up with a few that I can send to others who want to play as you and your husband do. Let me know.
Joan

Making Home Movies

Dear Joan,
My husband and I have been talking recently about how much of a kick it would be to make a home movie of us making love. It feels a bit scary to me, but I think I'd like to try it. The idea of seeing myself is really exciting, but I also know I won't look like those women in the porn movies. I don't know whether I'll be able to look.

Anyway, we got a video camera recently to videotape the kids, but I'm not sure how to go about making an erotic film. Can you

help, give us some pointers on where to put the camera and stuff? Thanks in advance.
Debbie

Dear Debbie,
Let me address your concern about your body first. No, you won't look like a porn star. How many women actually do? Very, very few. Even the porn stars don't all the time, and I'll bet they never eat a full meal. That's life. Just remember that the woman your husband sees on the tape will be the wonderful woman he's married to and loves and who is brave enough to play at making a movie. That makes it all wonderful.

I can certainly give you some tips about making a video from personal experience. Ed and I made a movie several years ago, and I think he still has it tucked away in his closet somewhere. We had fun making it, and got ourselves into a few strange positions, too. Let me give you some pointers based on our experience.

There are two ways to do the filming. You can just go directly to videotape and then watch it later (or not, as you choose), or you can hook the camera up to the TV so you can watch yourself live and capture the action on tape as well for more viewing later. The advantage to watching while you're filming is that you can adjust the camera position and move around on the bed to improve the quality of the movie. The downside is that you might be really embarrassed watching yourself, as I was. Eventually I did get used to the view and learned to enjoy the eroticism of it all.

Once you've decided whether to watch, begin slowly, maybe with a few scenes of you completely dressed mugging for the camera. Get comfortable with the machine and the idea of being on tape. Bounce on the bed, giggle, have some fun with it. At this point you might slowly strip for the camera. Let your partner direct the action, or just do it for him. Pretend to be one of the porn stars you see in the movies, or just be yourself.

Eventually you might want to masturbate for the camera, letting your husband have fun panning and zooming. If you want to film the two of you making love, that's a bit trickier. You can prop the camera on the dresser using books and such to get it aimed at the bed, or use a commercially available tripod. Now the trick is to stay in the frame—in the area that the camera is photographing. That's not as easy as it might appear.

You'll come out with some good shots, some not, but the fun's in the doing, not the results. With practice, you can manage to make some pretty enjoyable videos. Take care to keep those videos hidden. You don't want the kids to invite their friends for Cinderella and end up seeing more of Mommy and Daddy than you ever imagined.

I've received letters from couples who've tried it, with varied degrees of success.

Dear Joan,
My husband and I are the proud owners of a large number of porno movies and we really like to watch them to get us in the mood. We even fast-forward to our favorite parts and emulate what's going on in the film.

A few years ago we decided to make a movie of our own. I'll admit that I had to be talked into it. I am very body-conscious and felt embarrassed by the whole situation. Well, needless to say, he convinced me, and set everything up. I was quite intimidated by the camera at first, and kept my face from view for most of the time. He got shots of my naked body and of us making love. We didn't set it up so we could watch while we taped, so I didn't see anything.

A few days later, he watched it, alone, and told me how excited it got him. I tried to watch it with him, but I couldn't deal with the idea of watching myself having sex. Over the last few years we have appended more "scenes" to our movie, adding more props as we went along. The most recent scene is one that I didn't even know I was starring in. My husband blindfolded me, tied me to the bed, and brought me to orgasm before he even entered me. It was wonderful. It wasn't until after he had untied me, still blindfolded, and made love to me, that he told me that I was being taped.

He has since told me that that scene is the best we've ever done, because it was so uninhibited. He watches it often when I'm not around, and although I still won't watch it, I'm glad we did it because it brings him so much pleasure. It's amazing and very gratifying for me to realize that my husband would rather watch me on tape than some porn star with a perfect body.
Eileen

Dear Ms. Lloyd,
Both my wife and I are writing to you about making erotic films at home. If you have a friend you can trust, ask him/her to film you and your partner. How did we do that and why? We had tried to make films with a tripod and such, but they never came out the way we wanted. We always rolled out of view or had our backs (or butts) to the camera.

We were kidding about it with another couple and they offered to hold the camera for us if we would do the same for them. It was really awkward at first, but with a few beers and lots of trust, we did it. What turned out to be really kinky was when the other guy started to play director and told us how to move and exactly what to do. That was really hot.

Another day we returned the favor and taped them in their bedroom. That was really kinky too, and when they were done with the movie, we ran into the living room and came pretty close to making love right there.

We often watch our film, and it never fails to get us "ready."
Leo and Amy

Dear Joan,
My ex-boyfriend and I tried to make a home movie of us making love, but it didn't turn out too well. Oh, the lovemaking was great, and the movie turned out okay, but when I watched the film I was really disgusted by how fat I looked. He said that he

loved me and thought I was beautiful, but I just couldn't bear it, so we taped over the movie.

Now I'm really sorry I did that. I've given it a lot of thought, and now I realize that his excitement should have been enough for me and to heck with how I thought I looked. He's history now, and I hope that a new boyfriend will want to repeat the evening. I've got a whole new outlook and I'd like to try it out.
Emily

So, Debbie, make your movie and enjoy.
Joan

Fellatio

Dear Joan,

I know my husband wants me to go down on him, but I have a real problem with it. I don't think it's dirty or anything, but it's just, I don't know how to say it. I just don't want to. What can I do?
Mindy

Dear Mindy,

Most important, don't do anything during lovemaking that you find repugnant. I know you want to do things to make him happy, but there's a limit. If you find things you're doing during sex really difficult, you won't enjoy it and you'll put off the next encounter for as long as you can. What a perfect way to kill all the good things about sex.

As for oral sex, if it's something you want to try, let me give you a few tips about how to begin.

Many women have a problem with the idea or the actuality of oral sex. There are unfamiliar smells, tastes, and textures that seem really scary. She worries that she'll smell something really repugnant and gag or be repelled. She is afraid that he might ejaculate in her mouth, an equally frightening prospect for many. But, despite all that, she wants to give pleasure. Most men find oral sex very pleasurable.

The most important thing to do before considering playing with oral sex is to forget the Linda Lovelace syndrome. The movie *Deep Throat* did such a disservice to both men and women that it's really a shame. Women see that movie or the dozens like it and think that in order to perform oral sex, fellatio, she has to take a man's entire penis as deeply into her throat as possible, risking gagging and loss of control. Nonsense.

I remember when I was new to oral sex and I simply didn't know how to do it. I had the idea that there was some important talent I was lacking, something wrong with me because I didn't like the idea of sucking on a man's penis very much. "Does she give good head?" I heard the question in my nightmares. I knew I was doomed because I didn't know exactly what "good head" was. Therefore I was afraid to try. I knew that my partner would know that I didn't "give good head" and drop me like a brick. So I never did it.

What garbage. You've got to start somewhere. Like every other form of sex play, no one was born knowing how to enjoy it or what to do. It's an acquired taste, if you'll pardon the pun.

Okay, so you've gotten past the problems and you want to give it a try. Let's begin slowly. Have him lie on the bed, on his back, so you can explore. I know he'll cooperate, since he's anxious for you to try something new. Ask him to help you understand what gives him pleasure by purring or moaning. That's the best reward you can get, knowing you're doing something that he's enjoying.

Talk to him about your fears. Share with him that you've never enjoyed it, but you love him and want to do this. Help him understand that it's really scary for you.

Then start by touching. Learn his body, what makes him giggle, what makes him groan. What makes his penis erect and what does he seem to pull away from. Explore. It's amazing how few women actually know their partner's genitals really well.

Now, when you're ready, continue by licking the shaft of his penis like a popsicle. Just lick. Don't go anywhere near the tip right now, just touch with your tongue. You'll find it smooth, warm, and rigid beneath the skin. And, as you lick, it should become more rigid, showing his enjoyment of what you're doing. Don't forget your hands while you're tasting and playing. Touch him, squeeze gently, stroke, scratch lightly. Cup his testicles and stroke their surface. Explore and see what he likes.

That's enough for your first time. Don't go any further unless you really want to. He'll be quite willing to proceed in another way as long as you're left with good feelings.

Okay, what comes next? The tip of his penis will exude a drop or two of thick fluid, usually called precome. It's a natural lubricant and is often the first thing that stops the delight of oral sex. Touch it. Spread it around the tip of the penis. Taste a bit from the tip of your finger. You'll find it tastes a bit salty or tangy. When you feel brave, lick just a bit from the tip of his penis.

Okay, you've advanced past the licking stage and want to take him into your mouth. Discuss it with him and ask him to be very sure he doesn't ejaculate. If you can't trust him to be able to keep his word because he's too aroused, don't play right now. Try again another time, when he's not so excited. Tell him how important it is to you that he not come. Warn him that if he does, it might be such a turnoff that you might never want to play this way again. This shouldn't be viewed as a threat, just the truth. This next part might not be easy for you and he must cooperate if you're to succeed.

Once you've put his penis into your mouth, don't go too fast. Don't try, first off, to ram his entire erection down your throat. Many women just can't do that. Those with strong gag reflexes or those who are trying with men with large equipment will have difficulties. That's okay. A man can get just as much pleasure out of less forceful fellatio. Wrap your hand around the base of his penis and squeeze a bit. Then use your mouth on only the part that protrudes above your fist. That will help you control the depth of penetration.

Again, explore. Do what feels comfortable. Lick, suck gently, cover your teeth with your lips and bite softly. Form a vacuum with your mouth then pull back just a bit, then draw his penis in and withdraw it, simulating the movements of intercourse. You'll quickly get the hang of it. Gauge his reactions and do what makes him crazy. Since every man is different, I can't tell you exactly what will drive him crazy, but it should be evident. Hopefully he's still helping you with moans, groans, and body movements.

If you want to go to the ultimate extreme, you can suggest that you're ready for him to ejaculate in your mouth. This part gets messy, but for some men it's the best part of oral sex. For many women it's a delightful experience, both for its own sake and because it's a testament to your ability to please him. Do you have to swallow? Not at all. You can let the fluid dribble from your lips or swallow.

That's really all there is to it. Play. Enjoy. You might find that the pleasure of taking a flaccid penis into your mouth and sucking it as it gets hard a particular delight. And if it doesn't work out for you, that's fine too. Your sex life will not be forever doomed because you just don't like fellatio. There are lots of other toys to play with.

A word of caution here. As we all now know, semen, even precome, is a high-risk fluid. If he is HIV positive, that fluid is filled with the AIDS virus. And if you have an open sore in your mouth, even one you don't know about, you have just created a pathway that can allow the virus to infect you. So don't engage in fellatio unless you are sure about your partner's health. There are products, called dental dams, that work like oral sex condoms. I don't know much about them, but I'm told they work. However, if you're not sure of your partner's sexual history, maybe you shouldn't be playing at all!
Joan

Dear Joan,
I want to give my husband a blow job, but anytime I get close to his genitals, it smells really bad. I don't want to insist that he get up and wash himself, but I just can't get close to him that way. What can I do? How can I tell him without him getting mad?
Carla

Dear Carla,

How about this? Next time he's in the shower, climb in with him. Tease, play, wash him all over, then, maybe even with the water still running, try fellatio. He'll be squeaky clean and there should be no smell.

But if you have to tell him, do it. I think you'll find that he's more than anxious to please you. Being honest is the best cure for just about anything.

Joan

Dear Joan,

It's Carla again. Some time ago you helped me out with learning how to give head. I just thought I'd let you know that I did it! And it was really great!

I tried it in the shower and that was really nice, but then we decided to dry up and continue in bed. I just love his "squeaky clean" penis, as you said. As I was sucking him he moaned real loud and pushed my head away. At first I was afraid I'd done something wrong, but then he came. I watched his semen squirt out of him and it was wild knowing that I'd given him that much. I was so happy, and he held me and told me that it was great.

Afterward, I told him about the smell problem, and he was really good about it. Now he takes a quick shower before we make love, and he's always good-smelling. Since then we have been having lots of oral sex, at least twice a week, and he says he has the most intense orgasms in my mouth. Of course, I do love doing it the old-fashioned way too. Thanks so much for your help.

Carla

Dear Joan,

I like giving head, but I just can't swallow. I just can't. It makes me sick to my stomach just thinking about it. Am I crazy?

Fran

Dear Fran,

No, you're not crazy. Many women can't, or just don't want to swallow semen. I thought I'd send you a copy of a letter I got recently from a visitor to my website. I hope it helps you.

> Dear Joan Elizabeth Lloyd,
> I am a forty-two-year-old divorced woman. My ex-husband told me that he loved oral sex, but after we were married, it took me a while to do it for him. One day I tried it and found that I liked it. I particularly liked the texture of his soft cock while it got hard in my mouth.
>
> The only thing was that I couldn't swallow. I have tried and I just can't do it. I thought he'd be angry but he really understood and never tried to force me. He never made me feel like I was shortchanging him.
>
> Since my divorce, I have had a couple of affairs, and I let the guy know that I can't swallow. I was surprised at how many men are very understanding about this. Maybe someday I will be able to do it, but until then, I will give my man all the pleasure of oral sex that I can.
>
> Ladies, don't worry about not being able to swallow. If you treat your man like he is the best thing since sliced bread, your not being able to swallow won't matter. Go for it.
> *Wanda*

Fran, I think this woman has the entirely right idea. Enjoy what's enjoyable. Men understand and want us to be happy with our sexual relationship.
Joan

Dear Joan,

I'm a thirty-seven-year-old female. I used to love going down on a man, but my ex-husband would hold my head against his groin, forcing his cock into my mouth until I gagged. Fortunately, he's my ex now (smile).

My new husband has told me how much he enjoys getting oral sex, but I find that my past experience has made me reluctant to do something I used to enjoy. He promises not to hold my head, but I can't get past it. Can you help me?
Sandy

Dear Sandy,
How about loosely tying his hands to the headboard of the bed? That way he can't hold your head, and it might give you the freedom to enjoy oral sex.
Joan

I was so pleased when I received this letter a week or so later.

Dear Joan,
I can't thank you enough for your help. Last night I asked my husband whether he'd let me tie his hands, and I explained why. He agreed and I did it. It was fantastic. I enjoyed sucking his cock so much and (giggle) so did he. Thank you, thank you, thank you.
Sandy

Dear Ms. Lloyd,
I don't know who to ask. I can't ask my family or my friends, so you're my only hope. Can my girlfriend get pregnant if she swallows while performing oral sex on me?
Tim

Dear Tim,
If there has been no contact between your penis and her vagina, then no, she can't get pregnant. However, if, while you're playing, either before or after oral sex, some of the fluid from your penis gets into her vaginal canal, those little sperm might just find a way to swim upwards and result in pregnancy.
Joan

Dear Joan,

My wife tells me that she had many bad experiences trying to give a man oral sex. Her first husband knew that she did not like it, and so used it as a way to punish her. I guess you could call it a form of rape. I really want to punch him out for it, but that was more than fifteen years ago.

I know she wants to give it a try from time to time, and I let her call the shots, but she just can't go through with it. I don't think I'm pressuring her, but I can't deny that I'd like her to do it for me. What can I do?

Tom

Dear Tom,

Just relax, and if it happens, it happens. You say you want her to do it for you. She should be doing whatever she does for both of you.

If she talks to you about it and says that she really wants to, you might ask her whether there's anything you can do to help. Have you tried chocolate sauce or maple syrup? It has become such a joke, but it does work. The smell and taste are deliciously familiar and cover any smells and tastes that might bring back those bad old memories.

Joan

Dear Joan,

Last night my boyfriend lost control while I was giving him head and he shot into my mouth. It really tasted nasty. I've had men come into my mouth before and it never tasted that way. Do men taste different? Isn't it all pretty much the same?

Kate

Dear Kate,

I'm not really an expert, having only had two men come in my mouth, but I do know that there are things that affect the taste of all fluids, including semen.

Here are a few suggestions from people who've written to me.

Dear Joan,

I'm a thirty-one-year-old married woman and have always loved giving oral sex. I have never had a problem with taboos or with focusing my attention on what I'm doing. Having his member in my mouth is truly wonderful.

However, ejaculate just doesn't always taste so good. Before I was married I had lots of experience with oral sex and found that each person tasted a little different. I always prided myself that I swallowed, every time. But then I had a boyfriend who always tasted rancid. It really turned me off, and needless to say, we didn't last long.

I have a theory that a man's (and maybe a woman's too?) taste is affected by diet. The sweetest, most wonderful taste I ever remember was from a very healthy man who didn't drink caffeine or eat meat. The guy I mentioned before was a junk food junkie who lived on high-caffeine sodas. I don't know whether that has any relationship to the taste, but that's all I can guess.

Lizzie

Dear Joan Lloyd,

I'm a forty-year-old man and I love to have my girlfriends go down on me. I have found that the taste of ejaculate is related to diet. Red meat makes it bitter, so I tend to stick with chicken for my protein intake. One girlfriend also claims that if I eat cinnamon several hours before oral sex, my ejaculate will taste like a liquid candy cane and she can't get enough. Another advised me to use Equal, that artificial sweetener in the little blue packets. She said it made me taste wonderfully sweet.

I have also realized recently that certain foods also affect a woman's lubrication, because on some occasions the taste seems different.

Guy

Dear Ms. Lloyd,

I just wanted to say that a great way to make a man's semen taste better is pineapple juice. Any kind of citrus juice is supposed to work, but I have tried drinking several glasses of pineapple juice the same day as the lovemaking and my fiancée seemed to enjoy giving me a blow job even more than usual.
Craig

Kate, it might be interesting to discuss this with your husband and see what you two can come up with. Experimentation can be fun! Let me know.
Joan

Dear Joan,

I hope you remember me. I wrote you about the taste of my husband's semen. You were right. I couldn't let him come in my mouth, but when he came in my hand after fellatio, I tasted a bit. When he eats garlic or asparagus, he tastes nasty. When he eats lots of fruit, it's sweeter. I don't want this to sound like we're making some kind of scientific study. It's just fun to see what changes, and it's made oral sex so much more fun too.
Kate

Dear Joan,

About oral sex. I think my boyfriend gets off on it because it shows his power over me, and that's a real turnoff. Do men really get excited by the power aspect of it?
Marge

Dear Marge,

I'm sure some men do get turned on by power. By "making" a woman perform oral sex on him, a man may feel he's demeaned her in some way and that he's "shown her who's boss." I'm not a psychologist, and I don't want to speculate on the reasons for what anyone does, but if you feel you're not being treated as an equal in your relationship, maybe it's time to rethink the entire structure.

Lovemaking should be just what the name says: expressing your love and sexual desires for each other in a *mutually* satisfying manner.
Joan

Dear Joan,

This isn't a question, really, just a statement about oral sex. I absolutely, positively adore giving my boyfriend a blow job. I used to hate the idea of fellatio because I felt it was an uneven power play that benefited the man more than the woman. That was until I met my current boyfriend. I love him very much, and the love I have for him extends to all parts of him, especially his cock. The look on his face as I take him in my mouth, the feel of his hand on my head as he gently guides me, the soft moans and whimpers that he makes as I lick him, suck him, nibble on him, they all drive me wild. I get very aroused when I give him head, which never used to happen to me.

My first two experiences with oral sex were distasteful. The first man had the indecency to come in my mouth without warning while trying to shove his penis down my throat. I gagged pretty badly and I was sick to my stomach for hours afterward. The second man was always begging for it, and since I knew he didn't love me, I felt like a prostitute. Performing on him left me feeling used.

My current boyfriend is a wonderful, caring human being who originally objected to oral sex because he also thought that it was wrong for women to do it, that it used them somehow. He was quite adamant that I not go down on him, so, just to be stubborn, I told him to close his eyes and pretend like it wasn't happening. He found that he loved it, and to my surprise, I found that I loved it too.
Opal

Dear Joan,

I know that my husband would very much like me to go down on him, but I just hate doing it. I want to please him, and I have tried

doing it a number of times, but it revolts me and turns me completely off. Does that mean I don't love him enough?
Lisa

Dear Lisa,
Although many women have written to me that they have been able to overcome their initial reluctance and have learned to enjoy giving oral sex, some, like you, have not. It doesn't mean that you don't love him, only that your sexual tastes are different and that this particular activity is repugnant to you. No two people have exactly the same tastes, in food, sex, or anything else. Sex often involves a negotiation to find activities of mutual enjoyment. There are things that drive you both wild. There are things that drive one of you wild but are just okay for the other. And there are things that are totally repugnant to one or both of you. If you care about each other, you can satisfy each other's desires to a great extent. But sometimes the reality is that you can't give your lover what he or she wants, no matter how much you love each other. So give what you can and enjoy what each has to offer.
Joan

Dear Joan,
Let me first say that I am a twenty-seven-year-old female and I think that I must be just weird. I love to perform oral sex on men. But that's not the weird part. The really weird part is that I can reach orgasm from it. If I take his penis deep into my mouth, stroking with my tongue, I eventually bring myself to climax. I have had several boyfriends tell me that it is not possible for me to do this, so I show them, much to their joy and amazement. Am I really strange?

I'm multiorgasmic, so I can come again later when we do it for real. Am I depriving him of something?
Nellie

Dear Nellie,
I think it's wonderful. Does your partner feel deprived? I doubt it, but

be sure to check it out with him. Otherwise, have a blast. It sounds fantastic.
Joan

Cunnilingus

Dear Joan,

I have had lots of relationships, but now I've settled down with one woman with whom I want to spend the rest of my life. I love to perform oral sex on her. It gives me so much pleasure, both because I enjoy it and in knowing that I'm pleasing her. However, my partner doesn't like it. When I do it she lies there and seems to be allowing me to do it, not because she enjoys it, but because I do. It ruins my pleasure knowing she's not enjoying herself. What can I do?
Hank

Dear Hank,

There are two ways to go with this. The first is to just admit that she doesn't like to receive oral sex and forget about it. The other is to try and find out why she doesn't like it and change her attitude. When there's something holding a woman back, it becomes impossible for her to relax and just take pleasure. And there are many things that might account for her attitude.

She might, like many women, feel dirty and smelly—like she isn't "kissing sweet"—and therefore she doesn't want you near her genitals. That's solvable with a lovemaking session in the shower.

She may have feelings of subjugation or vulnerability when you go down on her. There are women who feel that the act signifies a man's mastery of her. Or parting her legs might feel like a giant, perverted step, and a wrong one. Women are still taught that knees should be kept together when sitting. Proceeding slowly and easily, with lots of reassurance, might work here.

She may feel that your performing oral sex on her is a barter arrangement, that you will then require "repayment" in the form of her performing fellatio on you. If she's really reluctant to do that for you, she might not want to enter into what she feels is an agreement: "I'll do this, but then you'll have to do that."

She may feel that it's selfish to just take pleasure. It can be difficult for a woman to relax and allow you to perform cunnilingus merely for its own sake, without feeling like she's "taking." It's an unfamiliar role for most women.

She may feel bad about her body. Body image is an overwhelming problem for some women. As good-looking as she might be, she might not want such intimate contact between you and the body she feels isn't as wonderful as she wants it to be. Have you tried making love in the dark, for starters? That might make her more willing to relax and enjoy.

She may feel that it's wrong. Oral sex, both cunnilingus and fellatio, has been labeled as taboo by many churches and parents. Early on, many religions were against any form of sex that didn't produce children, the next generation of followers. So oral sex, along with homosexuality, anal sex, and many other practices, were forbidden. That teaching goes deeply into our subconscious, driven along by our parents. That can be a high hurdle for you to jump.

There are women who believe, as many were taught as recently as when I was young, that a woman is a vessel and isn't supposed to enjoy sex. Women were divided into two groups—prostitutes (bad girls), who enjoyed sexual relations, and good girls, who were wife material and didn't enjoy sex at all. These good girls allowed men to slake their lust in order to produce children, then their husbands went elsewhere for sexual enjoyment. I hear you scoff, but that attitude is more prevalent today than you might believe.

There's one more possibility. I was about to write, "Are you sure you're doing it right?" but there is no real "right" and "wrong." I guess the question is, Are you sure you're doing it in the way best guaranteed to give her pleasure? Does she like being stroked? If so, build on that. Just touch, making a mental road map of her body. Notice the places she particularly enjoys being touched. Those are the ones to touch with your tongue.

With cunnilingus, it's important to realize that a woman's body's reactions change as she gets excited. I think my reactions are pretty typical. Early on, the clitoris is, for me at least, negatively sensitized. I don't like to have it touched or licked until I'm a bit aroused. Touching before I'm ready makes me want to just push away. Once aroused, I love to have my genital area stroked or licked, but it must be done gently, with pressure increasing as excitement builds. Once I'm really excited, the pressure must lessen again. I become overly sensitive, and too much pleasure is almost painful.

Of course, every woman is different, and your girlfriend might react differently. It's up to you to gauge her reactions and guide yourself accordingly. Don't think that what worked for a former lover will necessarily work for your current lady. Start slowly. Learn. Take lots of time and build from stroking to a few light licks. Don't neglect your hands while you're using your tongue. Continue to touch and explore. As a woman can tell that she's pleasing a man by noting that his erection grows, you can gauge your lady's response from her lubrication. Is she getting wet? You can certainly tell the difference between your saliva and her fluids. Hers are thicker and taste totally different. Are her nipples erect? That's another way to tell that she's getting aroused.

The moral to all this is to take baby steps, all with encouragement and the agreement that at any moment, if she says stop, you will. Let her call the shots and you might get what you want.
Joan

Dear Joan,

I'm a thirty-one-year-old married woman and I can say that I really am uncomfortable receiving oral sex. When my husband asks (more like begs) for it I feel obliged to give in, but I really don't like it. Don't ask me why. I wish I knew. Friends tell me that if I don't like it, he isn't doing it right. I'm not so sure. Either way, I love giving, but don't like getting. I think my husband should consider himself lucky that he doesn't have to perform. All he has to do is sit back and enjoy.
Luanne

Dear Luanne,

If you don't enjoy it, that's that. I'm responding to your comment that he should consider himself lucky that he doesn't have to perform oral sex on you. Many men truly enjoy performing oral sex, not just because it excites a woman, but for its own sake, for his own pleasure. Obviously your husband is such a man, since you say he begs for it. If you deny him, which is certainly your right if you don't enjoy it, you just need to realize that you're depriving him of something that gives him pleasure.

I thought I'd quote from a few letters I've received from men on the subject. They get a bit graphic, but it might help you to understand.

Dear Joan,

I have been a fan of cunnilingus for many years, finding it the most exciting form of foreplay, or perhaps even the finale. I recently introduced my second wife to the joys of oral sex. I say introduced because, although she had experienced it before, she never really enjoyed it.

I am fascinated by the female sex, and to me, the scent of an aroused woman is a powerful aphrodisiac. I enjoy lightly moving my tongue up her thighs to her sex, across, down, and back, slowly licking. The moment my tongue touches her clit and I feel her respond, I continue to lick softly and slowly, tasting her sweetness. As she gets more excited, I do as well. My slow actions turn into fast flicks of the tongue, and the gentle nibbles of her love button give way to sucking. Her wetness flows and her hips begin to buck. I reach up and finger her nipples, maybe give them a slight pinch. She squeezes my head with her powerful thighs, and I love it. My wife is difficult to bring to orgasm, but this seems to do it for her. Just writing about it makes me want to grab her and make love to her. I can't wait until she gets home!

Mike from Maryland

Dear Joan,

I thought I'd just write to you on the subject of oral sex. I think men sometimes believe they know it all and don't pay enough attention to their lady's desires. Since you're not a man, Joan, maybe this letter will help you to understand, too.

My girlfriend and I dated for several years before I finally learned how to properly perform oral sex on her. I think many guys make the mistake of trying to pleasure their women in the way that they would like to be pleasured. That's a mistake. Women require different attention than men do.

At first my girlfriend had a hard time accepting the fact that I wanted to lick her. She was used to sucking me until I came, but she somehow thought that licking her vagina was less appealing. She didn't understand how wonderful it is for me to do that.

To get her used to the idea, we showered together. Once she felt clean, I could get her to relax while I licked her, but, although I tried, I just couldn't bring her to climax. And I really wanted to.

My next step was to let her know how much I wanted to make her come with my face between her legs. Actually, I was a bit of a tease, and it makes me grin when I remember what I did. I picked an evening when we were going to a party, and in the car on the way I told her how much I wanted to give her oral sex. During the evening, I constantly whispered into her ear how much I wanted to eat her wet pussy. I told her how I could not be satisfied until her juices soaked my face. She kept asking, "Really?" and I kept assuring her that I really did want to. I guess eventually she began to believe me.

Needless to say, we went home early that night, and her entire outlook had changed. She was hot for me, and for my mouth. As I licked her, her hips went crazy, and she forced herself into my mouth. Eventually she came over and over again, until my entire face was soaked. I just loved it.

Once she became confident that I really enjoyed her that way, our sex life took a new turn. At that point, I really learned how to satisfy her orally. Instead of trying to make her come in a hurry, the way I like oral sex done on me, I slowed down and licked her entire area over and over, until I could identify which part made her feel the best. I was surprised how much that varied from time to time. Sometimes she wants my tongue on her clit only, sometimes she likes long, slow licks, sometimes she can't get off without a couple of my fingers inside her. The key is that I now know not to hurry her, but to respond to her body.

Of course, the most important part is for me to let her know how much I want her ahead of time. A simple note in the morning or a phone call during the day telling her how much I want her makes all the difference in the world.

I hope this helps some of the people who write to you to understand how it is from a man's point of view.

Thanks for listening.

Alan

So, Luanne, the answer to your question is yes, many men do enjoy performing oral sex just for its own sake.

Joan

Shaving

Dear Joan,

I'm a thirty-nine-year-old woman and my husband and I have been discussing shaving. We both think that it would be wonderful if I could be smooth down there, but we don't know how to go about it without the nasty stuff I remember from when I had my children. I remember that for a week afterwards I itched and there were red bumps all over the area. It wasn't pleasant at all. Is there any way I can shave my genitals without those aftereffects?

Julie

Dear Julie,

I've never shaved my entire genital area, except when I had my children, more than thirty-five years ago, and my recollection is about the same as yours. I have gotten letters from many visitors to my website who have successfully kept that area hairless and have serious suggestions which I'll include for you. I recommend, however, that you begin slowly. Start with your bikini line, the insides of your upper thighs, and your belly, maybe leaving a small area unshaven the way the porn stars do. That's supposed to be very sexy. That way you'll be sure that your skin responds well before you go all the way.

If you have any skin allergies, you might want to forgo this pleasure, as this area can be a nightmare if it gets inflamed. Everything will be an irritant, including your slacks and panties. If you want something different, trim your hair quite short or use a regular hair conditioner to give it a soft feel and delicious smell.

If you're determined, take care and let me tell you what others recommend.

It might make things easier if you first clip your hair very short with scissors or clippers. You might see what this "hairdo" does to your sex life. It's really delicious.

When you're ready to take the big step, clean the area really well in the shower. Use lots of antibacterial soap. If you haven't trimmed the hair very short, do that now to make the shaving easier. Then use a new razor and lots of shaving cream. Try to find products that have no perfumes or other additives, since those can be irritating.

Go over the area with only two strokes, one with the grain and one against. If you continually scrape the area it will certainly irritate the sensitive skin beneath. If the two strokes don't completely remove the hair, wait a day or two and then try again.

Take extreme care to avoid nicks and scratches, especially on the most sensitive skin of the mucous membranes on the lips and beneath. Rinse with cold water to close the pores, then dry the area and splash liberally with an aftershave, alcohol, or witch hazel.

If you can, leave yourself bare for a few hours, without panties and especially without confining jeans. Give the area time to dry and heal without the buildup of sweat and fluids that occurs beneath your clothes. If you do it at bedtime and sleep without covering the area, that might lessen the possibility of razor rash.

Many who've written say that it's easier just to avoid the "growing out" time by shaving every two or three days. That way the hair never gets longer than slight stubble.

One particular warning. Any kind of rash or the small nicks and cuts that might result from shaving make having sex a more high-risk activity. Remember that for disease to be transmitted there must be fluid-to-fluid contact. With any open injury or skin rash that might be exposed to semen, disease transmission becomes that much easier. If you're not with a regular partner, I would advise not shaving.

Here are a few of the letters I've received from visitors, both pro and con.

Dear Joan,

I'm a woman of thirty and I've been keeping my pubic area clean for several years, just leaving a small triangular area unshaved, as I like that look more. I have tried many different products, and have finally settled on the following.

I use a women's Excel razor because the head seems to swivel easily and the sides, with the bumpers on each side of the blade, don't have as much tendency to nick skin. Edge shaving gel now comes in an unscented "therapeutic" version, which helps too. I change blades often and since I have trouble seeing what I'm doing, I just go by how it feels. I change the direction of the stroke if I can feel the hair is not coming off, and shave about once a week so it won't get too long.

By the way, I have tried depilatories, and since I'm not coordinated enough to keep them off my mucous membranes, I've had very painful results.

Hilda

Dear Joan,

I have shaved since I was eighteen. I was not having sex and was still a virgin, but shaving made me feel very clean and sexy. One of the first times I visited my doctor for a regular female exam, an older nurse who was helping acted irritated and asked me why I shaved. My smiling response was, "Because I think it is beautiful." Frowning, surely thinking of her own body, she left the room. I hope she thought about this for some time and maybe shaved, herself.

Now that I am older and have experienced a great sexual relationship, I know it is not only the way it looks, but also how great it feels not to let anything stand in the way of seeing and feeling this beautiful part of my body.

Lynn

Dear Joan,

Here's my shaving story, and it just might discourage others from trying it.

I wanted to shave my pubic area, since I spend a lot of time at the beach and my heavy hair stuck out of the openings of my bathing suits. So I shaved my entire area.

For about a day it looked good. Then, not only did I start getting stubble, but also I got those little red bumps and the skin got really irritated. I thought perhaps it was a one-time thing, so when it healed up a bit I tried again. Same problem.

A while later I tried depilatory cream. Same problem, so I let it all grow out—a nightmare for a week or so.

Then I got a new boyfriend, and he mentioned that he was interested in seeing me with a hairless crotch. Well, I had heard good things about waxing, so I bought some of those double-sided wax strips. That method didn't get all the hair. It got maybe half of it, and I had to remove the rest with tweezers. Ugh. In addition, the strips were really awkward to use, and the irritation was even worse and showed almost immediately. I found that aloe worked pretty well on the irritation, but I gave up.

I'd really like to be hairless, but I've decided that my boyfriend can just get used to me the way I am. If he doesn't like me this way, he'll just have to find someone with better and barer skin.
Elana

Dear Ms. Lloyd,
I have a delicious idea for those women who want to shave their genitals. Let your partner shave you. Give him all the guidelines and warnings, then let him begin with a small part. It's an amazingly intimate sharing and can build the excitement for a wonderful time afterward. If you try this and make love, let me suggest that you wash again and reapply alcohol or whatever.

My boyfriend and I do this about once a week, and it never fails to lead to great sex.
MaryLou

So, Julie, if you want to give shaving a try, do it. Just take care.
Joan

Dear Joan Elizabeth Lloyd,
I'm a twenty-eight-year-old man and I really want to shave my pubic area. My wife agrees with my desire, and also thinks it will make oral sex much nicer. However, I'm really embarrassed at the thought of going to the doctor afterward. I'm sure either the doctor, who's a man, or the nurse, who's a woman, will notice that I've shaved and think I'm really kinky. How long does it take to grow back, and what should I do?
Nate

Dear Nate,
I'm sure that doctors and nurses have seen it all before, and after all, it's your body and you are allowed to do with it what you want. If it gives you a kick to shave, that's great. If you want to regrow it, it will

take several weeks for it to get to a reasonable length. But let the doctor and nurse eat their hearts out over your fabulous love life.

Here's a copy of a letter I received recently.

Dear Joan,
Regarding the "problem" of dealing with a doctor or nurse once you have shaved your vaginal area, here's my opinion. If you are experiencing a more rewarding sex life with your partner (and my wife says that being shaved enhances her sensitivity to oral lovemaking), that will have to be the medical folks' problem rather than yours! If you're asked why you do it, is there a need for any more of an answer than "Because my husband or wife prefers me this way" or "Because sex is more satisfying for me"? If your doctor has a problem accepting that, then perhaps he has a problem accepting other aspects of your being a normal, sexual human being, and therefore maybe you ought to find a physician who has less trouble accepting you as you really are.

My wife and I both shave, and for us it's a nonissue, because nobody in the medical profession has ever commented on it one way or the other.
Tony

I hope that opinion helps with your decision.
Joan

Hi, Joan,
I've tried shaving and it just doesn't work for me. Is there any other way to remove hair? Do the porn stars shave or do they use something else? Can I use Nair or another depilatory?
Angela

Dear Angela,
Many of the letters I have received on the topic of shaving recount other methods of hair removal. Some say that Nair works, and it probably does work for them. However, if you read the label, it

specifically says that it's not for use on mucous membranes. I'll send you a few of the letters and let you judge for yourself.

Dear Joan,

I have dark, thick, naturally curly hair on my head, so the hair on other parts of my body is also thick. I only trim my pubic hair, because removing the hair totally is pure agony for me. Believe me, I've tried all methods! I sometimes get ingrown hairs on my legs and underarms, but the bikini line is the worst.

I did find something that works best for me on the bikini line, though. I bought a depilatory called "Magic." It's a shaving powder marketed for black men to use on their faces to eliminate or prevent razor bumps. It comes in a powder form you mix with water and use just like Nair or any of the other hair removal products.

I followed the instructions on the container and I never leave it on for more than five minutes. It works for me on the inner thigh area, which is my main concern. Maybe you might pass this on to anyone who's interested.

Carol

Dear Joan,

I love the feeling of my shaven body, and once I finally did it for the first time, I couldn't keep my own hands off. I did have a problem, though. The shaved area grew back fast, and it became really dense. I didn't have very much hair to start with, and it was very fine, but once I began shaving, the pubic hair grew like a beard and I needed to shave every day.

So I began to try other ways to remove the hair. I tried creams, including Nair and the one advertised on TV called Epilstop. They didn't work, and irritated the inner areas.

Finally, I tried waxing. It hurt at first, but then it wasn't bad, and I love the results. It has been three weeks and the hair that is growing back is very fine, and some has not come back at all, at least not yet. I feel so sexy this way that whatever I have to do I'll never grow it back.

Eve

Dear Joan,

I am a thirty-two-year-old female, divorced, and now engaged again, who recently began shaving at the request of my fiancé.

I have to say that until he asked me, I had always thought shaving was pretty sick. I thought that the men who wanted it were into the "little girl" thing. I discussed that with him and he laughed. Darling, he said to me, there's no way you will ever look like a little girl to me. I guess that's probably true, since I'm a very big woman. When I pushed him for the reason he wanted me to shave, he told me that he loves to give me oral sex, and we would both enjoy it more if I shaved.

So I tried it. First of all, let me say that getting it done was a major pain. If you've ever thought of using one of those cold wax deals, don't even bother. The hair has to be really long for it to work at all, and in my case, I guess I just have too much body heat, because the wax never hardened at all—it was just a big runny, sticky, oozy mess!!!

Finally I just shaved it with a razor and soap, and I maintain it with Nair, except around the inner edges, which have to be shaved daily because I can't stand any stubble there at all.

Here's the good part, though. From the minute I finished shaving, I was really turned on. Wearing clothes felt different, and I constantly felt like I had a "dirty little secret." This is cooler than the hottest lingerie I've ever worn. The best part is that my fiancé went nuts. When he first saw it, I got oral sex for half an hour straight, until I was bucking and screaming for him to stop!

Now I feel everything more intensely. It's like the hair was preventing some of my nerve endings from being exposed enough to feel what was going on. Regular sex is better, oral sex is better, everything is better, and I've never felt this sexy in my life! In short, I LOVE IT!!! I will NEVER grow hair there again!!

Betsy

Hi, Joan,

I'm a woman with lots of pubic hair. I discussed shaving with friends, and one, who is married to an African-American man, suggested a product called Denby's. It comes in a sensitive skin formula that I use on my pubic area. The product is a shaving powder for African-American men who can't shave with a razor. It costs about a dollar fifty a can, and you mix with cold water to a paste consistency. I have an old small spatula that I spread it on with and I use cotton balls in my slit so it doesn't run everywhere. It takes about five to seven minutes to soften up, then you scrape it off.

I know that sounds painful, but it's not. Just wet the spatula and run it over your skin. I find doing it while I sit on the edge of the bathtub so I can spread my legs wide works best. Unfortunately, it doesn't smell too great, but if you are careful and take your time, it works really well.

Manda

Angela, take care, and test any product on the skin on the inside of your arm. Use it and leave the area as untouched as you can for forty-eight hours. If there's no adverse reaction, try the insides of your thighs before you use it on your most delicate tissues.

Joan

Going Still Further

Chapter 9

Toys

Dear Joan,
My husband and I recently decided that we wanted to buy a toy for the bedroom. He asked a friend at work about it, who lent him a catalog with lots of stuff. Actually, we looked through the catalog and didn't have to buy a thing. Just browsing improved our sex life. We do want to get something, but we don't know what to buy. Any suggestions?
Claudia

Dear Claudia,
I have lots of suggestions, but ultimately you and he will have to pick something and just try it out. It depends entirely on what you two enjoy.

I have a few dildos of different sizes that Ed and I play with from time to time. I also enjoy using a vibrator, both for love play and for masturbation. They come in both plug-in (pardon the double entendre) and battery-operated models. I have an electric one and I think the vibrations are stronger. You're limited, however, by the length of the cord. I also have a battery-operated vibrator, and it's wonderfully portable, but not quite as powerful. That one came with lots of sleeves that fit over the base unit, supposedly for different kinds of stimulation. A few looked like devices dating from the Spanish Inquisition, and I didn't find any of those more pleasurable than the basic unit, so don't waste your money at first.

A while ago I got a set of ben wha balls. You're supposed to insert them in your vaginal channel, and when they bump together, they are said to cause wonderful vibrations that are really arousing. I had read a really sexy scene in a romance novel and wondered whether inserting these little cuties would get me excited, too. Well, I tried, and they didn't. All I found was that while I was lying down they did nothing and when I stood up like the character did in the book, they fell out. Maybe I was doing something wrong, but I didn't have the patience to work at it.

Several years ago I got the Venus Butterfly, a device that straps onto my thighs and supposedly presses against my clit and vibrates without being held. It didn't work that way for me. I never got it positioned quite right. With Ed's hands helping, of course, it performed just fine.

I don't know whether you consider sexy lingerie a toy, but I have lots of really outrageous undies, including a waist cincher and a bra and panty set with four-inch fringe. Silly, but it sends a specific message that I'm in the mood for some lovemaking that's a bit less serious.

I thought I'd include some of the letters I've gotten from visitors to my website about the toys they particularly enjoyed. Maybe these will help you decide.

Dear Joan,
My husband and I have been married for more than fifteen years. We are very happily married and just recently explored the

use of sex toys during our lovemaking. This is all new to us, and we both like it a great deal. Boy, what we missed all those years.

As any woman would know, oral sex is great, but we found that when you add vaginal stimulation in the form of a dildo, it's heaven. So far we've tried only a few toys, a six-inch vibrator and an eight-inch-long vibrating dildo that I got for my birthday from my coworkers. Both are wonderful and we enjoy them. Depending on the mood, we will use the short vibrator in addition to my husband's tongue to bring me to the ultimate, but at other times, when I'm really hot, we use the longer one. I am not a big woman, but when I get really aroused I go wild and am able to take the whole thing into me! Wow, do I soar!

Jeanette

Dear Joan,

My name is Greg and I'm a guy who loves to add toys to my lovemaking with my wife. I always wondered whether a bigger dildo was more exciting for women, but recently my wife seems to have given me the answer.

My wife and I occasionally have a mild bondage session during which I tie her up lightly and comfortably. Sadly, I often lose the erection in the process of making sure she is both secured and comfortable. Maybe I make too much of her comfort, but that's important to me. Well, I recently bought a gigantic dildo as a joke, and when she unwrapped the package we both laughed and kidded about her ability to take it all inside. Recently, I got her tied up and teased her until she was thrashing around on the bed. Unfortunately, I wasn't hard, so I got the giant rod and slowly pushed it inside of her. Well, to my amazement, and hers too, I guess, she took it all, and it led to one of her best climaxes. By the time she was through, I was hard, so I replaced the toy with my erection. I worried that, since I'm not that big, it wouldn't feel the same, but she came again like crazy. I don't think she'd be as willing if she wasn't already really aroused, but when she is, wowie. Now that's our favorite toy.

Greg

Dear Joan,

Hello, Joan. I'm a forty-three-year-old married lady and I wanted to write and tell you about my toy collection. Actually, my husband and I have three toy collections, mine, his, and ours.

My favorite two toys are both vibrators, one called the Scorpion, and the other the Jack Rabbit. The Scorpion is really nice in that it has dual vibrators, one each for front and back door, and a pair of clitoral stimulators (antenna-looking things that rub in just the right places). It comes (pardon the pun) with a set of elastic straps so it can be held in place without the use of hands, or for the more adventurous, it can be worn under clothing!! I've never actually done that, but it's sort of a fantasy of mine.

The Jack Rabbit also has clitoral stimulators, but has a rotating shaft that is filled with little beads that move and grind around each other. The actions send me flying in many directions at once. I can heartily recommend both of those. I use them alone, but I'm sure they can be made part of great sex with a guy, too.

Marnie

Dear Joan,

Oh, yes, we certainly have toys, especially dildos, both for playing together and for me to masturbate with while he watches. But let me tell you what I've discovered about them. By the way, I'm fifty-one, and my second husband and I have delved into the world of toys extensively. My first husband wasn't into playing games in bed, and I really regret all those lost years.

Anyway, hubby number two and I have quite a collection of dildos, but aside from the size, they all feel pretty much the same. That was true until I got one made of this soft, jellylike stuff that's just a bit flexible and not so cold. Let me say that I don't mind the cold of the harder plastic ones; that can be a really exciting contrast to a hot body. But these are curved and ridged and feel just great. We got a set of three to start, and now we have just about every shape and size we can find online or in catalogs.

Try it, you'll like it.
Donna

Claudia, I got a letter from a man who had read that I didn't like the butterfly I tried. Here's his take on it.

Dear Joan,
We just received an order from Adam & Eve. In it was the "butterfly" vibrator strap-on for the woman, the one you said in your letter that you didn't care for. Well, we, my lady and I, decided to give it a try. We giggled a little at the awkward task of strapping it on her, but when it was in place and turned on, so was she! The very intense vibrations jolted her, as she repositioned it for maximum pleasure.

As it purred on, I sucked and played with her breasts. In a short time she was bucking and squirming, I sucked harder while my hands roamed all over. I can't remember her having such an intense orgasm, she came and came, and I never let up playing with her breasts and touching her. Well, as she was coming, I was ready. I couldn't wait for her to remove it (straps and all), so I just shifted it so I could enter her while it was still buzzing. It was a great feeling thrusting into her wet body while the butterfly was still humming against my erection. They claim it can be worn under clothing, and she can't wait to try that! We like that purple butterfly a lot!
Jimmy

Dear Joan,
I am a twenty-four-year-old guy and I have several girlfriends I play with. Since each woman knows I'm not monogamous, I think it's all okay. I don't cheat. Also, before you start yelling, I always use the best-quality condoms.

Sometimes I pack a "fun kit" for the bedroom. It has three

of my favorite compact discs, a good supply of personal lubricant (I like one called Wet Platinum, which works just wonderfully) and condoms, several toys (a dildo and several different kinds of vibrators), and a few scarfs which work for blindfolds, restraints, and such. I also have a few menus from nearby restaurants that deliver, just in case exhaustion overtakes us (big smile).

Oh, and if you brush your teeth and perform oral sex afterwards, your partner will have a wonderful reaction. Pepsodent has quite a following. Almost cultlike among the scene.
Bill

Dear Joan Elizabeth Lloyd,
My wife and I love playing in the bedroom. We have tried lots of different toys, with good and poor results. But we've learned from experience that when something doesn't work out one evening, we put it aside and try again another night. It's funny how something that's really a yawn one night will be an orgasmic experience another.

For example, several months ago we bought a set of Chinese anal love beads. There are about six, strung on a long nylon cord with a large ring at the end. You insert the beads, then pull them out, one at a time using the ring and cord as he or she climaxes. Supposedly wild stuff.

We tried them on me first, and though I enjoyed them, it wasn't earth-shattering. My mate seemed to appreciate them a bit more. I kept tugging on them lightly while performing oral sex. Okay, but not as good as lots of other things we do. Well, the beads ended up in the back of the "love drawer" for a while.

I was browsing the Net recently and read an erotic story about a couple who really thought these beads were the greatest, so I "pulled them out" (pun intended) of the toy box for another go. Well, something was just right this time. She pulled them out during my orgasm and I came so hard I thought I

would turn inside out. This just proves that if at first you don't succeed, keep going—and going and going.
Jack

So, Claudia, take a chance and buy something. If you don't like it, try again. Actually, just browsing the catalog and deciding what to order can lead to great sex all by itself.
Joan

Dear Joan,
My wife and I have only tried a couple of toys, including a small vibrator, which I love to use on her or watch her use on herself and bring herself to orgasm. Here's the fun part. We have discovered that if you take one of those long thin balloons, the strong ones that the clowns use to make animals, and fill it with just a bit of warm water, it works a little like a dildo, but I can squeeze and release the part that is outside of her, which forces the water in and out! If you want to have your husband try this, get creative and fill one with warm water and one with cold water and alternate. It will drive you nuts. Just be sure to get expensive balloons. You don't want to have one break, then have to get the pieces of rubber out.
Oscar

Dear Oscar,
What a wonderful idea. I can't wait to try it.
Joan

Dear Joan,
Someone told me that ben wha balls are good for exercising your vaginal muscles. I've tried doing Kegel exercises but I haven't felt any results yet. Has anyone tried using ben wha balls for this? Does it work?
Hilary

Dear Hilary,

I got a letter just recently about ben wha balls and Kegel exercises.

Hello, Joan,

I gather that you haven't found any way to get excitement with ben wha balls. For me they work just fine. When I place them in my vagina and rock back and forth with my knees up I feel a slight stimulation. But I've found another use for them.

Like many other women, I do Kegel exercises to tighten the PC (pubococcygeal) muscle, the one that squeezes my lover's penis. The exercises are really easy to do. While I am urinating, I stop the stream for five seconds, then release. That's it. Once you've isolated those muscles, you can do the exercises any-where, anytime. And the stronger those muscles are, the more you can play with him in bed.

Anyway, I found that the ben wha balls were great for keep-ing those muscles in good shape. I like walking around the house wearing them for ten or fifteen minutes, working my PC muscle. The longer I wear them the stronger the muscle be-comes. Sometimes I even wear them on a car trip, and do my Kegel exercises. That does great things for my love muscles.

Basically I find that they teach vaginal control and help with bladder control, you know, those sudden leaks as you enter the bathroom. I think it's called stress incontinence. I love them!
Margery

I hope that helps, Hilary.
Joan

Threesomes

Dear Joan,

My husband and I sat down about a month or so ago with a bottle of wine and talked. During a long and frank discussion, he told me he would like to try swinging, bringing another girl or guy into bed with us. I'm not sure about trying this because of a fear I have of losing him. I don't know which would be more likely to drive him away, if I said no or if I said yes and it went wrong.

I have also heard that a lot of relationships are better off when swinging or threesomes are brought into the picture. We have a very beautiful marriage and a young son. I don't want to do anything that might mess everything up. What do you think?
Cilla

Dear Cilla,
First and most important, don't do things only "to make him happy." Period.

As for threesomes, in general I'm against them. I think that it's taking a great risk for a few moments of excitement. Later on, when the excitement cools, there are often jealousies, comparisons, and bad feelings. "Does he like her body better than mine?" "Did he enjoy her lovemaking more than mine?" "My husband's now asking for a repeat. Does that mean he liked it better than when we make love just the two of us?" It's really dangerous, especially for anyone who tends to feel jealous or possessive, or who struggles with negative feelings about his or her body or sexual performance.

Here are a few letters from folks, both pro and con, to help you with your decision.

Dear Joan,
I know how you feel about threesomes, but I thought I'd share what I've learned, too.

I'm a twenty-seven-year-old woman and I have had several threesomes with my boyfriend, sometimes including another man and sometimes another woman. In my opinion, those threesomes provided some of the most erotic experiences possible. They have kept our relationship alive and passionate.

In my experience, in order to make it work and not leave feelings of jealousy or animosity, two principles must be applied:

First, the third person must not be a physical threat. If my boyfriend and I are inviting another man to play with us, my boyfriend must not have any insecurities about the way the other man looks. This works the same way for me. I don't want to feel threatened by another woman's appearance either. The difficulty here can be finding someone that neither of you are threatened by, and is attractive enough to be a turn-on. However, this fine line must be understood and accepted to keep your own relationship healthy and safe.

Second, you have to establish clear boundaries in advance. Acceptable sexual behavior must be established before the sexual encounter begins. Knowing each other's exact boundaries and not crossing them are key here.

There are certainly other factors that can affect the outcome of the experience, but I think those two rules are the most important.

Marlene from Washington State

Dear Joan,

About a year ago my husband I agreed to invite an unmarried woman, a friend of mine from college, into our bed. At first it was an exciting thought, and just talking about it led my husband and me to great sex. We talked for a long time before the actual date, and each time we thought about what it would be like, we couldn't make love fast enough.

Then the weekend came. She was visiting from out of town for a class reunion, and after dinner and wine, we got to talking. It turned out that she had always been attracted to my husband, so we did it.

At first it was okay. I was really hot and the three of us rolled around on the bed and had a great time. As the evening passed, however, it got more and more difficult watching the two of them together.

Now I wish I'd never done it. Although I feel secure that he loves me and wouldn't ever leave me for her, I can't help wondering about her motives. Does she still want him? It was an experience, and it was a good one at first, but frankly, I'm kind of ashamed now. In hindsight, it would have been better if it wasn't with a friend, someone who runs in the same circles as I do and can't be avoided. It's a constant reminder.

Connie

Dear Joan,

When we got married in the early seventies, my wife was a virgin, and I had very little sexual experience. After we had been married for five or six years, in the late seventies, I convinced her to try swinging. If you remember, those were the days of free love, key games, and much playing around.

Anyway, we did a lot of swapping and we enjoyed it very much. Since then, I have encouraged my wife to have sex with other men. I love it when she tells me about her escapades while we make love. At no time have we felt that her activities were threatening our relationship. She says that sex with others is just sex, not love. You seem to think that bringing other people into a couple's relationship is dangerous. In this regard, we do not agree with you.

Burt

Dear Joan,

Several years ago my husband and I established a sexual relationship with another woman. We would take advantage of the opportunity every chance we could, including getting a babysitter for all the kids so we could get in some "quality" time. Months of passion and play passed and I began to feel that I was getting the "short end of the stick." I felt left out and unimportant in the threesome. Everyone would be satisfied except me, and I was never the first recipient. I became bitter and jealous and angry. It seemed to me, in my own mind, that my husband had a girlfriend, and I'd given them permission. I would just join in part of it.

Eventually I told him how I felt and he immediately talked to her and we ended it. We haven't done anything like that again, for obvious reasons. Never again. I've had enough.
Patti

Dear Joan,
One evening several months ago, several couples and a single girlfriend of mine were playing a game of truth or dare. I chose dare, and my husband of ten years dared me to let my girlfriend go down on me. Since we all had been drinking, she didn't hesitate, and fulfilled his wish. That was brief, but later, after everyone else left, the three of us ended up in the bedroom. It was fantastic—exciting and different. I never thought I'd enjoy the touch of another woman so much, but I did, and I had to admit that. And the excitement it brought back into my marriage—WOW!
Cynthia

Dear Joan,
I think the idea of a threesome is disgusting and degrading. I know my husband wouldn't think of such a thing—he thinks too much of me. He wouldn't want any other man touching me and I wouldn't want anyone touching him either. Why would anyone jeopardize a good marriage for a few minutes of frolic? It's immoral and dangerous.
Nancy

Dear Joan,
Originally I thought it would be a gas to add another person to the bed I share with my wife. I pictured another woman and my wife pleasuring each other and, of course, me. The other woman would do some of the things my wife wasn't interested in doing.

Well, the more I think about it the more I agree with you about adding a third or another couple. I've tried to be honest with myself and I guess I wanted to do it as a way to play around with another woman with my wife knowing about it and giving me permission. As I considered, I thought about how I would feel if the tables were turned. What's sauce for the gander is good for the goose, and I thought about how I would feel if some young stud were making love with my wife and she was really enjoying it.

To tell you the truth, it made me think twice, then three times. I began to feel a pang of jealousy and realized that she would have bad feelings too. So in the end, I decided that I wouldn't try it, however wonderful it might be to consider it.

To confess, occasionally I think about a third while my wife and I are making love. I have never told her, but it does make sex more erotic if I picture another woman in bed with us.
Denny

I hope these letters help you sort out your feelings. In the long run, it's really a matter of emotion, and you and only you can make that kind of decision.
Joan

Dear Joan,
My name is Suzy and I'm twenty-six. My boyfriend has been asking me to think about having a threesome. He says that it doesn't matter if the third partner is male or female, he just wants to try it with me. I think I want to try it, but I don't know how to go about deciding on a person and figuring out if they would be interested. I don't want to do it with a complete stranger, but I'm not sure how to find someone that would be willing. Can you give me some advice on this?
Suzy

Dear Suzy,
If you want to make it happen, most threesomes occur with someone you already know and who already turns one or both of you on.

Discuss it with your boyfriend and see whether you know of someone who might fit the bill. Then get together in a neutral spot, a club, over a meal, and gently mention that you are both interested and see what the third party says. Realize that asking something like this might ruin things with your chosen third. It would be really difficult to continue seeing someone to whom you've admitted sexual feelings and who's said no. It might be just as difficult to continue seeing the "other woman" afterwards in social situations, especially if the threesome eventually ends.

I got a letter recently from a woman who's been involved in several such relationships. I thought you might learn a bit from her letter.

Dear Joan,

I'm twenty-seven, female, single, and have a pretty active sex life. I thought I'd write about how couples can get involved in a threesome from the point of view of someone who has been the third person.

Over the last few years I've been approached several times, in one way or another, to make up a threesome. I've accepted twice. Both times I've been with the couple on several occasions. In fact, I've just gotten back home after spending a fantastic week staying with one of them.

In both cases things got started because I had some sort of connection with the wife. The first time, I had already gotten to know the wife at the gym. (It's amazing how much goes on at my gym!) Anyway, soon after, I met her husband. He was a very nice guy and I had no problems agreeing when she asked me to spend an evening with the two of them. The experience was really great, and we all agreed to continue from time to time.

The wife of the second couple is someone I used to work with. Back then, we kind of liked each other, but weren't really close. I met her and her husband a few times at social events. When she approached me, we decided to have dinner together before anything got started. At dinner, things crackled, if you know what I mean—really hot. A few weeks later I spent a Sunday with them and we sort of seduced each other. We still get together a few times a year for "fun and games."

In the cold light of day, of course, it is a big risk for any woman to approach another about making up a threesome, but it *can* work. Women have women friends, and every now and then something just clicks—a trust and attraction that says "Let's try it." It's not too hard to recognize if you're looking for it. It is like seduction; it goes one step at a time. If you take a step and the other person comes with you, then you can take another step. In the end, it's not so risky to take the final step.

I can't imagine that I'd ever agree to anything because a guy approached me. Actually, I was approached on two occasions by men, and I've said no. I think the reason is that I won't get involved unless I'm 110 percent sure that the woman is committed and really wants it. I know that most guys fantasize about being with two women and sometimes try to drag their partners into something. I wouldn't want to be part of anything like that. It would just be too embarrassing if she were to get upset or back away when things started to happen.

Just to add a final thought—when it comes to the mechanics, things always seem to work best if one person remains passive and the other two work on pleasing the passive one, at least to begin with. If everyone is trying to do something to everyone else, then it just gets too complicated.

I hope this helps others who might want to try.

Babs

Suzy, take care, be sure it's what you want to do, then just look around. You'll probably find some interested woman, someone you already know. As I said before, becoming involved with a friend or business acquaintance is risky in itself. If it doesn't work out, how will you feel about this person? Will you be able to work together and see each other every day? Only you can answer this.

Joan

Dear Joan,

I know how you feel about threesomes, but my wife and I have figured out how to do it without any risk. We simply include other partners, both male and female, in our fantasy life. Although I think it turns me on more than her, it excites us both. We have not ventured into reality with these exciting thoughts, but I think I would be willing to give it a shot. I am not worried about my ability to deal with an extra partner, but I'm not so sure about my wife. This way really works well for us.

Tom

Dear Tom,

What a great idea. Tell stories in the dark about the third person, discuss what you're doing and how it feels, all in the imagination. How wonderful!

Joan

Fetishes and Other Charged Issues

Dear Joan,

I've been surfing the Net and I've stumbled upon sites devoted to the kinkiest things: panties, whips, teens, cross-dressing, urine, and, ugh, so much more. Isn't there a limit to anything? Shouldn't we be trying to separate fetishes from what's normal?

Jill

Dear Jill,

Many people who write to me end their letters with the questions, "Am I abnormal?" "Am I weird?" or "Am I unusual?" People are frightened of anything that is not "normal." We tend to think of abnormality as the same as diseased, sick, or bad. But a sexual turn-on is about taste, not about normality. It doesn't matter whether your sexual tastes are normal, unusual, or weird, as long as they coincide with those of your partner. You may be abnormal, weird, and unusual because you like to eat pickles with ice cream, but if you enjoy it, should you not do it because other people don't like pickles with ice cream? IMHO, nothing done between consenting adults is wrong, bad, or abnormal if no one is hurt by it. If both parties get pleasure, terrific! Let me take a moment to clarify what I mean by a consenting adult.

A consenting adult knows that no means no and will stop any activity when that word, or a key word that means stop, is used. No questions, no comments, the end!

In addition, a consenting adult knows and accepts that it is his or her responsibility, note the word "responsibility," to say NO when things get the least bit uncomfortable. It's not a choice, it's mandatory. This is necessary for the enjoyment of both parties. If each partner knows that the other will stop things at any time for whatever reason, either partner is free to suggest and try new things without concern. This part of the definition is most important.

You use the word "fetish," but that word has lots of negative connotations. A fetish is merely an object that takes on a strong sexual meaning to a person or persons. It might be anything from a picture of Betty Grable's legs or a bikini photo of a sweetheart to a leather blindfold or a pair of used panties. Kinky is in the eye of the beholder. If material offends you, don't look.

Joan

Dear Joan,

I have noticed that my boyfriend is into feet. He likes to caress my feet and touch and kiss them. In the summer he enjoys it if I go barefoot, and I catch him looking at my toes. I think he even gets aroused.

Is this normal? Should I be worried? I don't mind, but maybe this is a sign of something that should concern me. And if it's harmless, then is there some way I can participate?

Missy

Dear Missy,

Many men are turned on by feet, which is why there are so many catalogs and websites devoted to feet and shoes. It's harmless, and hooray for trying to make it still more delicious for him. How about getting a pedicure, so that you have deliciously painted toenails? Even better, let him give you one. Get a bright red polish, something really sexy, then let him wash your feet and clip and polish your nails. I think he'll be in heaven. Can you find some very high heels—the strappy kind, in bright red or gold? You might find a pair in a catalog or on a website. If money's a problem, try garage sales and flea markets. I think he'll go nuts, especially when it becomes obvious that you're not troubled by his interest in feet.

You might also put your bare foot in his lap like that wonderful scene from the movie *Flashdance*. Rub his erection with your sole and tickle him with your toes. Have fun with it. That's the most important thing.

Joan

Dear Joan,

My question's very simple. I get really hot at the thought of women's panties, especially ones that have been worn. I know it's not so unusual, but it's unusual enough to have me scared. If I have some trouble getting erect for my wife, I think about making love to her around her panties and I get really hard. Can I tell her that I'd like to touch her and make love to her with her panties on? It's so scary.

Phil

Dear Phil,

I know it's scary to you, but enjoying panties is one of the most common of fetishes. Your love of silky underwear is shared by lots of men. Below you'll read some of the letters I've received from those who share your enjoyment of ladies' undergarments.

Dear Joan,

Panties!! Well, I have a pair in my desk drawer right here with me and I love just knowing that they are close. I don't consider my-self weird, I just admit what I enjoy and that's that. My wife knows about my love of silky underwear and she loves it when I put a pair between us while we make love. Sometimes she even puts a pair on and we make love around the edge of the crotch. Wow!!

So, with her encouragement, whenever I feel down while I'm at work, I reach into my desk drawer and just touch those panties. They remind me of her and of the fun we're going to have later on.

Will

Dear Joan,

I am a totally heterosexual man and I live with my lover. A while ago she bought me a couple of pairs of men's thongs, which I have worn and like.

One day I was folding some laundry she had left in the dryer. I couldn't help but notice the similarity of her thong panties to mine. I was curious, so I tried on a pair of her silk ones to feel the difference. I must say, they felt so much nicer than the ones that I wear. They fit more tightly in the genitals and were smooth and sexy-feeling.

I don't have any interest in any other articles of her clothing, but the feeling of those panties was great. I have never let her know about this because I'm afraid of her reaction. However, I have taken to wearing my thongs more often and I'm always looking for men's underwear that could give me the same feel as hers did. I wish makers of men's undergarments would in-clude sexier cuts with smoother material like that.

Thanks for letting me spout off like this.

Roy

Dear Joan,

I am a man who loves women's panties. I love to wear them

under my clothes. It's like I have a secret that no one knows about. I think they feel good and it's really sexy for me.
Craig

Dear Joan,
I have always had a thing about women's panties. When I go with my wife to shop, as we walk through the lingerie department I get a hard-on. I help my wife pick out her panties, always the fancy, sexy kind. She has dozens of crotchless ones that I love to see her wear. All of her undies are revealing.

Recently she's gotten into a new habit. She enjoys trying to embarrass me by holding up a pair of panties and asking me how I like them. She'll do it in front of a woman salesclerk or with other women standing near. They think I'm picking something out for her, but for us it has another meaning. I'm not really embarrassed, just excited, but if I tell her that, she'll stop, and it makes me smile.
Danny

So, Phil, you can certainly mention this all to your wife. You might try finding an erotic story about a man who enjoys making love to his wife with her undies on and give it to her. Check out her reaction. If she's not totally turned off, say, "How about I try that with you?" and see what she says. It just might work. And think of all the pleasure you might gain.
Joan

Cross-Dressing

Dear Joan,
I am writing about my husband. It may seem weird, but he likes wearing my underwear, especially satin panties that feel so smooth. Recently he admitted that he likes wearing my dresses when I am not home. His favorites are the ones made of either satin or rayon

and he says that likes the way they feel on his body, all sexy and soft. He also told me that he fantasizes about being tied up and blind-folded while wearing my dresses and skirts.

Well, one day I tried it on him. The fact that he seems to want to pretend to be a woman, and also knowing that he cannot see what happens to him when I touch him, it is a great turn-on for me and for him.

I've been thinking, however, that maybe I'm just contributing to his kinky obsession. I really don't mind, but shouldn't I be trying to discourage him? Are we both really weird? Is he really gay and I'm just fooling myself?
Clara

Dear Clara,
You've asked quite a number of questions, so let me try to help you, one issue at a time. First, cross-dressing is much more common than you might think. True figures are difficult to come by, but from what I read, a significant portion of the male population enjoys the feel of ladies' undies. We really do wear much more sensual lingerie than men do, don't we?

Second, there is no necessary connection between cross-dressing and homosexuality. Many men who enjoy women's clothing are not, have never been, and won't ever be interested in men as sexual partners. Some are gay, of course, but your husband seems to really enjoy having sex with you. What more can you ask?

Should you discourage him? Why on earth would you want to do that? He's shared something so personal with you and you've both benefited from the great sex. Go with it and enjoy.

As for his fantasy about being tied up in women's clothing, that's quite common too. For many men, this fetish is so kinky that they want to feel "forced" to dress as a female. It's amazing that a woman can dress as a man and it's hardly noticeable, but a man? And isn't that too bad. For him, however, it has led to some wonderful sexual encounters with a loving wife like you who can participate, share, and enjoy.

I received a wonderful letter recently from a man who discovered his love of female attire quite by accident. I thought you might learn quite a bit from reading it.

Dear Joan,
I know how volatile a topic cross-dressing can be, but I had to write and try to help those men who are really troubled about this. I am a cross-dresser who has the help and approval of my spouse. I know this letter will get a bit long, but I wanted to tell it all.

Several years ago my wife and I were invited to attend a masquerade party given by the lodge that we attend. It was for a charitable purpose at Christmas, and my wife suggested I go in drag, and I agreed. Let me say this: I had never cross-dressed or even thought about it before that episode. We searched through her wardrobe, and since I'm a rather slightly built man, it wasn't difficult to find a few things that would fit.

I was a bit shocked when she brought home some new pink panties and other lingerie from our neighborhood Wal-Mart. I couldn't imagine myself wearing anything like that. "Why should I? No one will know what I'm wearing beneath my clothing," I asked her.

She reminded me of the projection TV that had been donated as a prize for the best costume. She maintained that if I was wearing feminine things under my clothes it would help me act the part. I finally agreed. She spent considerable time teaching me to walk in high heels, and she drilled me on female gestures and such. How she did it, I'll never know, but she also convinced me to shave my legs. That was quite a process, but for a great prize, I agreed to cooperate.

The night of the party she helped me put on the silky pink panties, and when they slid up my legs and I felt them around my hips, I got an instant erection!! I could not believe how sexy I felt. I was embarrassed, but with my wonderful wife, all things are okay. I have to tell you that she was really enjoying the fact that I was cooperating so willingly, and was smiling from ear to ear. I think I was really hooked that night and didn't realize it, and I think she knew it.

When we were finally finished adding makeup and a long blond wig, I was amazed and really turned on when I saw the young female looking back at me from the mirror. My wife kept saying how I could pass for a woman anywhere. While I considered how much I was enjoying dressing in women's clothing, she got into her costume. She quickly and calmly dressed as a man, and I was surprised at how much easier it was for her to become a man than it was for me to become a woman.

We arrived at the affair and started quite a buzz. People who didn't know us were really confused by who was who. Let me just say that we won the prize.

That was three years ago. Now, when I'm home, I dress in women's clothing, and I wear sexy lingerie beneath my business suits. Am I gay? Not in the least. My wife and I have a great sex life. She loves knowing that it's my masculine body beneath my frilly outfits. From time to time we go out with me "dressed," and no one really notices.

That's my story and I hope other men will stop being afraid of who they are and just enjoy.
Allen

So, Clara, I hope this letter will help to clarify the feelings of men who enjoy the kind of thing your husband enjoys. It's especially wonderful since you are able to share it with him. Go for it, girl.
Joan

Dear Joan,
I've never talked about this to anyone, but maybe you can help me. I'm terrified that there's something really wrong with me. I fantasize about something so weird that I'm afraid I'm not normal. I think about being diapered. There, I've said it. My fantasy is that my wife diapers me, then doesn't let me go to the bathroom. She tells me

what a good boy I am not to wet my diaper, but she won't let me pee in the bathroom. It's torture to try to hold it, yet I get really excited just thinking about it.

Now I've even found a website that shows photos of men in diapers. Please help me.

James

Dear James,

Just the knowledge that there's a site out there devoted to diapering should tell you that you aren't alone. Fantasies aren't bad or good, they just are. Do you think you might want to act this one out? Maybe writing to me and getting this out into the open will make you brave enough to mention it to your wife. Granted, it's a risk, but you might consider it a risk worth taking.

Joan

And Further Still

Blindfolds

Dear Joan,

I'm writing just to tell you a bit about myself and my love of blindfolds. Have you ever been blindfolded during sex? If you haven't, you really should try it. Not knowing what's going to happen is such delicious torture. I especially like it while I'm tied up, or forced to sit in a chair in the middle of the room trying to figure out what sensational thing my husband is going to do next. My husband figured out at one point that I could see down below my blindfold, so now he puts a cotton ball on each eyelid before he blindfolds me. Yummy.

Corine

Dear Corine,

I have certainly tried it, and thoroughly enjoyed it. I find that when I can't see I seem to be able to feel so much more. Thanks for the cotton ball trick. I'll tell Ed.

Joan

Spanking

Dear Joan,

I'll bet you get a lot of letters with the question Am I Weird? Well, here's another one. My husband and I have developed our love of erotic spankings to an art. It started with a quick swat on the ass at the moment of climax and slowly evolved into playing "Bad Girl" games. If I transgress, and I do often (smile), he lowers my panties and gives me several hard swats on the bare ass. Are we really weird? Should we stop? Is this eventually going to destroy something? I guess maybe that's overkill, but we're starting to worry. We're afraid to tell our friends because I know they will all freak. I'd really appreciate your input.

Shelly

Dear Shelly,

No, you're not weird. I can't quote statistics, but from the letters I get I can assure you that you are far from alone in enjoying the "heavier" side of sex play. Let me quote from some of the letters I've received.

> Dear Joan,
> My husband of almost fifteen years and I have used spanking in our sex life since before we started having sex. I know that experts have given a ton of reasons for the pleasure that a spanking gives, increased blood flow to the pubic area and stimulating nerve endings in that area are among them. However, in my personal relationship, what makes spanking such an intimate act is the ultimate trust that I place in my husband when we get in those moods. I trust him to not be too hard and to stop when or if I want him to stop. Sometimes it is the trust that he will know my limits at the time even if I don't recognize them. That trust and the pleasure that my "stimulated" bottom gives my husband really turn me on.
>
> Sometimes, like last week, I want to feel the warmth and

sting of his hand on my flesh and forget the intercourse. However, any couple who indulges in spanking has to be able to talk about it openly. The ability to communicate with your partner about your needs and desires makes a spanking even more pleasurable.

Darleen

Dear Joan,

My husband and I have been married for over twenty-five years and have just recently discovered spanking as a means to add excitement and variety to our lovemaking. It was something that I'd fantasized about for years, but I'd never seriously considered trying it until my husband and I got to the point where we could communicate our sexual desires more openly. And, our children are all way from home, so we have the privacy we need, too.

One evening, I casually mentioned my desire to be spanked, and he jumped on it. Instead of thinking I was some kind of pervert, he admitted that he had had similar fantasies. What a revelation. We laughed about how silly we had both been, not sharing sooner. I still lament the missed years of pleasure.

The first time we tried it, we began by having my husband give me a full-body massage, during which he incorporated the occasional slap to my bare behind. Let me explain that we had already talked it through, had established limits and agreed that he would stop if I asked him to. I trusted him completely, and still do. Anyway, as his slaps became more frequent and a little harder, I got more and more aroused, until I was extremely turned on and so was he. He ended up bringing me to a very intense orgasm using his fingers from behind me. He came almost as quickly when I used my hand on his penis. It was so surprising, we never did have actual intercourse that night.

Since then, we've added a wooden paddle and a standard vibrator to our spanking sessions for some added variety. He places the vibrator inside me or against my mound as he uses his hand or the paddle on my ass. Or he lays me over his lap, where he can easily manipulate any area he chooses with one hand while using the other for striking.

If anyone has ever toyed with the idea of spanking, I'd highly recommend it with a partner you care for and trust. I know that if I say stop, he won't go any further, but so far, I haven't needed or wanted him to. He knows me better than I know myself.
Janette

Dear Joan,

My husband and I engage in erotic spanking. For me, this kind of foreplay heats up more than just my bottom. I can't really explain the what or why of the turn-on, but it's mind-blowing.

We've gotten into it so much that we recently purchased a small whip (one suitable for my breasts or his penis), and he uses that on me. He can be gentle or harsh depending on how I react to it. My husband reads me so well that he always knows.

Another part of the erotic spanking is talking while engaging in it. He likes to pretend that I'm a very bad girl in need of punishment, and of course I always play along. I tell him what a bad girl I've been and how much I deserve and need to have a hot red behind. Somehow, anal sex seems to go along with the spankings. For me I guess the heat in that area causes my body to need some relief, and anal stimulation seems to do that. All in all, I'd say I have the perfect husband—one who understands my needs and fulfills all my fantasies.
Betty

Dear Joan,

I have a lover who's quite far away, so we don't get together very often, but we hot-chat over the Internet a lot. Recently I was caught off-guard by an offhand comment about spanking. It's lucky that we were online at the time. I think that if we had been in the same room, I would have stormed out. As it was, we signed off and I had some time to think before I responded. By the time we met online again, my anger had disappeared and I found myself intrigued by the idea.

At our next face-to-face meeting we enjoyed a romantic dinner and relaxed with good conversation and a nightcap, then went to our motel room, where the fun began!! We were making love like two starving animals, when all of a sudden, he began to hit me on my ass. Wow, it wasn't like when I was a kid at all.

The motel room had one of those big mirrors over the dresser so, as he spanked me, I could see the ecstatic look on his face as his hand rose and fell. I hadn't realized just how excited I was until I climaxed. It was amazing. Nothing had touched my groin at all. There were just the spanks, and the look on my lover's face. That was enough to drive me over the edge. We both thought that this was the sexiest, most erotic time that we have shared yet.
Gail

So, Shelly, I hope these letters help you to understand that you're not weird at all. If you both enjoy it, wonderful. Treasure the sharing and trust, and, of course, the fun and excitement.
Joan

Dear Joan Elizabeth Lloyd,
I just had to write on the subject of spanking. It's sick. It's a woman's way of feeling like she's forced, or that she's a little girl again under the control of her father. Ugh. How can anyone get pleasure out of something like that!!!
Sally from Tampa

Dear Sally,
Why we get pleasure from the things we do is for psychobabblers to try to explain. For me, if it feels good and hurts (I use the term in the emotional sense) no one, it's none of anyone's business. If you don't want to play, great. There are so many other ways to get joy

from good sex, that this game needn't be any part of your sex play. However, what others do is their business.
Joan

Dear Ms. Lloyd,

I've always wanted to indulge my fantasies about rough play in the bedroom, but I've found it really difficult to find a man who's willing. I am a mature woman with a lot of experience with many men through the years. Whenever I thought I had found someone who played a little rougher than the others, I would encourage it, but it always seemed as though it was the first rush of passion that caused the roughness, and after that first excitement was over, the guys seemed to need to prove how very gentle they could be—not what I had in mind at all. Or maybe they had just indulged me, doing something they just didn't enjoy. I can understand that, but I want to play rough!!!

I remember one man who misinterpreted my hints. He decided that I wanted to tie him up! The only time I actually voiced the truth in plain English, the guy seemed to pale visibly and I never heard from him again. Why can't I find someone? Is it because I don't live in New York City, home of everything kinky? Is there no one here in rural America sophisticated enough to understand? Or is it a form of sexual political correctness, that the "new man" is supposed to show his feminine side? Frankly, I have given up. What do you think, Joan?
Jan

Dear Jan,

I think you've just been unlucky. It's difficult for someone to assume the dominant (or submissive role) unless that idea had been kicking around in his brain for a while. It takes some time for the pleasure to overtake the automatic "Not me, honey." Be patient and don't give up. Maybe you should frequent some of the heavier chat rooms and at least indulge your fantasies with cybersex. And maybe you'll luck out and discover that someone you meet there is local enough to visit back and forth from time to time.

And if it matters so much to you that rough play be part of your sex life, be honest right up front. Discuss your needs so that your would-be partner has a chance to join or withdraw. And most of all, have faith!

Joan

Bondage/Dominance–Sadomasochism (BDSM)

Dear Joan,

I've heard of situations where the wife is totally under the control of her partner. Sexual slavery, I'd call it. I gather there are women who do this professionally. I think it's disgusting. Why in the world would anyone want to do that? What's your opinion?

Martin

Dear Martin,

If you've read any of my books, you already know the answer. If two consenting adults agree and mutually enjoy a lifestyle that hurts no one, that's just fine.

Let's define our terms here. True slavery is not consensual. The "slave" has no choice. Sexual submissiveness is a lifestyle that two people choose, and either is able to call it off at any time.

Why? Power games are a tremendous turn-on for many people, either for an hour's entertainment or as a full-time thing. It would seem that the one in charge has all the power. Not so if you examine it a bit more deeply.

Let's assume it's the man in charge, just to get me out of the "he or she" bind. Okay, he calls all the sexual (and maybe other) shots, makes all the decisions. It's wonderfully liberating for him not to have to worry about a partner's pleasure, just give free rein to all the desires he has ever had.

Notice I say that it would seem he has all the power. In reality, she does. She's the one who has the veto power, just by saying "stop." He must cease the moment she says the magic word. In reality, then, she holds all the cards, but it's the illusion of loss of control that's so powerful. She doesn't have to worry about what she's "supposed" to do or feel. She has no choices, so she can lie back and just take. Here's a letter that might explain.

Dear Joan,
In my house, I'm the heavy-handed one. My husband is the stereotypical executive with a highly stressful job where he's responsible for multimillion-dollar projects. He comes home totally wiped out and ready to be relieved of all responsibility. I gladly do that for him. It may seem strange, but when he arrives home, he's only too happy to follow my orders. I used to have him make dinner and clean up, but I've discovered I much prefer to have him bring home takeout so we have lots of time for play.

Ahhh, having a sex slave is so wonderful. If I want him to perform oral sex on me for an hour, he does. If I want a bubble bath, he fills the tub, adds lots of my favorite oil to the water, lights candles, and turns on some soft music. While I bathe, he waits for my instructions. Sometimes I'll have him wash me, sometimes I'll just let him wait while I luxuriate. Afterwards, if I want a massage, he's only too happy to oblige. In bed, it's the same thing. Whatever I want I get. And he loves it too. He's got no responsibilities, no worries. What could be better?
Annie and Luis

So, Martin, you see what's in it for her and for him. Maybe you want to reconsider.
Joan

Dear Joan,
I've had a control fantasy for a very long time. I'm a twenty-six-year-old woman and I dream about being hypnotized my some magnetic guy with flashing black eyes. Once I'm under his control, he tells

me to do the most outrageous things, and I can't help but do them. Wow—I'm getting excited just writing this.

I have a wonderful and understanding husband, but I just can't bring myself to tell him about my desires. Can you help me?
Sandra

Dear Sandra,

How wonderful that you've decided to share something so delicious with your partner. There are several ways to go about it.

How about finding a scene in a book or a story on the Web that depicts the kind of encounter you're dreaming about? Give it to him and let him read it while you're not around. He needs to be alone so he can get around any knee-jerk reactions he might have. Later, ask him how he liked the story. If he's turned off by the idea, drop it, then try again another time. If he liked it, there's your opening to ask whether he'd like to try something like that with you.

Another way to get into a control fantasy like yours is to play a game for forfeits. Any game, like poker or gin rummy. Then, when you lose, suggest that instead of the usual forfeit, you'll be his body slave for half an hour. Wink and say, "I'll do anything, absolutely anything, you want." A great opening for him. If he panics and stammers, suggest that you could begin by undressing for him. Or whatever you and he would enjoy.

Still another idea is to get into the fantasy the next time you're making love. Again, the line might be, "Baby, I'm so hot, I'll just do anything you want me to. Anything!"

Go slowly and build up to it.

If you give this a try, drop me a note and let me know how it goes.
Joan

Dear Joan,

It's me, Sandra, again. I hope you remember that I wrote to you about a fantasy I have about being hypnotized. You gave me some really good suggestions and asked me to let you know what happened. Well, I did it. I found a story about someone who hypnotizes a woman and makes her do wonderfully awful things. I copied it off the website and gave it to Jimmy to read. I hate to admit it, but I hid in the bathroom while he read. Later he asked me why I had given the story to him.

I almost chickened out, but I decided to take control (evil grin). I was really shaking, but I told him that I had a fantasy of that happening to me. I asked him how he felt about it, and he leered at me. Actually leered. We talked about what he could ask me to do and what would be off-limits. I was really nervous, and at that moment I couldn't think of anything I wouldn't do if he would just take control that way. So I said, "Try me and find out."

That was all he needed. He asked me whether he could "own me" for the next hour, and the fun began. I could tell you all about it, but I'll leave it to your fertile imagination. I can't thank you enough for giving me the courage to try. Our sex life is going to be verrrrry interesting.
Sandra

Dear Joan,
My husband of four years just told me that he would like to tie me up. He assured me that he wasn't thinking about anything sadomasochistic, just being the one to call all the shots. He showed me some pictures he had printed from a website, of a man standing over a woman who was tied, spread open, on a bed. At first I was horrified, but all the time I huffed and puffed and knew I shouldn't want it, I was getting excited too, picturing myself on that bed. Well, we talked about it and he finally got me to admit that it's an exciting idea. Now he wants to try it. Help me. Should I do it? How do we get started?
Marcy

Dear Marcy,
My advice is that if it excites you, let him do it; if not, don't. It's really just that simple. Don't confuse yourself with what you *should*

want, just think about what you *do* want. And if you want to give it a try, why in the world not? You can always call it off at any time, as can he.

You two need to set a few ground rules first, however.

You need privacy and lots of it. If you have kids, make sure you're not going to be interrupted. Send them to Grandma's or get a sitter and get a motel room. And you should talk about any games that are off-limits. If you don't, under any circumstances, want to be forced to perform oral sex, for example, tell him. Agree on the boundaries.

One of the fun parts of being tied up, and I speak from lots of experience, is yelling stop and knowing he's not going to. To be able to do that, however, you two need to establish a safe word. Select something you'll both understand. It could be an unusual word like *mustard,* or you can use the one used by many in the bondage community, *red.*

He must agree that if you use that word, he'll stop. Immediately, without question.

You must agree that you'll use the word if you get the least bit uncomfortable with what's going on. If you're not sure you're enjoying what's happening, say red. If your leg cramps, say red. If you can't agree to say that word without feeling like a party pooper, don't play.

You might be wondering why the emphasis on your saying red, but if you think about it, it's pretty simple. If he can be sure you'll call things off at any time, he can feel free to do just about anything he wants, knowing you'll be the one to call a halt. You're really the one in control, but you're both having all the fun.

If you say red, then you need to talk about the situation and agree on some change in what's happening. Maybe you just need a rope loosened, or maybe you need to change the game's boundaries. You two must communicate if it's going to work.

For tying, you can use a few old neckties or stockings, or just some strips of soft cloth. If you want to go to the store, get some soft cotton clothesline. You can buy some bondage gear from a catalog or from a website, but you might want to try something plain the first few times to be sure you both enjoy acting out the fantasy. But whatever you use, just be sure that it's comfortable. You don't want to say red because your wrists are beginning to chafe.

Turn the heat up in the bedroom so you're not cold. Once you've played a few times, try different positions. The typical way a person is tied at first is spread-eagle, but try tying ankles to upper thighs with knees bent and legs spread, or tying wrists and ankles to a belt around the waist. Get creative. Look over some websites together and get ideas. Talk about it. That's almost as exciting as actually doing it.
Joan

Dear Joan,
Jeff, he's my husband, likes to tie me up, and it makes me crazy. I just love it. We recently bought some soft rope in the hardware store and cut it into pieces. He ties my wrists and ankles to the legs of the bed, and, well . . . it's dynamite. We're now interested in getting more creative about bondage. We've looked at websites and catalogs, but the bondage stuff is sooo very expensive. Have you got any inexpensive ideas for things we can use? Thanks so much in advance for any help you can give us.
Danielle (and Jeff too)

Dear Danielle,
How wonderful it is for two folks to indulge in such delicious bedroom play. I have some ideas and I've gotten more from some letters from others who enjoy bondage, which I'll attach below.

Let me give you a few suggestions first. Go to the pet store and get some of those heavy choker collars sold for dogs. They are nothing but long chains with big rings on the ends. Then pick up some padlocks at the hardware store. Need I say more? While you're at the pet store, check out the leather collars for dogs and cats. They can be used on wrists or ankles, or get a large one to strap around your neck. They usually have rings to which you can attach other chains and locks. I actually have some chains and collars, and the cold leather and steel really heat up the bedroom.

You can also buy Velcro in strips at a fabric store. With a minimum of work your husband can Velcro you in some inventive positions. I got a few letters about homemade bondage gear, and I thought these folks had some really great ideas.

Dear Joan Elizabeth Lloyd,

My wife and I believe that staying in the mood is important in good lovemaking, and we find that keeping that mood can be tricky when using toys or props. For the past few months, we've been trying a bit of mild bondage, but we have found that the restraints you can buy in stores are rather hard-edged. They are also clumsy to work with and they always seem to come in "dungeon black." That's not our style.

I've always been handy with sewing. I know that's not supposed to be masculine, but who really cares? I enjoy it. So several weeks ago I took matters into my own hands and made some very nice cuffs. They are white and soft, all trimmed in lace. They wrap tightly around each wrist, attach with Velcro, and have a silver ring sewn in as part of the design.

I remember the day I went to our local variety store to shop for the first time. I found some heavy white strips of material that's usually used for making belts, Velcro in thinner strips, and lots of wide lace. There was an awkward moment when the saleslady asked in passing what I was making. I just told her I had orders from the wife and tried not to grin. I found rings in the hardware section and I added an assortment of snaps and hooks. It took me a while with the sewing machine to assemble the cuffs, but when I was done I had exactly what I wanted at a fraction of the price you would pay for comparable store-bought items. The evening I surprised my wife with them is one that will go down in the record books for most violent orgasms.

Now my lovely wife wears her restraints while she gets ready for bed when I tell her to, or when she wants to tell me she's in the mood for this kind of sport. Once we're undressed, I can hook the cuffs together or fasten them to something without a lot of fuss. They also look nice and feminine, something I have never seen in the commercial stuff. My mind is now working overtime, filled with ideas for more items I can create.

Maybe there's a business here (wink).
Just Call Me Stitch

Dear Joan,
My husband loves to tie me up, and I enjoy it too. A lot!!! Recently he made me a gift. He took an old belt and cut it into sections long enough to go around each wrist. He attached a ring to one end and cut a slit in the other that the ring can push through. He wraps the cuff around my wrist, pushes the ring through the slit, then passes a rope or scarf through the ring to secure it. He made a similar pair for each ankle. Needless to say, we are exploring all the joys and possibilities of these cuffs often. He recently bought bungee cords in a variety of lengths and hooks them to the rings. The slightly stretchy bands are wonderful when wrapped around my waist and thighs. They can be tight enough to feel restraining without being too constricting.

I thought people might enjoy these as inexpensive alternatives to purchased items.
Carrie

Dear Joan,
For homemade "playclothes" I take ordinary clothes that I'm ready to throw out and use them. With some, I let my husband know that they are being discarded. It can lead to a delicious evening during which he ties me up, fully clothed, and then cuts my garments off, slowly, while teasing me unmercifully.

At other times, I go out with him wearing something he's seen often, but I'm ready to get rid of. What he doesn't know until we're in the mall or at friends, is that I've cut the crotch out of the slacks and panties. I cut carefully, so no one can really see,

but when he uses his imagination, well . . . I remember one evening at a restaurant when I told him my slacks had no crotch. We were sitting side-by-side and he reached under the table and played with me right there. It was fabulous for us both. He loves teasing me in public, and of course I couldn't react to his fingers for fear that the waiters and other diners would know what was going on. I was a wreck, but a delicious one.
Mimi

Well, Danielle, I hope this gives you lots of tempting ideas.
Joan

Dear Joan,
I've read a great deal about bondage, and at the beginning it sounded exciting, but so heavy, like old castle dungeons and stuff— not my idea of fun at all. Recently a new boyfriend suggested something sort of different. He wanted to tie me up and tickle me. It's funny, tickling has always been something really erotic for me, so I let him. It was great. I couldn't get away and he just tickled my feet and my sides and underarms. I laughed, but got really excited too. Last evening he showed up at my house with a huge feather. Well, I don't think I need to tell you how wonderful that was.
Janette

Dear Janette,
To each his or her own, I guess. I absolutely hate being tickled, so I guess that lets me out of that game.
Joan

Dear Joan,
I was sexually assaulted when I was a teenaged girl, almost fifteen years ago now, and I was in counseling for quite a while. It was only after many years that I was able to tell my counselor that I had sexual fantasies about being dominated. Well, it was quite a revelation to me when she said that it's not uncommon and that I should think

it all through and relax, stop worrying about what was right and wrong and just let my mind be whatever it is.

She taught me one really important thing. Fantasies don't hurt anyone. They're a great way to play mind games.

I now have a wonderful husband and we explore dominant/submissive games in the bedroom and it's all wonderful. I can allow things to happen without worrying. I know he would never hurt me.

I hope you don't mind me writing to you. Maybe my letter will help someone else.

Darcy

Dear Darcy,

Thanks for your enlightening letter, and I'll share it with anyone who writes and seems to have similar issues. I thought you'd be interested in these letters.

Dear Joan,

I'm a rape survivor. It's been almost two years since I was raped by an acquaintance at a party. I was in counseling, both one-on-one and group, but this was a topic I was always too shy to actually talk about. I thought I must be crazy for having these types of fantasies after being raped, but I continued to fantasize about being submissive, and the idea wouldn't leave me alone.

Until I met Nick, soon to be my husband, I thought that even considering being submissive was wrong, because I assumed that most rape survivors would want to be in control, especially in the bedroom. Nick is so understanding and he finally convinced me to open up. I told him about my fantasies, and we discussed them and even found a few books about rape victims and control issues.

In the end I decided that everyone's different and individual, and for some people it's okay to be submissive, as I am now with him. I know that, with a loving partner, I am really the one in control and can stop at any time. I'm confident that he cares about me and would never do anything that I didn't want.

Kristin

Dear Joan,

I'm a thirty-seven-year-old male and I discovered one night that my wife had been raped when she was in her teens. She hadn't even mentioned it before because she was so ashamed. We spent several hours talking and I tried to make her understand that she had been in no way at fault.

Having no experience in this area, I got a number of books, including a particularly good one, *The Courage to Heal Workbook*. It took me a while, but I learned to understand the patterns of a rape survivor. I noticed that when she and I were having sex, it turned her on extremely to have me pull her hair while I was thrusting or "forcing" her to perform oral sex. When we discussed it, she was really embarrassed. She thought she was sick, but I showed her the book, and the more we talked, the more she opened up that she'd had these ideas for many years. I explained that I was uncomfortable doing these things to her, that I liked the softer, sensual side of sex, but to help her I would try to role-play as much as I could.

Let me tell you that over the years, I've really gotten into it, and I've even convinced her to be the dominant from time to time. Actually, that was quite a revelation for her, to be in control. Now we swap roles occasionally, although she does prefer for me to dominate her. It's become a large part of our sex life and we both like it a lot.

David

Isn't it sad that so many people have to reach conclusions the most difficult way, and are caused so much unhappiness and worry in the meantime?

Thanks so much for your letter, Darcy, and I will certainly share it with others when the situation warrants.

Joan

Dear Joan,
I have read about clubs where there's a lot of heavy sexual stuff, like BDSM. Do these places really exist, and what are they like?
Michelle

Dear Michelle,
I have no direct experience with clubs like that, but one person I've spoken to has been to several and they are pretty much what you've probably read. In most there's no exchange of body fluid, just lots of rather impersonal pseudosexual activities: slapping, tying, some whips and such, too.

The best information I can give you comes from this letter.

Dear Joan,
A friend recently sent me your address since you helped her understand her desire to be dominated, prompted by the fact that I "came out" to her that my husband and I are into BDSM. I thought you might be interested in my experience.

I am thirty years old and first experienced the lifestyle in my mid-twenties. My husband, who's a bit older than I am, introduced me to it because he wanted me to be the dominant. He had played the role of submissive with his ex-wife and wanted to continue playing with me. Little did I know then how much I would enjoy that role.

Now we not only play together at home, but with others at bondage-play parties at local BDSM clubs. I must admit that I enjoy going to the clubs and I find it even more sexually stimulating because there are no emotional ties with the submissives I deal with. I find that I can really let loose as a dominant while my husband is off with someone else.

For the most part I find that male submissives are often men who are executives or businessowners who need to switch roles to balance out their lives. There is just something about having a complete stranger beg you to tie them up and torture them, and then have them lick your shoes, that gets my juices flowing.

When that happens, my husband and I go home and I order him to service me. It's fantastic.

I freely admit that this lifestyle isn't for everyone, and quite frankly, I have come to believe that most of us who indulge in this were born with these unique appetites. It just takes us a while to develop our skills. That isn't to say that there aren't those who are just dabbling to see what the big deal is about, but I find that they don't hang around long.

Well, I hope this helps you understand a bit better. Thanks for listening.
Marge

That pretty much says it, I think.
Joan

Rape Fantasies

Dear Joan,
I'm a thirty-two-year-old female and I recently saw a movie in which a woman is kidnapped, tied up, and, although we don't actually see anything, obviously raped by several hunky-looking gang members. I know rape is totally disgusting, but I found myself intrigued with the idea of being held down and sort of lovingly forced. It's been going around in my head for weeks, and I'm beginning to worry. I can't imagine actually having anything like that happen to me, but it still intrigues me. Am I weird?
Dolores

Dear Dolores,
Not in the least. Being overpowered by some good-looking guy and forced to do all the terribly wonderful things he has in mind is a common fantasy, and a delicious one. Actually, I have had fantasies similar to that for as long as I can remember.

What's so sad these days is that it seems to be so difficult for many people to understand the difference between fantasy and reality. Folks, and there are sooo many, who have power/control fantasies would never consider actually committing rape, or being raped. That's abhorrent to anyone with a conscience.

That doesn't prevent us, however, from having fantasies in which we are either in complete control of a sexual encounter or completely devoid of any control over what's happening. I'm not going to try to play shrink here, but just let me say that I think those of us who were brought up on the "good girl–bad girl" myth would love to feel we aren't in control, that someone else is "forcing" us to have fun. Think about the common theme in romance novels. He makes slow love to her, for the first time, and she's reluctant. But "her body takes over" and she can't think, can't resist. This is the same thing, really, and it used to be still more blatant. Remember Rhett carrying Scarlett up those wide stairs? She's kicking and yelling, but the next morning she's delightfully satiated and happy about it.

So relax and enjoy your fantasies. And maybe you can figure out a way to share them with your partner and actually act one out.
Joan

Dear Ms. Lloyd,
I'm really worried about myself. I'm a forty-three-year-old man and I want to rape my wife. I mean really rape her, hold her down, have her fight me, maybe tie her up. Part of me is sickened that I would actually think about such a thing, but it also makes me really hard. I need your sane reaction.
Clay from Canada

Dear Clay,
Rape is an abhorrent crime and I'm sure you wouldn't think of raping some poor innocent stranger. I assume you mean that you want her to fight you, but it will all be with her permission.

You described the typical dominant fantasy in which you are in complete control of every aspect of a sexual encounter. You can do what you want, when and how you want, and there will be no con-

sequences. I think that in one way or another most of us have a similar fantasy, or have the mirror image, one in which we have no control. Control fantasies are perfectly normal, and you can have a lot of fun if you can share one with your partner and maybe play it out from time to time. Just be sure to check with your wife frequently while acting out this fantasy, to be sure she's comfortable with it.
Joan

Anal Sex

Dear Reader,
Anal sex is a particularly difficult topic for many people to discuss. There's a deep taboo that seems to come with our first suck of mother's milk. Maybe it was the Church that so severely discouraged anything that didn't lead to procreation, maybe something else. But wherever it started, it has prevented so many people from engaging in this pleasurable form of sex play.

Readers, if you don't have any intention of trying anal sex and the mere idea is a turnoff, skip this section. If you're at all curious, or just titillated by the idea of anal intercourse, you might benefit from the opinions of couples just like you who really enjoy this activity.
Joan Elizabeth Lloyd

Dear Joan,
I'm a forty-one-year-old wife and mother. My husband of seventeen years has always wanted to try anal sex, but the idea scares me to death. It's not really a turnoff for me, it's just that I'm afraid that there will be lots of pain and that I'll panic or just disappoint him. What can I do?
Laura

Dear Laura,
Most important, if you don't want to do something, don't. It's just that simple. If you're willing to experiment, however, let me help you

Totally Private

begin. Anal intercourse, actual insertion of the penis into the anus, should be the final step, not the first. It's probably where your husband wants to end up, but it really should begin much more slowly.

First, in the bath or shower, touch yourself. See how it feels. With lots of soap and a long reach, you'll feel what your anal opening is like. Does touching it repel you? If so, maybe you should go no further. If it's not so bad, then you might suggest to your husband that he touch you there during really hot sex play, when you're really turned on. Nothing more, just touching.

Let me give you this strong warning. Do not let anything that's been in contact with your anal area come in contact with your vagina or the surrounding tissues. There are really nasty bacteria lurking in and around the anus that will give you a really serious infection if they get into the warm, moist vaginal tissues. If your husband wants to touch your anus, he must either refrain from touching you elsewhere with the same hand, or wash thoroughly with an antibacterial soap. Another way to prevent contamination is to have him slip a condom over his finger, play with your "backdoor" as long as he likes, then remove the condom before he uses his fingers in other places. A rubber glove works even better, especially if you're going to move on.

The next step is to try slight penetration with that finger. Use lots of water-based lubricant, like K-Y Jelly or Astroglide, both available at your local store. Remember that anal sex is a high-risk sexual activity, and a petroleum-based product like baby oil or Vaseline will eat through condoms and rubber gloves, allowing disease organisms to pass through the microscopic holes. Read labels and be sure the lubricant you use is water-based!

Use lots of lube on both your anal area and on his finger. Then ask him to penetrate slowly, only half an inch or so. Agree that if you say stop, he will, and be sure you say stop if there's pain. Let him back off and try again another time if you feel severe discomfort. It will certainly feel a bit strange, but real pain is a reason to stop.

When your body becomes accustomed to slight penetration, you can try a bit more, and still more as you see fit. Remember, you are in charge here, and your husband must obey your wishes and take his time. Full-finger penetration might not happen on the first try, so you both need to be patient.

By the way, the joy of anal penetration this way isn't limited to women. Men enjoy anal play just as much as we do. As a matter of fact, as you'll see below, prostate massage can generate some tremendous orgasms. If you're going to try it with him one evening, the steps are the same, although you can be a bit less careful with where you touch afterward. Just stay away from the end of the penis or your own body.

If you find you enjoy this play, you can purchase an anal dildo. These differ from vaginal ones in that they are usually slimmer (until and unless you want something wider), and they have a flange at the base to prevent unintentional deeper penetration. The vagina is a closed channel, so nothing can get really lost inside. If you've removed a tampon, you know how to find something that slips too far in. The anus is merely the opening of the large intestine, the far end of the digestive system. Therefore, an object inserted too far won't be retrievable. Ending up in the emergency room after an overzealous bout of anal play is a really lousy way to end an evening. So be sure anything you use for anal penetration has a wide base that won't allow the object to slide all the way in.

When you're ready to go for full anal intercourse, remember to use a condom; better still, use two. Anal intercourse is the ultimate high-risk activity. There are always minuscule injuries to the internal tissues, usually nothing of any consequence. However, if your partner carries the HIV virus, his semen and precome will be filled with it, and the tiny tears will provide a perfect avenue of transmission. I would advise you to use a condom and take particular care if you have hemorrhoids. Use lots of water-based lubricant.

If and when you finally decide to try anal intercourse, let me suggest a few positions. Lie on your stomach with a pillow beneath your hips to raise your behind, and let him try that way. Usually it's more comfortable, particularly early on, with the woman on her side, curled up with him behind. This can give you some control of the action.

If you're worried about the depth and comfort of his penetration, let him lie on his back and you straddle him. You and he can guide his penis to the right area and you can control the depth and frequency of penetration from your position on top. Take care that the penis doesn't slip and come in contact with your vaginal area. If it does, wash thoroughly to try to avoid nasty infections.

Once you've tried it, decide whether it should continue to be part of your sex play. If so, great. If not, fine too.
Joan

Dear Joan,

I don't know whether you will remember me or not, but I wrote to you some months ago about anal sex. You wrote back with some hints for us to try, and I just wanted to let you know your hints helped a lot. We have been able to make this part of our regular sex life, and we both think it's great. It was something that I was totally against for almost seven years. Now it's great, and we both enjoy it often.

So let your readers know it may take a little time, but it's worth it once you get there, so don't give up trying if you want to do it.

Thanks for your help.
Laura

Dear Joan,

My husband wants to try anal sex and I'm willing to give it a chance. My question is, though, why is it such a turn-on for guys? Is it power? Is it because it's forbidden?
Eunice

Dear Eunice,

There are thousands of nerve endings involved in sexual excitement, and many end in the anal area. The spasms that are felt during orgasm echo throughout the genitals and anus and can be felt on the penis. In addition, as the years pass, a woman's vaginal muscles weaken and the passage enlarges. Inserting a penis into an anus makes a tighter, and for many, a more exciting, fit.

Is it power? Probably for some, but who cares what psychobabble you put on top of it? Suffice it to say that for those who are into it, it's extremely pleasurable.

Is the pleasure enhanced because it's forbidden? Probably. It's sort of deliciously evil, something taboo that's really harmless.
Joan

Dear Joan,
My husband wants me to try anal sex, but I worry that, if things get painful, he won't be able to stop and he'll hurt me. What can I do?
Marge

Dear Marge,
Don't play! The statement that he "won't be able to stop" is nonsense. No man gets to the point that he can't stop any time he wants to. Trying anything new involves trust. If you can't trust him to stop when you say stop, don't play!
Joan

Dear Joan,
I'm a forty-two-year-old man and I've just remarried. My ex-wife and I always engaged in anal sex, and she seemed to really get off on it. Of course, I did too. Now I want my new lover to enjoy it too. What can I do to help her get used to it?
Phil

Dear Phil,
I'm so glad you say that you want to help her get used to it, not make her try it. That's a wonderful attitude. As an "old hand" at anal sex, you know the ropes and you know that it's her call. If she wants to give it a try, go for it; if not, forget it.

If you want her to enjoy it, go slowly and let her call the shots.

In addition, while you're playing with the anal area, don't forget to do the things you have done in the past that excite her. Caress her breasts, play with her nipples, stroke her clit. Remember, excitement is an all-involving process, so don't just concentrate on one thing.
Joan

Dear Joan,
My husband and I are ready to enjoy actual anal penetration. We've had great orgasms during play with toys and such, but now it's going to be the real thing. I'm worried about the mess. Should I use an enema before? I don't want any embarrassing icky stuff.
Pam

Dear Pam,
You can use an enema if it will make you less hesitant, but I've never used one and I've had anal sex many times without an unpleasant experience. I guess that's a matter of personal taste.
Joan

Dear Joan,
Do women really enjoy anal sex? It seems so painful and degrading. What do you think?
Janice

Dear Janice,
What is degrading is a question for each woman to answer for herself. Although we don't often have anal intercourse, Ed and I sometimes play that way with hands and toys and we both enjoy it. I don't find it degrading at all, nor do the many other women who enjoy this kind of play.

Let me share some of the feelings in letters I've received, both pro and con.

Dear Joan,

As a lady, I know that, according to many people, I'm not supposed to enjoy anal sex. Far from it, though!!

When my husband suggested that we try anal sex, I thought about it quite a bit. He promised that he would stop if I didn't like it, but he thought I'd really enjoy it. I trust him totally, so I finally agreed.

The first time we tried it, anal sex was a surprise for me. I knew he'd be very considerate, and let me guide him, and I did all the moving till I was comfortable. Well, wow! Ladies, if you try it, be prepared for tremendous orgasms!!

Ginny

Dear Joan,

I am a twenty-two-year-old female and I've been married for almost two years. My husband and I had tried anal sex several times, but it was very painful for me. I wanted to do it with him, so I thought I'd try something. I had a friend who told me that she had ordered an anal-ease cream for about nine dollars that dulled the sensation a bit while still leaving feeling. I didn't want to spend that much on something that might not work, so I bought an anti-itch cream. He applied it to my anus before we tried again. It was amazing. For only about two dollars a tube, it eased the pain tremendously! It was the most incredible sex we have had yet!

Samantha

Dear Joan,

I am a female, aged thirty-seven. My first experience with anal sex was with my husband. I was really hesitant, but I gave it a try anyway, since I thought I might enjoy it too. He used a lot of lubricant, but he pushed too fast and the pain was unbelievable! I almost passed out. He felt terrible.

It was several years before he thought about asking again, but even after that long I still would always say no. I was so afraid of that pain. Well, when I was in my last months of pregnancy the kid was huge and it was getting a little uncomfortable to have vaginal sex. I had read in a few women's magazines about trying anal sex in the last couple of months of pregnancy as an alternative to vaginal sex, so we decided to give it a try.

We were fooling around and I was really turned on (which I think helped a lot), and my husband was very concerned about not hurting me, so he went very, very slowly. He caressed me and talked to me, helping me to relax. This time he didn't hurt me at all.

Now, every time we do it, it gets even better for me! So it is definitely worth trying, but you need to do it right. You need trust, patience, lots of lubricant—and go slowly! Let her guide you and do the pushing. The spooning position has been the best for us.

Sally

Dear Joan,

My husband and I just discovered something new about anal sex. We have been playing this way for years, and we both love it, but recently, I bought an anal sex toy. We were fooling around and my husband grabbed the toy, lubed it up well, and inserted it. It was such an intense feeling. He then stood me up and leaned me over the bed and started thrusting into me hard with the plug still in place. Phew! Oh my—what a feeling. It was like being loved in my front and rear at the same time. We both had incredible orgasms. Anal sex is so erotic. I love it.

Glenda

Dear Joan,

I've recently had anal sex for the first time, and if you don't do it the right way, it can really hurt. It's not that big of a deal now that I finally tried it, but it is fun because it's "forbidden." It is pleasurable, but not as much as vaginal sex.

Missy

Dear Joan,
It's very simple. Anal sex hurts! Don't do it!
Leslie

I thought I'd include a letter from a man, too.

Dear Joan,
Speaking as a man, it feels great!!! I mean certainly the sensations are intense, but what makes it even better is that a woman is giving something of herself. Something that is out of the ordinary and requires an immense amount of trust. I often feel most close to my wife after anal sex.

From her perspective, there is often some discomfort at first, but usually the sensation takes over and she has had some amazing orgasms. She enjoys the sensation of extreme fullness and surrender.
Jeff

So, Janice, I hope this helps you understand people's feelings about anal sex a bit better. Just like other forms of sex play, some like it, some don't. It's really up to you and your partner.
Joan

Dear Joan,
Let me address the question of anal sex from the man's point of view—not the man who's penetrating a woman, but the one who is being penetrated. So much of anal sex seems directed at the man inserting his penis into the woman. However, my wife loves to use a well-lubricated, latex-gloved finger to penetrate my rectum, too. And it's one of the most exciting things, maybe even better than intercourse. Sometimes I can come that way and no other.

Here's how it often goes. She tells me I've been a bad boy, and she'll have to "punish me." I know that's probably a bit sick, but I don't care. It's so erotic. Anyway, I stand in front of her as she pulls on a pair of gloves, very slowly. Then she makes me watch as she uses lots of K-Y on her fingers. I lay across her lap and she does it, talking to me all the time. Sometimes I rub myself against her thigh until I come, other times she insists that I masturbate while she does it. If you've never had a prostate massage when really hard, let me recommend it to any man who reads this.

I've read enough of your writing to know that you believe that things done between consenting adults are all okay, and for us, this is great sex.

Jake

Dear Jake,
What more can I say than bravo! You're right about my opinion about great sex, and you seem to have found it. And if the power structure of that role-playing game gets to you, another bravo!
Joan

Dear Joan,
Okay, I give up, what's a prostate massage and how do I give my boyfriend one? I know it has something to do with anal sex—we do that lots and it's great. It gives me such fantastic orgasms, and someone told me that a prostate massage can do the same for him. Can you help?
Ginger

Dear Ginger,
A man has a gland that borders his rectum and urethra called the prostate. It spasms during ejaculations, just like the rest of his penis and testicles. That's also the gland that causes much of the trouble men have with sex in later life, enlarging and limiting the flow of urine and causing difficulties in ejaculation.

During routine physicals, a doctor might examine his prostate to check for abnormalities. Amazingly enough, that exam often results in a spontaneous erection, because the prostate is such an intimate part of the sexual apparatus.

You can use that gland to give him great pleasure. Insert a lubricated finger deep into his anus and press gently toward the belly-side of the passage, about as far in as you can insert that finger. You should feel a solid, dome-shaped structure. Don't press hard, just stroke it—you should notice an immediate excited reaction from him. Rub gently and let him guide you. Men differ in the intensity of their reaction and how hard they want to be touched.

Of course, if there's any discomfort, stop and suggest that he see his doctor just to be on the safe side.

If you're thinking of trying prostate stimulation, you might be interested in this letter.

Dear Joan Lloyd,
I'm a thirty-three-year-old man with a great wife and a wonderful sex life. I bought a vibrator for my wife a few years ago. You probably know the type—a little five-inch hard plastic bullet that can be pressed against her or inserted. Sadly, she promptly put it in the back of her nightstand.

This summer, while she was away on business, I decided to take it out, put in a fresh battery, slide a condom on it, lube it up, and slip it in my back door while I masturbated. Holy cow! When I turned it on I exploded! Since then, I bought a jelly anal vibrator, and I'm hooked. I like the feel of the little probe, and when the vibrations start I can't control myself. If you guys like a little pressure on your prostate during sex, this is the same, only much better. Oh, I discussed it with my wife, and she said that if I wanted to do it when I was alone, that was fine with her, but she wasn't interested in playing with me—more's the pity.
Ralph

It's amazing how many people play this way, and sad that some can't share the fun.
Joan

Dear Joan,
My husband and I have tried anal sex several times. We've read all

the advice and tried everything, but it still hurts. We've agreed not to try it again. It just hurt too much.
Meg

Dear Meg,
I read your letter and you're right to give it up. It's not worth the pain you seem to be experiencing. If you were really excited and used lots of lube and it didn't work, forget it. There are so many other things you and he can do for fun in the bedroom—and elsewhere.
Joan

A Totally Unscientific Survey of Sexuality and Lovemaking

Dear Reader,

I know you've enjoyed *Totally Private,* and you've also probably learned something, too. Maybe the book has answered a long-standing question, or just given you some new ideas for play in the bedroom. That's precisely what I had in mind when I wrote it.

My next book will contain more questions and answers about love and sex, based on the responses to the survey below. I'd love to include your feelings and experiences. Please take some time to fill it out; use lots of extra paper and tell me all about yourself and your sex life. As in *Totally Private,* all answers will remain completely anonymous and your submission becomes property upon receipt without compensation, to be published or not in my discretion. Send all surveys (and, as always, any questions, answers, comments, or opinions) to me at Joan Lloyd, PO Box 221, Yorktown Heights, NY 10598, or e-mail me at survey@joanelloyd.com

For an expanded version of the survey, please visit my website at www.joanelloyd.com. If you don't have access to the Internet, please send a self-addressed, stamped envelope to me at the above address and I'll gladly send you the longer version. I look forward to hearing from you and reading and using your facts and fantasies.

There are only four pieces of information that I really need to tabulate the results:

Your age? ___ Your sex? ___ Gay or Straight? ___

Are you permanently partnered right now? Y/N ___

Please answer all of the questions that interest you.

About You and Your Partner

1. What part of your body do you like most?   Least?
2. What part of your partner's body do you like most?   Least?
3. What attracts you to a partner at first meeting? Looks? Be specific. Attitude? Be specific.
4. What attracts you to a partner as time goes on? Looks? Be specific. Attitude? Be specific.
5. Do you masturbate? How often? What makes it feel particularly good? Do you have a routine? Describe it for me.
6. Do you remember the first time you masturbated?
7. Do you need pornography, music, erotic stories to get you in the mood or does your imagination suffice?
8. Do you use any toys?
9. Does your partner know that you masturbate? How does s/he feel about it?
10. Does your partner masturbate? How do you feel about it?

Questions on Sex

1. What was the best sex you ever had? Tell me every juicy detail. What made it so great?
2. What was the worst sex you ever had? What made it so bad?
3. Do you think your best sex is yet to come?
4. Tell me about your first time.
5. Tell me about your most recent experience.
6. Have you told your partner how many lovers you've had?
7. What's the most embarrassing thing that ever happened to you while making love?
8. What's the most wonderful thing that ever happened to you while making love?

About Lovemaking with Your Partner

1. What do you wish your partner knew about when making love with you?
2. What do you wish s/he would tell you?

3. Do you wonder whether you're a good lover? Have you ever asked?
4. Have you ever faked an orgasm?
5. Have you ever told someone s/he was great in bed when s/he really wasn't?
6. Do you usually make love with the lights on?
7. Do you usually make love at night?
8. Do you usually make love in the bedroom?
9. What is the most unusual place you've ever made love? Tell me all the delicious details.
10. What's the wildest thing you've ever done during sex?
11. Is there a sexual thing you've done that you now regret? What happened? Why do you regret it?
12. Do you have a favorite position for lovemaking? Describe it as best you can.
13. What is your partner's favorite position/activity? Do you like it too, or do you do it to please him/her?
14. Do you and your lover engage in oral sex? If not, why not?
15. If yes, do you enjoy it, or do you just do it to please your partner?
16. Do you and your lover engage in anal sex? If not, why not?
17. If yes, do you enjoy it, or do you just do it to please your partner? Do you think your partner enjoys it or does it for you?
18. How often do you and your partner play with toys? Never? Sometimes? Always? Describe.
19. Why did you decide to bring toys into the relationship?
20. Where did you get the toys? Were you embarrassed?
21. How do you approach someone new about bringing toys into lovemaking?
22. If you don't, would you like to? Tell me what you would like to play with.

About Playing Pretend Games

1. Playing pretend can add spice to lovemaking. Have you ever done it? Played doctor? Pirate? Kidnapper or prison guard? Tell me about it.
2. If not, would you like to? What do you think would happen?
3. How would you react if your partner answered the door dressed like a police officer or a doctor?

About Your Fantasies

1. Do you fantasize while you make love? Describe one (or more). How often do you fantasize? Have you told your partner?
2. Do you fantasize at other times? Describe one of those fantasies.
3. Do you fantasize about making love to another person? Who would it be?
4. Do you have a fantasy you haven't shared with your partner? Take some time and share it with me. Would you like to act it out, or should it remain just between us?
5. Do you dream about a threesome? With whom? Tell me all the delicious details.
6. Do you ever think about being watched while you're making love? Or watching another couple? Have you ever done it? How did (or would) the scene play out?
7. Have you ever fantasized about having sex in a public place?
8. Have you ever fantasized about being in control of, or being controlled by, your partner? How much control? Would you like to act it out? Have you ever? Describe.
9. Do you ever fantasize about pain being pleasure? How much?
10. Do you wish you could administer or receive the pain? Would you like to act it out? Have you ever? How would you like it to play out?
11. If you are straight, do you ever have homosexual fantasies? If gay, do you ever have heterosexual ones? Can you describe one?

And Lastly

The one thing I've never told anyone about my sex life is . . .

All the material received in response to this survey will become the property of Joan Elizabeth Lloyd and may or may not be included in any future work. All responses will remain anonymous and will be edited as appropriate.